# NOCTURNES

# NOCTURNES

## ON LISTENING TO DREAMS

PAUL LIPPMANN

THE ANALYTIC PRESS

2000    Hillsdale, NJ                          London

© 2000 BY THE ANALYTIC PRESS

PUBLISHED BY
THE ANALYTIC PRESS, INC., PUBLISHERS
EDITORIAL OFFICES:
101 WEST STREET
HILLSDALE, NEW JERSEY 07642
WWW.ANALYTICPRESS.COM

SET IN BASKERVILLE & BASKERVILLE OLD FACE BY
CHRISTOPHER JAWORSKI / QUALITEXT

INDEX BY LEONARD S. ROSENBAUM

LIBRARY OF CONGRESS CATALOGING-IN-PUBLICATION DATA

LIPPMANN, PAUL
NOCTURNES : ON LISTENING TO DREAMS / PAUL LIPPMANN
P.   CM. —
INCLUDES BIBLIOGRAPHICAL REFERENCES AND INDEX
ISBN 0-88163-243-0
1. DREAMS.  2. DREAM INTERPRETATION.  3. PSYCHOANALYSIS.  I. TITLE.

BF175.5.D74 L56 2000
154.6'3—DC21
00-048098

PRINTED IN THE UNITED STATES OF AMERICA
10 9 8 7 6 5 4 3 2 1

DEDICATED

TO FRANNY AND OUR MISHPOCHA
TO THE DREAMERS AND LUFTSMENSCHEN
TO MY PATIENTS

WITH GRATITUDE

# ❧ CONTENTS ❧

# Preface and
# Acknowledgments

Yiddish was the language of my childhood. I never knew a Yiddish word for "preface." But when I first heard the word "foreword," I thought it referred to *The Forwards—Der Forverts*, a socialist Yiddish newspaper, not read in our house because it was thought too reactionary compared with *Der Freiheit—Freedom*, the newspaper of the Yiddish more radical left. So, I begin with this Foreword, technically a Preface, and since my last chapter is on Freedom—Freiheit—this book is bordered by the names of two of the great Yiddish newspapers of days gone by, a means of education for the immigrant generation of my parents and their friends. I remember in early childhood hearing my father read portions of Freud's writings to my mother. I think it was about dreams translated into Yiddish in the *Freiheit*. Thus, my earliest Freud was in Yiddish, which was also the language of Freud's mother. When, in an early analysis, I would mention Yiddish words emerging from within my dreams (basic words for family life, for the immediate surround of childhood, for childhood emotion still remain primarily, for me, in Yiddish; *bet-gevahnt* still comes to mind before *sheets* and *blankets*), the analyst, a lively and creative psychologist from Vienna, turned up his nose, as did many Viennese Jews, at the Yiddish. Therefore I kept many of my dreams, particularly those referring to childhood language and emotion, to myself. This book is for all those whose early language has to be kept private, even in therapy. Also, this book is for students—undergraduate and graduate—therapists, analysts, and their patients, and for the general public interested in dreams and the way psychoanalysts think about them.

This book is a journey into the world of dreams and into the analyst's consultation room where dreams and therapy can meet. As we enter the 21st century, 100 years after Freud's (1900) *Interpretation of Dreams*, we are at another fin-de-siècle crossroads, in which dreams and their interpretation may be critical. In 1900, Freud opened the door into the 20th century for the psychoanalytic study of dreams. In the face of today's new economic and electronic global market, dreams again stand as a radical point of departure—REM in relation to RAM, imagination in relation to materialism.

In this book, I take contemporary relational psychoanalysis to task as I do classical psychoanalytic dream interpretation for often misusing dreams to suit their theoretic points of view. It should be stated that my work as an analyst draws deep inspiration from both points of view and I engage in criticism in the spirit of comradeship and respect. As an aside, although rooted in interpersonal psychoanalysis, in this writing I do not make a firm distinction between interpersonal and relational approaches, nor do I make a clear differentiation between psychoanalysis and analytically inspired psychotherapy. Such distinctions, although meaningful in other contexts, are not crucial for me in this work on dreams.

## ACKNOWLEDGMENTS

Here, I am happy to take the opportunity to express gratitude to those who have helped make this book possible. I am fortunate to live in a four-generation family. We live near each other, in the Berkshires—in the small rural towns of Stockbridge, Great Barrington, and Housatonic, Massachusetts. We often have meals together and there is lots of talk. We tell each other our dreams. We go through our lives connected—in good times and in troubled times.

This is called enmeshment, overdependency, and other bad names. But, it is the ground from which I come.

First to Frances, my wife and my closest colleague from the old days at New York University Graduate School in Clinical Psychology, 45 years ago, who shares every idea, who listens to every sentence, who knows my every dream, whose good sense, humor, and hard work have sustained all of us as it does the counseling service at Williams College where she is director.

My children, John Lippmann and Eve Lippmann Jennings, both educate and inspire me. John is an organic vegetable farmer, the "real McCoy," and his partner, Leslie Best, a psychologist and dance movement therapist, have been, throughout this writing, the best of critics—helpful, original, honest, straightforward. My daughter, Eve, a psychologist, and her husband, Sean Jennings, also a psychologist, and their daughter—my granddaughter Lily, and her stepbrother, my stepgrandson, Joseph, are like life itself—boisterous, colorful, imaginative.

My mother, Blimela Lipshitz, now 96, lives nearby. Her clarity, intelligence, and liveliness, her fighter's spirit, her lovingness, and her psychological know-how is at the center of our family. It is amazing at my age to still have, every day and in reality, my mother's love to count on. Her dreams are wonderful. The last was of a boyfriend from 85 years ago. She woke up smiling. My father, Meilach Lipshitz, was my soul's teacher, friend, and love. He died 30 years ago, but lives in every thought. He was a poet, a musician, a *luftsmensch,* a dreamer—and this book is dedicated to his memory. To my brother, Meyer Lipshitz and his loving family, my gratitude for his being the earliest inspiration for my wishes and dreams.

My patients are the teachers and the guiding spirit of this book. They have opened their lives and their dreams to me, and my gratitude is immeasurable. Thank you deeply. And thank you again.

My friends Morris Eagle, Yale Nemerson, and Andrew Morrison, who have shared the best and worst of times, are owed deep gratitude for their enduring friendship. Their interest in my work with dreams, as in my earlier explorations as a sometimes painter and klezmer musician, has sustained me, because if *they* were truly interested, then what I loved to play with might have some genuine worth outside my own fantasy. Also, the inspiration of my dear friend for many years before his untimely death, David Schecter, is present on every page.

I am deeply grateful to the William Alanson White Institute for more than I can say. The spirit of friendship, open inquiry, and intelligence that permeates the walls at 20 West 74th Street in New York City have sustained me from graduate school days. My teachers, analysts, colleagues, and students are fully present and alive in this writing. I am deeply grateful for the opportunity to have been teaching dreams at the Institute for many years. Everything in this writing, and in my work as an anayst, has been nurtured at White. Its spirit of independence, its respect for freedom of thought, its decency are at the core. The interpersonal approach has made it natural to integrate thoughts about the deepest inner world, as in dreams, with ideas about the social universe.

Other institutions have been most helpful during these years, in allowing me to teach on dreams, and thus have played a role in this work. My gratitude to the New York University Postdoctoral Program in Psychotherapy and Psychoanalysis, to the Massachusetts Institute for Psychoanalysis, to the Western Massachusetts and Albany Association for Psychoanalytic Psychology (WMAAPP), our local Division 39 chapter, to the Austen Riggs Center and especially to its fellows in psychiatry and psychology, to our ongoing Stockbridge Dream Study Group, whose participants—Freudians, Jungians, interpersonalists, relationalists, meet and mingle over the dream, and to members of private dream seminars over the years. My thanks also to the members of the Women's Therapy Centre in New York City and to the members of the Seminario de Socio-Psicoanalisis of the Instituto Mexicano de Psicoanalisis who listened to early parts of this book and taught me much with their generosity of spirit.

I would also like to honor the memory of two great psychologists and psychoanalysts whom I was privileged to meet and to know over the years, and whose work both on dreams and on social forces in individual psychology have served as a model and an inspiration—Erik Erikson and Erich Fromm.

Finally, my gratitude to John Kerr, psychologist, author, and editor for The Analytic Press. We survived each other's shyness, and he survived my writing and helped improve it and so here we are.

—Paul Lippmann
Stockbridge, MA

## C﹩ I ﹩ɔ

## INTRODUCTION

*When we tug at a single thing in nature, we find it attached to the rest of the world.*

—John Muir

She speaks quietly of her dream, a bit embarrassed. *"There is a road that goes through the woods. It's a dirt road. A crowd of people are on one side and they're all looking at a dead deer on the side of the road."* She looks at her hands and her voice becomes thinner. *"Blood all over the road. It's not clear but I think it was hit by a car, and they want me to cut it up and distribute the pieces for food. Something about doing it fairly. They know I'm a doctor and they want me to do the carving."* She looks over at me briefly and says, *"But I need someone to help, to take off the hide. I don't feel right about it. But I'm glad they ask me. I think I can see it's a female. I know some of the people."* She looks over again, smiles a small smile, and shrugs, as if to say "Beats me."

We have known each other for most of a year and often talk about dreams. We work together in analytic psychotherapy. The patient is a tall, willowy, dreamy woman in her late forties, but with a shyness and naiveté of a woman much younger. For many years, she has been a respected physician. And I am a psychologist–psychoanalyst in my mid sixties, thin, graying, Jewish, a bit rough around the edges. We meet twice weekly in 50-minute sessions in my office in the small town of Stockbridge, in the Berkshires of western Massachusetts. The psychotherapy is of the psychoanalytic variety, with an interpersonal shading. She is a troubled, often terrified, and yet tender soul—quiet, gentle, intelligent, inward. Secretly and guiltily, she is obsessed with things corrupt, sexual, and violent. Occasionally, she feels she is losing her mind, for a day or two at a time, especially when she is unable to survive the struggle between inner violent chaos and outward softness. Her guilt is monumental. She has been trying hard to hold her mind, herself, and her family together following the stillbirth of her daughter's infant and the sudden death of one of her favorite patients. She is possessed of a deeply silent and growing disappointment in life and in the possibilities of love. In her dreams, we have found a way to explore her troubled heart. In dreams, we have found a way to struggle through perilous times and to begin to weigh the meanings of things. Dreams can provide a way to look at things a bit "from the side" and thus permit breathing space for some terrible experiences that cannot be faced head-on.

There is a way of being with dreams that can be helpful to people in trouble. If one can develop a respectful capacity to allow the mind to play, if one does not force one's own opinions and thus take up too much psychological room at the expense of the patient or the dream, if one can be a naturalist and follow a dream and a dreamer wherever they lead, then it is often possible for dreams to unfold themselves in therapy and to reveal untold mysteries of the human heart. Often this unfolding can lead the way in easing psychological suffering. Psychoanalytic therapy, I believe, is particularly well suited to make good use of dreams because it respects the complexity of human experience, because it is rooted in an appreciation of the unconscious dimensions of mind, and because, at its best, it tries to listen deeply without knowing too quickly.

It is of interest that in our field, fewer and fewer psychoanalytic therapists use dreams well. Once upon a time, dreams were at the center of psychoanalysis. Now, in our journals and at our meetings, dreams are rarely discussed. And when they are, they seem to be used exclusively to elaborate aspects of the relationship between patient and therapist, to elaborate aspects of transference themes. Although often interesting and even useful, this approach hardly makes full use of the potential of dreams to open the discussion to unexpected vistas.

In what follows, I discuss the various phases in the 100-year relationship between dreams and psychoanalytic therapy in ways that I hope can renew interest in the dream and that can raise questions about the direction of contemporary psychoanalytic therapy.

## Catch Me If You Can

At night, in sleep, we dream. The mind, like heart and lungs, never stopping; whether asleep alone or in another's arms, whether happy or sad, mad or sane, rich or poor, the dreams pour forth in extraordinary buds and blossoms of creative thought. Within this most common, natural, universal occurrence, there is an endless variety and uniqueness that still causes me wonder and amazement.

A lot of work goes into these flowers of originality. There is evidence that everyone (REM) dreams for about 2 hours each night—more for infants, less for the elderly—whether the dreams are remembered or not. Therefore, in a week, a person averages about 15 hours of dreams, in a year, over 700 hours, and, over an 80-year lifespan, over 60,000 hours of dreaming. That amounts to almost 7 years of full-time dreaming in a lifetime. Or, if one thinks of time divided into the 40-hour work week, one dreams, on the average, for 25 years of work-week time. Worth a gold watch.

And yet, this most commonplace and extraordinary experience remains a mystery. Despite thousands of years of probing exploration, despite the efforts of philosophers and scientists, of machine and imagination, the mystery of dreams continues to fascinate and puzzle. From ancient biblical desert to fin-de-siècle Vienna, from the thrones of pharaohs to the couches of analysts, from Torah through Talmud to *Traumdeutung,* the dream continues to tease as it eludes our best efforts to grasp its essential nature, its purpose, its meaning.

Pursued though time, through night's experience, through day's fading memory, the dream slips away into its own realm: "Catch me if you can." Why so elusive? Why, despite thousands of years of effort, do we remain so mystified? It is truly amazing that the dream should have resisted for so long the weighty impact of millennia of interpretation, theory, superstition, and dogma. There is a crucial quality of "unwilled freedom" to be found in the construction and experience of dreams. We need enter the dream's own realm with the lightness and respect that are owed it. That is, we have to consider how, in exploring the mystery of dreams and their potential use in psychoanalytic psychotherapy, we may do so without harming the essential experience of the lightness of dreaming.

## A COUNTRY ROAD

Strolling, with my sweet yellow Lab, Odessa, on a dirt road through the woods near my home, puts me in mind of the experience of engaging with dreams in psychotherapy. Along the way, there is an extraordinary proliferation of vegetation: mosses, ferns, wild plants of every variety, berry bushes, grasses, small and large trees, in greens of every possible shade, all redolent with a recent rain's dampness. And hidden from view, announced only by the call of birds, above and beneath and behind the visible, lies an entire universe of living, breathing nature. Here and there I stop and look closely at a clump of mosses or a pattern of leaves or the light playing on two small yellow wildflowers. Time holds its breath and the world is instantly and completely encompassed in a small leaf and the minute red spider crawling along its stem. I look more closely in the vicinity of the leaf and see a few and then many more tiny red spiders scurrying about—a newly hatched family of baby red spiders.

Odessa stops a few yards away, farther into the woods, and is sniffing and nuzzling some grasses. I watch her a moment, speckles of sun around her; then she looks up and we decide to continue on to the nearby pond. She trots over and we near the bend in the road where what lies ahead is now hidden from view. My senses quicken, but I know that if there is a deer, a bear, or a coyote or other animal around the bend, Odessa will know about it first. So I keep half an eye on her as we continue. A month earlier, we had surprised a doe and her fawn at just this spot and we all took a good look at and a good smell of each other for long minutes before the deer and its young slowly walked off and my dog barked a farewell. But this time, there is no one on the road. We see the pond and it is time for Odessa, named for that city on the Black Sea where some of our family once lived, to take a swim and for me to look at the swirling fish under the lily pads. On such a walk, anything can happen; one can discover unknown worlds in an instant and surprises around the bend.

This sort of experience, of course, is not restricted to the countryside. A walk in the city, where nature is mostly of the human variety, can also open to surprises and discoveries. Anything can happen—a new love around the corner, a catastrophe down the street, a store window showing a piece of life long forgotten, a tiny piece of sky, a moment of slapstick. The city can be dreamlike, beyond one's will, a theater of happenings. Country or city, on the ocean or in the mountains, out of doors or in bed, if one's mind is open to each moment's chances, each moment's changes then one is in that frame of mind that is favorable for engaging well with dreams.

Dreams too are filled with unwilled surprises, sudden focusings, unfocusings. The experience of being told the dream can engage us in imagining its events and its moods, in discovering together its nature, its surfaces and hidden recesses, its flora and fauna, its surprises. The delight in working on dreams can be like the very discovery of nature. Why, then, should working with dreams in psychotherapy so often take place in an atmosphere of test and constriction? The development of this question and some possible remedies take up much of this book.

## ON A DREAM OF A RIVER

It is late in a summer vacation, and I am in a canoe with my wife, Frances, on the saltwater marshes of the Pamet River on Cape Cod. We drift lazily with the current around a long curve. The tall green and yellow grasses and reeds conceal all but the cloudless blue sky above and the green-gray-blue of the moving river below.

Suddenly, a hidden great blue heron startles us from our dreaminess with a rush of beating wings, as it explodes from the tall grasses, whooshes up and away, then turns and soars off, graceful wings spread wide, to a further part of the river. Perhaps we'll meet again later on.

How much like dreams are birds. They float in and out of our awareness. They fly where they will without our will involved. They float in air, the original *luftsmenschen.* But at times also, dreams are like fish. Fish live outside our immediate awareness in all layers of the sea, from the surface to the depths. Sometimes we catch one, mostly they go their own way, like dreams. Sometimes I have dreamed about birds and sometimes about fish. But can you imagine how pleased I was when I had a dream of a flying fish, emerging from the sea in short bursts of flight, fins spread like tight wings. It then dove back under the surface, and then up through the air again and under sea again until it flew above the dream boat I was in and hovered overhead for magical moments. I awoke with the thought that I might, after all, be *dreaming about dreams*. Of course, I was in fact dreaming about a flying fish (the dream experience, the manifest content) and not about dreams (an interpretation, an hypothesis, a latent content).

My earliest memory is of watching clouds. Outdoors in a crib or carriage, a soft breeze, looking up to the sky—so goes the memory—I saw clouds and watched and watched. Their movements, their shapes, their inner spaces and textures, their changes, all held my deep attention for long moments. I played with them in mind. I still marvel at their design. In an airplane, thousands of feet high, above the clouds, I see them from above. Miraculous perspectives. I imagine only in dreams could our ancestors, in dream flight, approach such a view from above the clouds. Perhaps we sometimes live what our ancestors could only dream. Perhaps experiences in our lives fulfill their dream wishes, as well as their nightmares. Perhaps our dream wishes and our nightmares are glimpses of what future generations may in fact experience in their daily lives. Is it possible that dreams glimpse long-ago and far-future experience? Do the generations touch in dreams? Watching the clouds, walking in nature, seeing a remarkable bird emerge from its own place, all provide spaciousness akin to the feeling of listening to and working with dreams.

## NOT ALL "DREAMS" ARE DREAMS

Peruse the book section of your favorite newspaper over a period of weeks, or browse through a bookstore, and you will be sure to find many books with the word "dream" in the title. These books are not about "dreaming" in our specific sense, but use the word as a general substitute for "wish" or "hope" or "fantasy" or "ideal" or "imagination" as in "The American Dream" or "Hoop Dreams" or " Dreams of a Seaside Resort" or "Capitalism: The Fading Dream" or "Women Who Dream of Independence." And in general conversation, one hears phrases like: "I never dreamed he would ask me out," or "Can you dream up a plan for us?" or "You don't have to take me seriously; I was only dreaming out loud," or "My dream came true! Two tickets to the playoffs!" or " He broke my heart; the dream is over," or "The Dream Team is in the Olympics."

But book titles, idioms, and catch phrases aside, talking about dreams as dreams, about the ordinary and regular experience of nighttime, is relatively rare in our culture. To be sure, if directly asked about dreams, or if the topic is overtly introduced, many people are quite forthcoming, interested, willing to talk about them, to ask about them, or are curious about the latest research. This observation does not apply to persons connected with psychoanalytic therapy as analysts or patients or their intimates. Such persons often seem to believe that dreams are like dirty secrets or might reveal pathology and are best kept to themselves or for their therapists' ears only. Although most people gladly open up about dreams if invited to talk about them, dreams, in most of our culture, do not enter ordinary conversation spontaneously. At school, at work, at the mall, at the gym, on the farm, it is rare to hear people talk about their nightly imageful musings. Perhaps because of their puzzling quality, their extremely personal and idiomatic nature, the relative importance of material things in waking communication, or a shyness about irrational matters—whatever the cause—dreams as dreams remain a topic most often unspoken in our culture. Given the ordinariness and ubiquity of dreams, this silence is all the more striking.

Let us contrast this curious reticence—unless invited—with the observation that in other cultures and at other times, talking together about dreams was a most ordinary and common occurrence. Especially in nonindustrial cultures, dream talk was common stuff, as people attempted to fathom their meanings and to better understand their lives—past, present, and especially, future. Moreover, tucked away within our own surface culture are many communities and persons where dream talk is still important. A middle-aged mother and sometime painter, of Haitian origin, living in South Florida, said in our conversation about the relationship between dreams and Haitian art, "Not a day goes by without somebody talking about a dream somebody had. It would be like a day without a drink of water to not hear and talk about somebody's dream. How would you ever know what's going on?"

I asked an elderly Italian man in Tuscany about the way dreams are regarded in his village. He spoke at length about dreams as predictors for his wife, his mother, and his grandmother. "Dreams tell the future, definitely," he said. "But in Pisa," where his wife came from, "dreams always mean the opposite of what they say. In the South," he went on, "dreams come from the Devil, so you have to be careful. You have to watch for the 'evil eye.'" The twinkle in *his* eye made it hard for me to discern how much he was kidding the American psychologist. He is the same person who said, with the same twinkle, "My father used to say that in America—I mean no disrespect—in America, you moved very quickly from a state of barbarism to a state of decadence, and in so doing, you passed over what here, in Italy, we call . . ."—here he paused as though searching for just the right word—"what we call . . . civilization." Talking about dreams was evidently part of what he meant by "civilization."

## Childhood Dreams

I do not come to dreams lightly, although I try to teach a kind of playfulness in working with them. When I was a child, many of my dreams frightened me enormously. I dreamed continuously of imagined Holocaust events, or so it seems to me in retrospect. During the daytime, in the early 1940s, my father—who worked for an organization called the Hebrew Immigration Aid Society, or HIAS—had early access to records of family members forced into various concentration camps, which ones were dead, which ones still alive. Tormented, he wanted desperately to travel back to Europe to rescue beloved sisters, brothers, aunts, uncles, cousins, friends. With equal desperation, my efforts were to keep him with us in America—alive and safe—even if staying meant his being beside himself and powerless with the impact of early knowledge of the growing nightmare in Europe.

    I remember some terrible evenings when he sat in black silence tearing at his clothes, covering his head in ashes, weeping bitterly, a letter in front of him on the kitchen table, telling of yet another murdered sister or brother. At night, I would awaken from terrible concentration camp dreams to make sure my father was asleep in the bed next to me, that he hadn't slipped away in the night to travel to Poland. I feared going back to sleep. I feared dreaming. If dreams were to protect sleep, I wished for neither. A few years later, when I slept in my own bed, I developed the habit of keeping a small radio under the covers right next to my ear. All night it played, drowning out dreams. But Holocaust dreams continued to slip through nonetheless. Murder, blood, horror beyond description. I visited, in my dreams, alleyway after alleyway in camp after camp as I ran after my father, seeing what he saw, as best a child could—every oven, every emaciated man and woman, every Nazi, every possible abomination and humiliation, every bloody crime against every Jew. I hated my dreams. I hated the night. I went to bed like a coward waiting for my next beating. And yet, while I tried to drown them out, to kill them, I felt nonetheless that it was my duty to dream them, to experience them, to remember them. It seemed the very least I could do to pay for the sheer luck of being an American child, alive, safe. So during the day, I played, studied, had crushes, had friends. I was good at stickball and skelly and ringalevio. I loved the piano and the boardwalk. During the night, I hid and ran and suffered and wept and bled with my dying relatives and my beloved tortured father in the camps in Poland.

Therefore, I came to dreams as an adult and as a psychoanalyst slowly and carefully. I had spent my life drowning them out, avoiding them, hating them, fearing them. I knew their power to bring pain and fear and horror. I did not approach them gladly or innocently. My interest, respect, and love of dreams have been most gradually developed. As an adult and as a psychoanalyst, I look back at the child in nightly torment and speak with him, in imagination, about better days to come. As an adult and as a psychoanalyst, I still dream of my father, long dead. I still try to comfort him. But I also have happier dreams of him, and of my son and my daughter, my wife and my granddaughter. It has been a long time since the radio was next to my ear. Now I listen to dreams all day long. Now I dream about dreaming itself at night, or at least about flying fish.

Dreams open to every conceivable human experience. The mind in sleep seems limitless in its range. It touches on every known emotion, activity, wish, fear, memory, anticipation. It opens the theater of time and space and, through its imaginative genius, shows itself capable of transporting the dreamer into every corner of the vast universe of human life. This potential for spacious range in the sleeping mind is of particular interest. Whether one dreams of the most minute details of a particular moment or of vast cosmic questions, the potential, in dreams, for spacious range is certain. We need go no further than to the realm of the manifest dream—the dream as dreamt—to observe its remarkable capacity for wide-ranging content, emotion, style, and activity. If we add to this the realm of latent meanings—the dream as interpreted—we enter a domain of limitless possibility. Our lives when we are awake are mostly contained by the finite nature of time, space, and physical reality. Our minds asleep, our "dream lives," open these limits enormously. As modern times seem to squeeze the soul out of much of life—many of us are too busy, too harrassed, too rushed—it is lovely that the experience of dreaming itself and a subsequent consideration of its many possible meanings can both open and expand a sense of spaciousness. All the more reason not to trap dreams into some preconceived and narrowed set of meanings.

## NOCTURNES

I take the title of these short essays on dreams and psychoanalysis, *Nocturnes,* from its meaning as "music created for the night—*Nachtmusik.*" The most well-known nocturnes are those short magical compositions created by Frédéric Chopin, which range from the simple, meditative, and peaceful to the passionate, always interlaced with a quality of yearning. These are among my favorite pieces of music for solitary listening. Their soulfulness speaks directly to the heart. The languages of art, sculpture, dance, theater, but especially the language of music, are well suited, I believe, to express some of the deepest and most private experiences that we struggle with in life as well as in psychoanalytic psychotherapy. Listening to and working with dreams is in the same realm.

Music, in the way it is shaped, sometimes takes on forms that seem identical to designs of thought and mind. This is perhaps clearest in Bach, but is also present in Sibelius and jazz and in Tibetan drumming and children's shaming songs. For those who are musically inclined, music and mind seem to share an architecture, also often made manifest in dreams. For me, they are linked in another way as well. My earliest and dearest wishes were those having to do with the desire to make music, to create music, to absorb and appreciate music deeply. Writing about dreams in this way is about as close as I can come to composing my own nocturnes. In this way, "infantile" or, more correctly, childhood and adolescent wishes are being partially fulfilled in this writing.

In addition, nocturnes refers not only to music, but also particularly to experiences of the night. It is in nighttime that dreams show themselves. They are fully creatures of the night and thus share with all other night life certain characteristics—notably, elusiveness, aversion to light, and an ability to see in the dark. The idea of "night" includes, for our purposes, the subjective experience of night, reproduced by the closing down of most of the external visual systems in going to sleep. But it also has relevance to ancient night, to a time before our species illuminated the night, to a time when our genes and brains were developing, to the earliest times when dreams were the only show in night town except for the stars and planets, the moon, lightning, fire. Night and the condition of closing one's eyes are closely related. The darkness thus created establishes one of the conditions for the creation and experience of dreams. Night is thus the medium for the dream as water is for the fish and air is for the bird. And so the detailed, careful, and imaginative study of nighttime as well as of sleep in the lives of our patients and ourselves can illuminate the context within which the dream shows itself.

I introduced this writing with references to nature, to music, to nighttime, to my earliest wishes, to my father and early fears of dreams, in part to invite the personal into our discussion. But there is a further purpose. If one of the functions of the dream is to open wide the possibilities of imagined living, and if psychoanalytic psychotherapy also functions to open the range of potential experience from the narrowed confines of neurotic functioning, then both dreams and psychoanalysis function along similar lines toward similar ends. This book is devoted to the opening of boundaries and the stretching of wings that is inherent in both dreams and psychoanalytic psychotherapy.

# ∽ 2 ∾

## WISHES AND DREAMS

*Oh how glad I am that no one, no one knows . . . . No one even suspects*
*that the dream is not nonsense but wish fulfillment.*
—Sigmund Freud

Sigmund Freud (1900) believed that in wish fulfillment, he had discovered a major motivating source of dreams. For the first half century following the publication of *The Interpretation of Dreams,* psychoanalysts linked wish fulfillment with dreams in every imaginable way. Although most contemporary neuroscientists and cognitive psychologists (e.g., Hobson, 1988) repudiated this hypothesis, particularly in its totalistic version, some are beginning to think that perhaps Freud had a good idea after all. As they chart the course of rapid eye movement (REM) events, a few now see the brain's involvement, during dreaming, with emotional and motivational pathways that could conceivably relate to the discharge of wishful impulses. Evidence from brain research, in today's climate, is often taken more seriously than evidence from the study of psychological experience. So maybe Freud did have something useful to say, some experts now begin to concede (Solms, 1999).

## WISHES AND DREAMS HAVE ALWAYS BEEN LINKED

But, outside of neurophysiology, in ordinary conversation, wishes and dreams have always been linked. She says, "My fondest dream is of a house with a porch and we two sitting and rocking together." He says, "If I could get into Cornell, that would be a dream come true." He says, "I dream of hitting the lottery." I ask, "Did you actually *dream* of hitting the lottery?" "No, no. I mean I want it." In our language, dream and wish are often synonymous.

But Freud had more in mind. He believed the wishes of childhood, particularly forbidden wishes, found their expression in dreams, if not in real life. But because it was a totalistic generalization (that all dreams are the fulfillment of repressed infantile sexual wishes) and because it was embedded in an emphatic theory, and especially because he emphasized the infantile sexual nature of the repressed wishes, the hypothesis became a lightning rod for criticism of Freud's view of dreams. But it was, and remains, a most interesting idea that dreams of adulthood reach back to childhood, back to long ago forbidden desires that still seek expression, and are allowed brief access to dreaming consciousness. The hypothesis implies, of course, that we never get over our early urges and that they continue to supply inspiration for our dreams, and for all of living. Also implied is that dream life is more suitable to such expression and partial gratification, whereas in waking life one is less able to achieve even such limited fulfillment.

Part of the brilliance of Freud is that he was able to hold to a grim realistic view of life and still see the possibilities for the experience of pleasure in diverse, complex, interesting ways, as in the artful compromises within the psychological symptoms of troubled persons, and as in dreams, taken to be the playground for experiences that cannot quite be fully realized in waking life. His grim realism is much preferred, in my own opinion, to the optimistic search for happiness in much New Age therapies. Although many in the middle and upper classes, here in the United States during much of the 20th century have had a relatively easy time of it, for most of recorded history, and even today for most of the world's population, life has been difficult, harsh, brutal, dangerous, arduous, frightening. Dreams, therefore, during difficult times, have often brightened and softened and been a glimpse of a better time.

Jung's (1933) notion of the compensatory and balancing aspect of dreams vis-à-vis waking life is also useful. For some, the nightmare of daily life can only cease in sleep and dreams. In dreams, wishes for a happier time and for moments of solace can be realized. The crippled can dance, the imprisoned can fly, dead loved ones can return to life, the old are young again, the soldier is home with family. Dreams can restore hope, lift mood, cause wonder. Dreams have provided for humans an extraordinary harvest of life other than the cares, toils, and sorrows of daily existence. My guess is that as life circumstances become more brutal, the wish-fulfilling aspect of dreams becomes more important, as compensation. Is it conceivable that the high degree of dysphoria in our dreams, in our culture, is in part an expression of the dream's capacity to show "the other side of life," to compensate for the "good life" enjoyed by many in our culture, to educate the soul about suffering?

Nowadays, most people who work with dreams think that dreams are motivated by a multiplicity of psychological forces in addition to wishes from infantile or adult life. Among the presumed uses of dreams are problem solving, memory consolidation, exploration of unknown possibilities, self-exploration, rehearsal, trauma healing, communication to the therapist, and so on. Freud would probably gather all these dream motivations under the broad rubric of "wish." After all, he did write that a wish to prove him wrong was the underlying wish of one patient's dream in which the manifest content seemed to contradict his theory (Freud, 1900). Thus, the wish-fulfillment theory was most broadly applied and could cover most all contingencies, including the central and significant wish to continue sleep in the presence of underlying excitation.

We could broaden the relation between wishes and dreams even further to include the wish to visit with dead loved ones, the wish to revisit one's past, the wish to see the future, the wish to learn, the wish to make connections and forge meanings, the wish to create scenes and stories, the wish to integrate parts of one's life. Hillman (1979) suggests an additional wish, the wish of the lonely inner being for the companionship of dream images. The possibilities are endless and imply that our dreams have meaning and that one part of their meaning is their capacity to fulfill wishes. This need not be their one and only function, because dreams may, in their inspiration, be as varied as all of life. But among their many inspirations, wish fulfillment, in both broad and narrow meanings, remains significant.

This psychological perspective is very different from the neuroscientist's view that dreams are brain events stimulated by brain events; that is, a dream is the brain at work. This outlook received enormous impetus from the ground-breaking REM discoveries nearly 50 years ago (Aserinsky and Kleitman, 1953) and has been part of a growing body of research and speculation ever since. There is no reason to dispute this conception. The brain does seem involved in all mental events. A walk in the woods is also a physiological–physical event: the knees moving, the lungs working, the eyes registering, the brain firing. But a walk in the woods is primarily, to most people, both other than and more than the sum of the physical events; it is largely a psychological event involving an experience and its meanings. And this, for psychoanalytic therapists, is the central area of study. The idea that the dream is a psychological experience within a psychological realm is not in inevitable combat with the neurological view, but there is no reason to relegate lived experience to the subordinate position of an epiphenomenon of the physiologic, as Hobson (1988) did so enthusiastically.

Our view is that the preconditions, experiences, and consequences of dream life do exist fully in the psychological realm and can be explored fully in psychological terms; they can be explored also in physical terms. It is certainly premature to attempt to translate one into the other. Better to have each illuminate the other. Better to have each generate hypotheses for the other. It seems strange to have to articulate such an old, obvious, and well-established point of view. But the contemporary domination of the materialistic-physicalistic realm in the study of human experience makes it necessary, once again, to emphasize the psychological.

In the current atmosphere, physical concepts and explanations dominate. The brain, genes, drugs—these are now in ascendance. Such a view corresponds with a political atmosphere in which the inner world is downgraded. Perhaps it is our comeuppance for the days earlier in the 20th century when the social and the psychological dominated within the ideologies of behaviorism, Marxism, and psychoanalysis.

Anything was possible. Nothing was beyond change. An interest in predetermined or causative physical patterns was equated with reactionary thinking as against the unbridled optimism of social and psychological causation, especially when coupled with the American Dream of endless possibility. Currently, New Age psychology, leaning on Hindu-Buddhist philosophy, has it that "the brain exists within the mind" or that "the universe is a creation of mind" as opposed to opinion in the scientific community, which has it that "the mind exists within the brain" or that "the mind is one grain of sand within the physical universe." Do we have to choose? I believe not. Both are intriguing, both illuminate ideas about the dream experience as well as about all of mental life.

## A BROADENING OF THE WISH-FULFILLMENT HYPOTHESIS

And so, to return, wishes and dreams may be related. Freud was predominantly interested in the role that wishes play in the psychological construction of dreams. I believe we can expand this correlation to distinguish wishes within the experience of having a dream, wishes in regard to the dream's aftereffects and consequences and, particularly, wishes in relation to the experience of telling a dream and of thinking about a dream with another person. In all of these, various kinds of wishes at various levels of awareness and with various significance may surround the experiences of dreaming and dream conversation.

For many, the mere experience of a dream is, in itself, fulfilling. This is not to say that all dreams are pleasant or enjoyable. Far from it. It has been reported that 75% to 80% of dreams are dysphoric in content or mood. When asked to explain this high number, in the face of Freud's hypothesis of wish fulfillment, one dream expert reported that dysphoric dreams are an exact reflection of the 75% to 80% of life that is dysphoric. This half-joking point of view may have its own merit.

It is not simply the pleasantness of dreams that fulfills the wish to dream and to recall them. It is, for many, the experience itself that is pleasurable and rewarding. No matter the content, for many, being in a dream, waking from within a dream, remembering or half remembering a dream, thinking about a dream, are all highly valued experiences. I have had more than one patient report that going to sleep involves wishing for dreams—and this before and apart from any therapeutic interest. Of course, once a patient realizes that I enjoy working with dreams, the wish to please or displease enters. I try to balance my own enthusiasm for dreams with the awareness that because only a very small portion of all dreams are recalled and reported, it is more natural to forget than to remember dreams. It may even be a kind of "perversion" to recall and discuss dreams; the "garbage hypothesis" of Crick and Mitchison (1983) implicitly entails this view. But Crick and Mitchison notwithstanding, some patients know I enjoy the perversion. And further, many patients think all analytic therapists want to work with dreams, an idea that has resulted from the decades during which an interest in dreams was to be found primarily in an analyst's office.

Some patients have, from childhood, treasured, recorded, thought about, worked over, their dreams. And for some, dreaming is a dreaded activity. In passing, a patient's general attitude toward dreams is an interesting, although often ignored, area for inquiry. The significance of one's relationship with one's own dreams, and more generally with one's own mind and its activities, cannot be overestimated, even though many contemporary therapies completely ignore this area.

In addition to one's feelings about dreams, there is the telling of the dream and the subsequent working on the dream with another person. Some wish not to tell their dreams to anyone. My sister-in-law, upon learning that I was to lecture on dreams near her hometown, mentioned that she would attend, and wished me well, but half-jokingly added that she wished we "shrinks" would "leave people's dreams alone!" She added: "They have taken everything from us. All our secrets. All our private pleasures. All our wacky stuff. But, please leave us our dreams! It's the last stuff we have!"

And so, some do not particularly derive pleasure in communicating and working on dreams. The deep personal privacy of dreams is their pleasure. But many do enjoy dream reporting. From early childhood on, there seems to be a motive to communicate one's dreams. The little child opens her eyes and says to Mommy with a giggle: *"Oh Daddy was talking to horsie and we were standing in the yard, high in the air, with all the horsies."* Or, in tears: *"Mommy! The monster came in the house and ate all the flowers!"* Mothers, usually, are the first "dream secretaries," listening to and remembering their children's early dreams—the earliest model for the analyst decades later. Throughout life, for many, the telling of dreams is akin to the most wonderful storytelling, except one need not create the story in the telling, one need only report the story that has already been created before one's sleeping eyes.

Of the many pleasures in psychotherapeutic work, engaging with dreams is among the very best. In this increasingly busy and complex modern life in which, unfortunately, more and more therapists work in back-to-back 45-minute hours, now harassed by managed care, and in which the possibilities for reflectiveness are severely reduced, it does the soul good to turn to the mysteries of the world of nighttime imagination.

The dream is an extraordinary work of nature. Flowering in the dark of night, and disappearing in the daylight back to its unknown origins. It leaves behind barely a trace, a wisp of mood or image. Or it can take possession and profoundly alter the day or an entire life. Such is this strange flower of the unconscious. To be trusted in the midst of our day's work with the occasionally remembered pieces of dream life emerging from the fevered brain of REM sleep in our patients is indeed a delight. Surprises, ambiguities, puzzles, streams of layered memory lit up like the aurora borealis, secrets, wishes, frightful ghost hauntings, ugliness and ordinariness and playfulness beyond measure—all of it lights up our work, like the dream itself illuminates the night.

Telling dreams and listening to them can gratify many wishes on many levels in both participants. For example, we often sense a patient's deep wish to have a dream paid attention to and appreciated. We can experience the listener's wish to be told stories, especially such original and entirely unique ones, akin to the wonder and delight of receiving Odysseus on his return from the ends of the earth bearing tales and sagas of wondrous, frightful, and mysterious adventure. And also we can imagine for both dreamer and listener the shared wish to discover meaning and coherence together in the midst of ambiguity, metaphor, and symbol, to experience together the creative workings of unconscious mind, to catch sight, at times, of the very architecture of mind. And along with all this, there is the wish to play together as we often can on the field of dreams.

Let us add to these pleasures, the experience of moving the therapy forward on the wings of a dream. The feeling, in analytic conversation, of giving into, submitting to, following the unwilled freedom of the sleeping mind at work, of allowing the unconscious mind to direct the proceedings, to point the conversation in *its* direction, is an experience I most highly recommend. The increasing push for goal-directed and concrete results provoked by the myriad of competing therapies, by the increasing popularity of drugs, and by the economic bullying of the insurance dominated healthcare system, all point in the direction of a call for oppositional contrariness. Such a character trait has always been important in creative psychoanalysis. In the ideal, psychoanalysis is not owned by the system, by the prevailing political, economic, social, or cultural trends. This originally "Jewish science" stands aside from the mainstream, the better to evaluate, understand, respond to major social forces as they impact on both patient and analyst. Our interest in what is not spoken, in "the shadow side," in Jung's term, in the defenses that turn us away from psychological pain, in conflict outside awareness, all of these are part of our contrary and oppositional interests. The concept of the *unconscious* is central in this project. That is, some of the deep pleasure in working with dreams derives from the very way one yields to the unconscious in the selection of therapy subject matter—oppositional and contrary to the dictates of the conscious mind, particularly in its social conditioning.

This yielding to the inner voice is, thus, of the essence in psycho-analysis. The fundamental rule of free-association for the patient, together with Freud's strong recommendation for the analyst to engage in "evenly hovering attention," advise the participants to let go of conscious judgment in determining what to talk and think about. Our current political interest in "consciousness raising" is replaced by an emphasis on "unconsciousness raising." And in this and other respects, dreams serve as a basic model for psychoanalytic and psychotherapeu-tic work and treatment. Both dreams and psychoanalysis involve "making connections in a safe place" (Hartmann, 1995).

### DREAMS CAN CHANGE THE TOPIC

No matter what is being talked about in therapy—for minutes, hours, weeks or months at a time—dreams will, more often than not, *change the subject.* They often seem to arrive from left field, with no apparent rhyme or reason, no connection or affiliation with any of the ongoing proceedings. They seem to follow their own logic, their own timetable, their own agenda, outside of the willed purposes of the dreamer. I believe this aspect of dreams is one of the most important for psychotherapy. If we are attentive to dreams and follow their stories with an open mind, we are almost always led into pathways that are quite different from those we have been following—a lovely way to correct for obsessional rigidities, for getting in a rut, and for the defensive safety of familiar territory. Also, of course, dreams will point in ways quite different from the preprogrammed therapeutic objectives of the managed care people.

For example, a patient and I have been talking for weeks about her resentment of her mother's infidelties as they connect with her own husband's philandering and her son's fickleness. They are untrustworthy, all of them. She vents, she rages, she sobs, she connects these again and again, but seems to be moving nowhere in her emotionally damaged condition. She is in a rut. Comments about our relationship in regard to trust are feeble and seem out of place—a therapist's ritual rather than a meaningful or helpful idea. Suddenly, as a postscript to a long and difficult dream, there is a snippet of Uncle Bill's farm. And we are instantly transported from infidelity, mother, husband, and son to Wisconsin 40 years ago—to cows, horses, cornfields, silos, barns, a kitchen table piled with ample food, and to a river in which the patient as a girl found herself and found her own, private, creative, imagining mind. Pouring out from the small dream fragment of *"a porch like the one I think was on my Uncle's farm house,"* was all the rich memory of a child's summer. I had not heard of Uncle Bill or his farm before. And I have no way of knowing if such memories would have found their place into our discussions in some other manner at some other time. But suddenly here was this dream, which led us to a prolonged consideration of her early and deep relationship with her own mind. Daydreaming and playing at the river, marking stones and placing them in the river for the next day's imaginings, naming the stones, watching sticks and leaves sail down the river, squinting her eyes so the light on the river became intoxicating, rubbing noses with the baby cows, tasting warm milk, dozing in her aunt's ample lap, playing games with her cousins—she was happier during these visits around age 8 than ever before. How could she have forgotten those visits?

The memories and their evident pleasure seemed so out of place with her current sense of victimization, just as her angry depression seemed so out of place with the wonderful child's mind that showed itself in reaction to this dream. She began to weigh these two opposite frames of mind. But, we also learned that she felt deeply disloyal because of these visits—disloyal to her home, her friends, her neighborhood, her parents, her siblings. The self-accusation of disloyalty had several other linkages to a number of experiences, mostly with girl-friends, with pets, and earlier, with dolls. The dream required no interpretation. The connection between feelings of pleasure and accompanying disloyalty, on the one hand, and her suffering at the hands of the disloyalty of others, was an interesting and fruitful one for us to think about together. Although this dream fragment led to memories and feelings that fit well and helped her open her mind in regard to her current preoccupations, the next dream, 2 weeks later, set us on another course, which fit not at all into current concerns, but rather opened a whole new window of observation. The pleasures of continual discovery, of new vistas, of deepening understanding, of surprises, all wait for the engagement with dreams.

## CONNECTING DREAMS AND DAYTIME THINKING

We often make great efforts to connect a dream with daytime activity, with themes previously developed in the therapy, with childhood experience, with early relationships, with the presenting problem, and so on. All of these activities can be relevant and helpful, as well as occasionally intellectually satisfying. In some, the connection of dream life with daytime life and with conscious concerns is crucial in developing and knitting together integrative processes in persons who feel disorganized, dissociated, unconnected to their own inner experience. Often, the connections between a dream and day life are obvious. And when they seem not to be, questions about day residues and associations to dream images both carry us quickly to daytime concerns. Thus, dreams can be translated and deconstructed to fit in with the known or the problematic. And both parties are often satisfied. The irrational fits in with the rational, the night with the day, the unconscious with the conscious.

But I believe, with Hillman (1979), we tend to make this translation of dream "stuff" into everyday conscious stuff a bit too quickly. It is often more enriching to go with a dream into its own territory, without too quickly turning it into a useful bit of therapy, or into what we presume are its daytime meanings. If a dream can be thought of as "a turning of the soil" of conscious thinking to expose the underside, the underearth, then perhaps it is mistaken too quickly to turn it back, without first living with the underearth—the colors, tastes, smells, the feeling of earth between the fingers, the tiny stones, substances, worms, bugs, shoots. If we turn it back over and pat it down to the familiar too quickly, we may miss the whole point of the dream, which might be to show us itself as it is, to show us sides of ourselves that are outside our usual awareness.

For example, a patient dreams of *driving slowly into the rear of an old VW bus*. We both chew on this dream for a while and fit it in to what we know, but something nags at us, until I ask for no apparent reason: "What did you see just as you were about to hit the VW?" I think I was drawing on my own experience just before a minor accident. Somewhat unexpectedly, there is a very specific memory of the next dream image, which helps as she reports seeing *the people inside, through the rear window, who are delighted and laugh at her and seem unaffected by the slight crash*. We go further and she identifies *two of the people and something about the particular laugh*. We go still further and she sees *what they are wearing, hears their laugh*, and we are launched into unforeseen territory in which these dream people remind her of dream people, just remembered, who have populated other dreams back to adolescence.

When we are careful not to translate these characters too quickly into aspects of the self, or of others known to her, or of the transference, we are taken still further into the nature and quality of these dream characters who, it seems, have a life of their own. As the patient reports aspects of these figures and their repeated appearance in her dreams, we are engaged in what could be called "staying with the image" in dream conversation. Thus, we are led into an unexpected realm that could easily have been closed to us, if we were too quick to translate this car accident dream into (a) her anger, (b) her destructive impulsivity and problems with psychological brakes, (c) her feelings about her earlier hippy life (the VW bus), (d) her feelings about the therapy and the therapist, (e) anal destructive preoccupations (rear-ending), (f) feelings about Germans (the VW), and so on. All of these may well be involved in the dream; all of these can, in the ideal, be woven together with her strange dream characters. But actually, the window opened by furthering an image inquiry and by not being satisfied with the summary dream description. This turned out to be a fortunate piece of work because the patient came to realize that she has, all this while, been living a separate life in her dreams, a life rich and mostly unknown to her. It was a mind-opening experience for this person, a meeting with the unconscious mind.

The pleasure in accompanying a person to such a meeting, the pleasure of helping introduce the unconscious, not as a concept but as a lived experience, cannot be overemphasized. For me, this is at the heart of an important wish of mine in my work as an analyst; its fulfillment is being able to follow a dream to an actual encounter with the unknown. But then, wish-fulfillment, in general, is a significant part of the experience of analytic work for myself, and I would guess, for many others.

Thus, while it is possible to debate with Freud's wish-fulfillment hypothesis as central to dream construction, I think he was correct in placing wishes and dreams in intimate proximity. And it is possible to extend his idea and to see that wishes may be involved, not only in the construction of a dream, but also in its experience, in its telling to another, and in its analysis. I understand that I am using "wish" in a more general way than did Freud in his hypothesis, but these kinds of wishes may be linked. I would like to add to them still another wish, a personal one—my wish that psychoanalysis reengage, theoretically and clinically, with dreams. This wish is a central motivating one for this book—a return to the dream.

# ca 3 so

# DREAMS FROM THE DAWN
# OF TIME

*If a man dreams of a particular spot in the river, he will fish there.*
—From dreams of the Temiar people of Malaysia

My personal wish to return to the dream in psychoanalysis requires us
to take a long look back. We need to consider the place of dreams in
psychoanalysis from the beginnings of their intimate engagement in
Vienna at the close of the 19th century, through the classical period, to
a gradual disengagement, until contemporary psychoanalysis has little
to say about dreams, preferring instead to shower its affectionate
interest on the therapeutic relationship. From a love of dreams to
relative disinterest, psychoanalysis has engaged in a stormy 100-year
love and hate story with dreams. Dreams arrived at the gate to the 20th
century on the wings of psychoanalysis and psychoanalysis arrived on
the wings of the dream. But dreams are now courted by others and
psychoanalysis acts as though it has better things to do. Although there
are many reasons for this change, I believe we are the poorer for our
disengagement with the mysteries of dreams, and I hope to bring us

one step closer to the spirit of the "old days" when the dream was, for psychoanalysis, a chariot to the underworld.

But the way dreams have fared in psychoanalysis is only part of a larger story of the way dreams have been regarded through history, from early civilization onward. Once, in many cultures, considered crucial for central aspects of living, dreams have fallen from an exalted position through the effects of the Enlightenment, the scientific revolution, the industrial revolution, and now, the postindustrial electronic age. In both the history of human thought and in the history of psychoanalysis, the dream once was considered central for knowledge, then declined in significance. Are these parallel developments related? Is it inevitable that dreams point the way and are then discarded? How did psychoanalysis come to oppose the general cultural attitude toward dreams at first, but then come more to mirror the general attitude? What is the complex relation between the contemporary age and dreams? Is there any value for psychoanalysis to renew its opposition to the general disregard for dreams?

For those of us engaged with dreams in analytic work, these questions serve as a background for our interest. We need not wait for the latest REM research to inquire into the relationship between psychoanalysis and dreams, between dreams and the cultural context, and between psychoanalysis and the contemporary cultural context. That is, an inquiry into the relationship between these three—dreams, psychoanalysis, and the social world—can inform and enliven our work. It can broaden our vision from a narrow and habitual preoccupation with the purported correlation between mother–baby nursery events and analytic consultation room events.

To begin to explore these questions, let us turn our attention much further back, to a consideration of dreams and their interpretation at the dawn of human history. Certainly our interest and work with dreams has a context in culture and history long before psychoanalysis made use of dreams in exploring and laying claim to the unconscious at the beginning of the 20th century. When we work with dreams, the dreamer sits in an ancient chair from which dreams were told to dream-knowers, and we analysts also sit in an ancient chair in which dream-knowers listened to dreams, both of us reliving a powerful relationship from earliest times. If we open our informed imagination, we can sense hope, fear, and expectation in the telling of dreams to the dream experts through the ages, now coming in our direction. We can imagine what has always been required of us: that we are well familiar with the world of dreams, that we simultaneously coexist in the underworld of dreams and in the visible world above, that we can move freely back and forth between these worlds, and that we are able to gather in the dream and to respond to it in the service of our discipline, our culture, and our dreamer. We can sense the ancient significance and the power of our task as dream-knowers. But also we can sense how small and unprepared we are in the modern relationship between dreamer and dream-listener as contrasted with those who came before. We need all the help we can get.

## DREAMS IN EARLY HUMAN HISTORY

When I teach about dreams to young psychoanalysts, I often invite, imaginatively speaking of course, their parents, grandparents, and great grandparents to the seminar table, because I think these forebears have a right to participate in our deliberations. I ask the students to identify their progenitors, the kind of work they did, their religion, the part of the world they come from, and so on. These students, after all, are the "dream come true" of their ancestors. Imagine how pleased many of the ancestors would be to see what had become of their descendents, these decent and hard working young men and women, professional people, gathered around a table studying, reading, thinking about and discussing human life and dreams and how to help people in serious trouble. If we are a dream come true of our distant forebears, the least we can do in return is to remember them and invite them to join us in talking about dream life. I understand that this may be a bit of a zany idea, but one that can help to begin to open our minds to the imaginative world of nighttime mental adventure. With the many generations in mind, we can begin to talk about dreams in early times.

These two ideas—that we sit in a large and ancient chair previously inhabited by all the dream-knowers from ancient times, and that we invite our ancestors to join us around the seminar table in learning about dreams—are two examples of the use of visual imagination that can carry significant information and that can be stimulated in analytic work with dreams. I believe we have unnecessarily abandoned this area of exploration, the fuller playful use of imagination, to Jungian analysts and to New Age practitioners. I see no reason to leave the field to these other dream workers. We can rediscover from Jung, his students, expressive psychologists, and New Agers the idea that in working with dreams, one enters the realm of complex play and imagination and that a capacity to go beyond linear rational conceptual thinking is required for part of the task.

Also required is some idea about the history of the human engagement with dreams, out of which the psychoanalytic tradition emerges. This history is highly speculative, as recorded history is only a few thousand years old as against the untold thousands of years of unrecorded experience. Yet, there are several good versions (e.g., Krippner, 1990; Rupprecht, 1990; Van de Castle, 1994). We learn of the significance and power of dreams and their interpretation in ancient Egypt, Greece, and Mesopotamia, in ancient India, China, and Tibet, from native populations in the Americas, from every corner of the world. Central to the birth of religions, and of philosophies of life, death, and rebirth, dreams and their interpretation weave through most all known civilizations. And for the rest, we again enter the realm of imagination. To approach an understanding of the role of dreams in early human history, we have to imagine a time in a world very different from ours. We need to pretend to gather around the fire to hear the story of dreams. Just as in dream seminars for psychoanalytic candidates, we need to call on our grandmothers and great grandfathers, on our ancestors and their ancestors, all the way back to the beginning of human time. We need to ask them about dreams. We need to ask them to help us imagine what dreams might have been for people before cities, before electricity, before night was diminished by our inventions, before mystery was diminished by our sciences, before modern life. What was it like to dream in the earliest days?

To create the setting, let us try to piece together what we know from reports of anthropologists, from recordings of dreams from early civilizations, from what REM science teaches, and from the use of our own imagination. First, the world of nighttime, in early human history, was much darker and quieter than in our contemporary world. There was often a moon, which moved and changed shape slowly as time passed. There was often a bright and abundant world of stars and planets that moved very slowly and were, for some, arranged in meaningful patterns. The night animals came out and sounded their sounds. In addition to moon and stars, the only light was an occasional comet, perhaps lightning, a rare volcanic eruption, perhaps a distant fire.

There was no rumbling from a subway underground or an elevator nearby. There was no television, no radio, no electricity—especially no electricity—no neon, no flashing signs. There were no 24-hour minimarts, no all-night shopping malls, no computers, no internet, no musical recordings, no books, no magazines with the latest commentary on the latest news, no Hollywood stars, no announcement of the latest stock prices. But there was a nighttime darkness that enveloped all, a vast and impenetrable darkness. In our modern night, when we close our eyes, we recreate some of the darkness of earliest life. And in that darkness, there was not much else but sleep. In the primeval darkness, there was the possibility that imagination ran free as sleep descended. Remember, no movies, no books, no television, no internet, just the stories of one's group, the culture's shapings of life's experience, and one's own sensations, one's thoughts, one's imaginings, until sleep. And then, dreams slowly moved in, at first something like the thoughts and imaginings before sleep, and then more and more creative until near morning when the dreams were most complex and dreamlike. So there was a progression from daytime, adaptive, survival-oriented thought and activities through the night to the deepest, most magical, most fantastical sleep imaginings lighting up the mind.

In ancient times, whoever we were—hunters, farmers, fishermen, children, teachers, warriors, wise old men and women, healers, fools, the sick, the stranger—we all, as far as we know, did not have much to distract from sleep in the darkness of night. In the light of day, one was awake and one performed the necessary tasks in the struggle for survival. Looking, seeing, thinking, planning, acting, worrying, feeling, anticipating, remembering, communicating, walking, hunting, farming, having sex, making war, all that was involved in living. But at night, mostly, one slept and dreamt. Also, there was more physical labor in ancient days, so physical rest and sleep were more necessary, rather than the restless sleep that follows from modern day work seated behind a desk, or in front of a computer. No wonder so many hours are spent by so many these days on exercise machines. An interesting piece of research suggests itself here: What is the relation between amount or kind of exercise and quantity, content, and quality of dreams, between the nature of work and dreams?

In today's world, in a night that has been diminished by our successful efforts to subdue, control, and dominate nature, sleep is only one of a menu full of activities that can occupy us at night. Whether or not we make full use of it, the menu is there in choices galore. But in this dark night within our imagination about the earliest of times, sleep is the major activity of the night with much less to compete with it. It seems obvious that dreams, in such a world, would take on far greater meaning and importance than in our contemporary situation in which sleep as an option is dwarfed by the multiple excitements available. Dreams, as the fruit of sleep, pale by comparison in today's world. Who cares what is dreamt by any solitary sleeper when the world is so crammed full of activity all around us? In ancient days, to continue with our story, the dreamer brought the dream outward to eagerly expectant others; the latest news from within had some import.

Perhaps in a world in which nature is not subdued, there are dangerous predators and other enemies that can emerge and threaten in the night. Perhaps dreams, in such a situation, keep the mental systems in gear so that if we awaken suddenly in some danger, we can, without delay, move into survival mode. For Freud, dreams participate in fulfilling a wish to sleep. Perhaps in early history, dreams participated in fulfilling a wish to sleep—but not too deeply, given the possibilities of life-threatening dangers from outside. For Freud, and in modern life in which nature has been "tamed," the dangers are thought to come more from within in the form of forbidden impulses. This relative safety is at the heart of Freud's dream theory in which the dream work modifies the dangerous latent impulse-thought, such that partial discharge takes place while preserving sleep. For early humans, the dangers may have come more from without in the form of predators, enemy warriors, storms, famine, and so on such that dreams may have had some relation to these real and external dangers quite different from the modern relation of dreams to internal states.

It is also possible that modern dreaming, like a vestigial tail, gives us the experience of early thinking, before the development of verbal-conceptual language—visual, imageful, less linear, more fluid, associational, emotional, more easily forgotten. If so, then what was the nature of early human dreaming? Direct and simple wish fulfillment of the sort Freud suggests for the dreams of preverbal children? Were these dreams rehearsals for danger? Did they connect old with new ways of hunting, farming, settling scores, gaining mates? Were they linking images with early verbal representations like a dictionary primer? Perhaps they were a prescientific exploration of hypotheses about the ways things work or were a prophetic view of the future. Perhaps they were the basis for early storytelling and mythmaking. Could they have been the repetition and relief of traumatic experience or maybe some entirely different and unknown mode of mind activity in sleep?

However we imagine our earliest ancestors in their dreaming, one hypothesis emerges. Their dreams probably meant more to them than ours do to us. Not only has the natural home of dreams, nighttime, been diminished, but in addition, we modern humans have access to so much external stimulation, so much information, so much diversion, so much passive entertainment, so much noise, so much to crowd out the dream, that it is a wonder that we can still pay some little attention to the dream's wisp of experience. Early human dreaming was probably of greater salience and greater significance in the lives and thoughts of our ancestors than in ours. I am also suggesting a correlation between the experienced importance of dreams and the nature of the external world, such that the more that nature is dominated and controlled, the less important is the dream in the psychological and social life of the dreamer. There are probably many intervening variables in such a correlation, for example, the quality and quantity of external stimulation, the nature of competing experiences, the social view of dreams in varying cultures, changes in the nature of night and sleep, the relationship between technology and self-initiated activity, the nature and sources of knowledge about the world including the self, and so on. On the whole, I am suggesting that people are connected more closely to their dreams in a world in which people live closer to their own bodies and their surround and in which dreams play a role in the development and maintenance of forms of knowledge.

I am assuming also that there is a positive relationship between the relative importance of dreams in early humans and in more contemporary, although fast disappearing, preindustrial and prescientific tribal, hunting, and farming cultures. Anthropological studies of such cultures (e.g., Kilborne, 1987; Krippner, 1990; Tedlock, 1992) suggest that dreams routinely occupy a far greater importance in daily life than experienced in our industrial and now postindustrial and electronic cultures. In these earlier developed societies, dreams were more likely to be thought about, talked about, lived out, dramatized, expressed, danced, brought into healing, religion, and ritual, than are our dreams. They informed and instructed, warned and advised, entertained and assisted, prophesied and explained. They were a feast, for such cultures, harvested from the night, a source of nourishment found in sleep.

Hunters used dreams to locate their prey, farmers to decide when and what to plant, warriors to find ways to defeat enemies, suitors to win their prize, healers to heal the sick, leaders to govern, and so on. And all of this is informed and shaped by the culture within which the dreaming is embedded. Simply put, we just don't think as much about dreams or allow them as much room in our lives as did both early and contemporary preindustrial humans. From this, it can be concluded that we are "asleep" in relation to dreams and their potential as revealed to our ancestors and to those who live in preindustrial cultures. Busy as can be with our extraordinary technology, we are small and alone with our dreams and hardly have a clue about how to live with them, or whether there is any longer a need to consider them at all.

In part, the relevance and importance that dreams held for ancient life has been replaced in modern life with knowledge gained through science and rational explanation rather than through the mysteries of dream experience. We no longer use our dreams to heal, to locate food, loved ones, or enemies, map unfamiliar territory, or anticipate the future. The Age of Enlightenment led us to a philosophy, a science, and a technology that replaced the magic and mysticism of the soul revealed in dreams. In a sense, knowlege of a certain kind replaced an ignorance of a certain kind that depended on dreams for information. Some students of the human condition would turn this last on its head and claim that ignorance of a certain kind (rational materialism) has replaced knowledge of a certain kind (practical and spiritual mysticism). Lost, however, in this gain of knowledge and predictable control of nature is the ancient and intimate affinity between the inner world of dreams, in which soul is revealed, and the exterior realm of real-world events. In other words, soul and world have become disconnected. Freud's effort, in a sense, was to bring these realms together again, to allow the ancient fascination with dreams into the modern world.

In psychoanalytic work with dreams, we return, if only for moments, to prehistory, to the earliest days, when dreams could be heard, when their message was not overshadowed by the enormous clatter of modern life, when they had their own power, when they had significant weight and consequence, when their experience and their message had an impact and made a difference in one's life. In psychoanalytic work with dreams, not only the dreamer, as Freud suggested, but the dreamer together with the analyst regress to an earlier time when dream talk was a major source of interest, inspiration, and education, when it mattered to dream and to inject life with the dream's import.

### IMPORTANT DISTINCTIONS IN DISCUSSING DREAMS

As dreams decline in importance in modern times, so do interpreters and their interpretations. To appreciate this decrease in significance, we must first distinguish carefully between dream and interpretation. There are four different aspects of a consideration of dreams that are often confused and must be separated. These are (a) dreams, (b) their effect, (c) their interpretation, and (d) the use made of dreams or of their interpretation. The conceptual confusion between these four, particularly in our field, has led to a considerable degree of misunderstanding and mistaken conclusions. It is not rare to hear an analyst report a dream interpretation, made by patient or analyst or both, as though it were the dream itself. And it is not rare to hear how useful for psychotherapy was a dream or its interpretation, as though its usefulness was in fact due to the dream or its interpretation rather than to other factors. Let us clarify.

First, there is the *dream*, that is, the actual experience of the dream—its images, its story, its details, as revealed in the sleeping state and more or less remembered on waking. Associations to the dream images together with related ideas are associations to the dream, linked musings, and connections; these are not the same as the dream, unless they occur within the dream itself. For example, *"I dreamt of a snake, and I knew in the dream that it reminded me of maleness."* Or, *"She was singing an aria from a Verdi opera and I reminded myself that Verdi means green."* These are examples of associations and linkages that occur within a dream and are, thus, in this stricter definition, part of the dream proper. Associations and related thoughts about the dream, developed subsequent to the dream's experience, are not part of the dream proper.

Analysts have found it advantageous to soften the boundary between dream and related musings. For instance, some believe all associations are part of the dream; some believe that an entire analytic session in which a dream is mentioned is part of the dream. This fuzziness of boundary brings more material into one's ideas about the dream; one then has more with which to work. In addition, such concepts are often rooted in ideas about the construction and deconstruction of a dream.

But I think it a good idea to maintain the distinction. A dream is a dream is a dream. All else may be connected to, but is not to be considered identical with, the dream. The dream, in the sense I am using the term, is the same as "the manifest dream," the dream as dreamt in the sleeper's consciousness, for which we have to accept the dream as remembered in the wakened state as the only extant version. The idea of the "latent dream," or the "real dream" below the disguise, or the associations and amplifications as the way to the real dream are all not the same as the dream and are not to be confused with the dream.

Second, there is the *effect of the dream*, primarily on the dreamer, but also, on occasion, on others. Dreams are often evocative; they give rise to powerful or subtle emotions, reflections, intentions, behaviors. The dream's effect is one of the more underemphasized, and in my opinion, one of the more important aspects of dreams. I am not discussing here the effect on the dreamer of a dream's interpretation, but of a dream itself.

> *She awoke from the dream of her dead husband in grief, pain, and tears, only to turn and find him fast asleep in the bed next to her. She was profoundly relieved and the day ahead of her was filled with a quiet happiness for what she possessed in her life.*

This is what I mean by the dream's effect or, better, aftereffect. Another example:

> *He told her his dream, in the interest of full honesty, with which they both prided themselves in their recent marriage. He reported he was sexually involved with a man and an old girlfriend, in this dream. She applauded his honest reportage but inwardly felt cold to him the rest of the day, worried that their marriage was on the rocks.*

Thus, the dream's effect on self and others is an important category for consideration.

Third, there is the *dream interpretation*. This is a vast area that, in its ancient form, will occupy us following these distinctions. Interpretation is at the center of Freud's work. *Interpretation* refers to ideas about the meanings of a dream, including hypotheses about the purposes of a dream. Because dreams are often ambiguous, confusing, disjointed, and not easily understood by the waking mind, they seem to call for clarification, explanation, elucidation. It seems entirely natural to attempt to transform a puzzling dream into a more coherent one. Ideas about symbols, hidden meanings, and hidden connections, advanced either by dreamer or by interpreter, are in the realm of interpretation and are not identical with the dream, no matter how good the fit seems or how helpful is the interpretation. In the Torah, the Pharoah's dream of seven fat cattle is not the same as the interpretation of 7 years of plenty. The point of view of the existentialist Boss (1958), which has gained increasing acceptance, is that the dream, in its manifest form, is in itself a significant experience that needs no translation. Joseph's dream that *his brothers' sheaves of wheat circle around and bow down to his erect sheaves of wheat* is very close to, but is not the same as, the interpretation in the form of a prophesy that the brothers will bow down to him. The image in a dream of the number zero is hardly the same as the interpretation that the dream is about the vagina, as concluded by several senior analysts at a recent dream workshop. This is not to disregard interpretations that have their own world of meanings; it is just that they are not the same as the dream itself. The interpretations can be dream-near or dream-distant, but they are meanings attributed to dreams and are not the same as the dream itself. Sometimes interpretations are made within a dream. As aforementioned, these are to be considered part of the dream and distinct from subsequent interpretation. This distinction between dream proper and interpretation will prove to be a significant one in our discussion of different ways to work with dreams.

Fourth, there are the *uses* to which a dream or interpretation are put. The Pharoah used Joseph's interpretation to change agricultural patterns in ancient Egypt such that the possibilities of a national famine with its attendant disasters could be avoided. In our own work, the potential uses of dreams are abundant for a host of usually unspoken purposes. We can use a dream to make a point, to work through old material, to find new paths, to subdue a patient's irritation, to show our "smarts," to assist in suppression, to direct attention to the transference, to suggest the use of the couch or chair, or to suggest additional sessions, or fee changes, or termination, and so on. A dream can be stupidly interpreted by a therapist, but the therapy is advanced; conversely, a dream can be well interpreted by a therapist, but the therapy founders. The way a dream is used is thus separable from the dream, itself, its direct aftereffect, and its interpretation. It would be convenient if a valid idea about a dream were highly correlated with its usefulness, but in the realm of psychotherapy, unfortunately, validity in interpretation is not identical with helpfulness or usefulness. In the best of all possible worlds, it certainly ought to be. But our field has in it plentiful evidence that wrong ideas, or fanciful notions, or untested speculation, or plain foolishness, is not necessarily a hindrance to persons being able to be helped by our procedures. People make due with whatever is at hand. Patients have the enduring capacity to use the best and the worst of what we offer in their efforts to alleviate psychological distress. A dumb idea strongly expressed may be more helpful than a good idea tentatively expressed and vice versa, all depending on the nature and needs of the particular patient. Thus, dreams and their interpretations are used in all sorts of ways in psychotherapy, and their uses and usefulness, therefore, need to be conceptually separate from other aspects of the dream.

## DREAM INTERPRETATION IN EARLY HUMAN HISTORY

Now that the distinction has been made between dreams and their interpretation, we begin to see how the realm of dream interpretation is as vast, varied, complex, and multidetermined as that of dreams themselves. These two, dream and interpretation, move hand in hand, like twins, like lovers, throughout history. The role of the dream interpreter is found throughout recorded time in almost every civilization. Whether called shaman, healer, elder, priest, magician, medicine man or woman, throughout the ancient and the preindustrial world, social organization has provided for the role of the interpreter of dreams. It need not be in the form of an actual person; it could be in the form of drawing, sculpture, dance, theater, and writing, such as the countless dream books that have translated dream images into meanings for entire populations. Although such books that contain dream images and their interpretation may seem foolish to the modern mind, it must be remembered that in more homogeneous cultures, certain dream images can be taken more easily to indicate certain common understandings and experiences. In our more heterogeneous situation, it may make more sense to request the dreamer's own thoughts about the dream *prior to* offering an interpretation.

Thus, the concept of the *latent dream* is not original to Freud, although its specifics may be. The latent dream is generally synonymous with the interpreted dream, that is, the meanings ascribed to the dream images, the underlying and hidden "truth" of the dream. It is no wonder that dream interpreters in ancient times were persons of considerable power, charisma, and influence. In a world before the contributions and authority of science, dreams may contain some of the most important information on the nature of life. Therefore, the "correct" interpretation of a dream is no small matter as it can conceivably lead to God, or to enlightenment, or to prophesy, or to life-saving healing, or to significant information on how to live safely or properly. In all of this, the dream interpreter is a cultural agent in that the private dream is translated by the interpreter into socially meaningful patterns. The dream's images and stories have woven into them, by the interpreter, the beliefs, customs, values, purposes, wishes, goals and philosophies of the broader community. This point is made most clearly in a recent scholarly work on dreams in the Buddhist tradition (Young, 1999).

As dreams have lost some of their earlier power, the dream interpreter has also lost power and influence. Science and modern times have replaced some of the authority of the dream to affect life, and have replaced the dream interpreter as well. I believe Freud was in between, a middle phase between the great tradition of the ancient dream interpreters and the modern REM scientist. The scientist, not the dream interpreter, now has the key to life in our times. In relation to dreams, the neuroscientists with their electronic ability to image our dreaming brains are currently in the ancient role of dream interpreter. They now tell us what our dreams "really" represent. In our times, the firing of neurons. In ancient times, the soul traveling or the gods instructing. New Age adherents are moving backward to embrace the more personally meaningful and helpful set of ideas. Scientists are moving forward to increasingly interesting physical ideas about dreams and the dream's near relative, consciousness. Can psychoanalysis integrate these two approaches?

The ancient importance of dreams and of the dream-knower has also been replaced in our culture by modern technology. I need only mention Hollywood as "the dream factory" to indicate the way the spirit of dreams in our times has been externalized and thus transformed from a private and individual experience to a social one. As recently documented (Gamwell, 2000), the earliest filmmakers were fascinated with dreams and consciously made an effort to depict dreams on film shown in darkened "public dream theaters." Certain questions come to mind in relation to this transformation of private dream to public dream theater: Have we been robbed of our private dreams? Are they less important to us because they have been drowned out and replaced by the enormous stimulation of movies, television, computer technology, and the internet, that borrows from the ways our own private dream experiences portray life on the internal screen? At the same time, is it possible that Hollywood returns to the dream experience, if not to the individual dream, the social nature of ancient dreaming, which became too privatized in modern times? Is it possible that the ways dreams once instructed and informed has been lost in modern life and is now being returned, but through the externalized, manufactured, and commercial art form and product of the external screen? Are films one way back to an earlier socially shared intimacy with our own dreams, or are they a further source of alienation?

Thus, the story of dreams in human life can be thought of as a found, and lost, and then found again process. Dreams and the dream interpreter were important in early individual and social history. In modern times, scientific knowledge and the control of nature led to a significant decrease in the importance, as well as in the social and spiritual cohesiveness, of dreams and their interpretation. But now, virtual dreams return on the external screen, restoring a social context, introducing social meaning into the private mind, as once the private mind yielded hidden meanings to the community. And where is psychoanalysis in all this?

# ∝ 4 ∞

# A STORY OF DREAMS AND PSYCHOANALYSIS

*. . . nor is there an interest alive in me in anything but the dream.*
—Sigmund Freud

Once upon a time, dreams and their interpretation were at the center, the very heart and soul of psychoanalysis. Freud (1932), in describing the place of the theory of dreams in psychoanalysis, wrote: "It occupies a special position in the history of psychoanalysis and marks a turning point; it was with it that analysis took the step from being a psychotherapeutic procedure to being a depth psychology." And, he continued: "the use of which decided who could become a follower of psychoanalysis and to whom it remained forever incomprehensible" (p. 7).

It is hardly possible for most of us today to realize or imagine the way dreams, in the early years of psychoanalysis, captured and held the ardent interest and enthusiastic devotion of our pioneers. It was inconceivable to think about psychoanalysis without thinking about dreams. From the central tool of his self-analysis, to the subject of Freud's favorite writing, dreams breathed life into our earliest efforts. Things have certainly changed dramatically, as we celebrate the 100th anniversary of the *Interpretation of Dreams* (Freud, 1900). Dreams are now hardly mentioned in our books, our papers, our meetings. When discussed at all, they are introduced briefly to elucidate some point in a particular therapy and, in general, have been crowded out and replaced by a myriad of other, more current, interests ranging from the intricacies of transference and countertransference, to the ethics of disclosure, to the politics of gender in the therapeutic relationship. Some might say that we have progressed considerably in expanding our range of interests. We have moved, it is proudly proclaimed, from a one-person psychology to a two-person psychology, even to a consideration of "the third." It certainly sounds like progress, arithmetically speaking. Many are proud of our "evolution"; they think we have grown from the passionate, although "misguided," "misinformed," poorly boundaried clinical efforts of our forebears, to the more complex, more sophisticated, although less passionate, clinical work of modern analysts. One idea frequently advanced about our forebears is that "of course, they made mistakes; they didn't know what we know." I think this idea is a conceit of modern times. We have certainly made many gains. But we may well have lost more than we won in the bargain.

I believe the turn away from dreams, in our theoretical and clinical work, has left us poorer, not richer. We are left deprived of a significant source of information about the creative workings of the unconscious mind, and we have removed ourselves from a central part of our heritage as psychoanalysts. It is not only the loss of a legacy and a tradition that matters. Of even greater significance is the loss of the underpinnings of the legacy in regard to dreams—the reasons why dreams and psychoanalysis were so deeply intertwined, the reasons why dreams and the unconscious were embedded within one another; we have lost what was once ours. Without dreams at the center of psychoanalysis, in my view, we are without a rudder, without a gyroscope, without a method of orienting ourselves within the unconscious. Without dreams at the center of psychoanalysis, we have turned back from being a "depth psychology" to being just another "psychotherapeutic procedure." The growth and development of ideas about transference, countertransference, and the therapeutic relationship are most valuable but are not sufficient to fill the vacuum left by our abandonment of dreams and the unconscious.

Nonetheless, dreams are of growing interest to large numbers of students. Bookstore shelves are packed with more new titles on dreams than at any time in the past. Jung's works and those of his students endure in popularity. The New Age interest in dreams and healing finds an expanding market. Shamanist, kabbalist, Buddhist and yogic philosophy, American Indian dream guides, feminist and ecologically informed thinking about dreams, dream groups based on the writings of Ullman (1988), all are finding eager adherents. Many dozens of web sites for the sharing of dreams grow daily. And science joins in as neuroscientists, cognitive psychologists, computer scientists, linguists, and others studying thinking and consciousness draw inspiration and hypotheses from 50 years of REM research and from the enduring mysteries of dreams. The Association for the Study of Dreams expands its activities each year; its high quality publications join together seemingly unlikely contributions from a wide and divergent array of participants, some from the science of dreams and some from the mystical. It is of interest that at the beginning of the new century, dreams are finding a large and growing body of students, in the midst of our increasingly materialist culture, in the center of the global market economy; all except for psychoanalysis.

Psychoanalysis remains relatively silent on the subject. Dreams are left for others. This is the psychoanalysis that, alone, ushered dreams into the cold, scientific, materialist 20th century, the same psychoanalysis that provided a warm home for dreams on the couches of its practitioners, the very psychoanalysis that saw, in dreams, a royal road to the unconscious, and the psychoanalysis that treasured dreams while other disciplines turned up their noses. This same psychoanalysis now has so little to say about dreams, while others press dreams to their bosoms. How come? What happened between the two old lovers—dreams and psychoanalysis—that they are barely on speaking terms, while increasingly looking elsewhere for inspiration? Is it that we have turned our back on dreams or has the dream turned its back on us? Like two old lovers, have we tired of each other? Did the spirit of dreams grow tired of the way psychoanalysis treated and mistreated dreams by imposing its theories in such a dogmatic and self-centered way, thus obliging it to move on to other, more respectful lovers? Have we, tired of the way dreams refused to yield to our designs, gone on to more malleable and agreeable interests?

If one begins to consider the question of our turn away from dreams, many influences show themselves: historic, cultural, economic, philosophical, psychological. For example, in the economic realm, who in this world of market-driven managed care disregard for the complexities of inner life can take the time to lean back and open one's mind and consider the enigmatic world of dreams? Who has the inclination to converse deeply about dreams, given the sort of once-weekly 45 minute, back-to-back sessions with increasingly troubled patients in which many analysts find themselves engaged? Are dreams and their interpretation in psychotherapy cost effective? Try informing a managed care clerk that the treatment relies, in part, on analytic work with dreams, and the utter disbelief on the other end of the telephone speaks volumes. Beyond economics, within the general culture there are forces that increasingly drown out interest in dreams and pull us away from the inner world and toward the fabulous doings on the external screen. But let us look within our own doings for a while. Let us consider the story of the relationship between dreams and psychoanalysis in order to understand some of the internal causes of our turn away from dreams, including our own, mostly unacknowledged ambivalence toward dreams and their interpretation—the love–hate story between dreams and psychoanalysis.

## In the Beginning

In the beginning of psychoanalysis was the dream. Earlier I wrote that dreams were ushered into the 20th century on the wings of psychoanalysis, and that psychoanalysis was born into the new century on the wings of dreams. These two were made for each other and began their relationship at just the right time—at the dawn of the 20th century. Dreams, the mostly visual, imageful, and dramatic reflections of sleep, could be thought of as the free associations of the mind without immediate regard for the concerns of daily survival. Without the checks and balances of ongoing sensory and perceptual feedback, without the world outside the mind imposing itself and requiring attention, the sleeping mind is free to range, safely but also boldly, through a rain forest of old and new connections. The rational mind is on holiday, and the dreaming mind, drawing inspiration from the unconscious, seems to go anywhere it wishes. Without conscious purpose or design, it roams about, within the safety of sleep, until it creates the scenes and the stories it alone requires for its own purposes. Hartmann (1995) called this aspect of dreams "making connections in a safe place."

And that exact function is to be found in the center of psychoanalysis, that is, making connections in a safe place. Dreams, themselves, thus, can be thought to be one of the inspirations for psychoanalysis. Moreover, within dreams in ancient life, one finds the beginnings and the models for many healing methods as well as for storytelling, theater, religion, and other essential social activities. It is interesting that in one of the most private experiences of human living (no witnesses, no audience, no actual other), we can find the origins of substantial aspects of social living. In this sense, the dream is seed for much of life; certainly, dreams are a crucial seed for psychoanalysis.

Dream interpretation goes even further, and alongside the dream, introduces each era's and each culture's deepest beliefs and all the ancient lore and wisdom of dream knowers from the beginning of time. All of this, the healing and creative functions of dreams, their ambiguity and puzzlement, along with the magic and lore of dream interpretation, all of this rag-tag collection of "refugees" from the four corners of the ancient world, stood quietly outside the doors to the 20th century, seeking entrance. But the 20th century would prove a formidable barrier to this ancient, slightly disreputable, crowd. They might seem musty, old, and harmless, but dreams could contain seeds of rebellion, oppositionalism, freedom of thought. Thus, in our story, the modern mind looked with suspicion and disdain, and also with fear, on all this ancient wisdom and foolishness.

## PSYCHOANALYSIS TO THE RESCUE

While looking for the secrets of nervous disorders, Sigmund Freud, a Talmudic Jew without the Talmud, a figure of the Age of Enlightenment from Vienna, began to analyze himself using dreams. This was not a particularly peculiar project. It was not unusual for Jews to analyze themselves. The religion is one of introspection, not only during the Days of Awe. And it was not peculiar for people to look into their dreams for understanding. It was known for some time that the irrational mind could assist the rational mind, and dreams were their meeting place. Freud used his dreams and his interpretations of their meaning to remember and to find himself, especially following his father's death. He certainly made extraordinary use of the assistance issuing from his own creative mind, from his own dreams and their associated ideas. Dreams and hysteria were interconnected and our infant science was launched. From a self-analysis using dreams to the *Interpretation of Dreams,* Freud (1900) pushed his new science of the unconscious forward into the 20th century. This is not just metaphor, because, as we know, he postdated his book from November 4, 1899, when it was actually published, to 1900, when it could claim to be a "newborn citizen" of the new century.

Thus did dreams and their interpretation enter modern times under the necessary cover and disguise of science. Under the white lab coat, all the ghosts and goblins of ancient superstition and folklore flooded into our colder, rational, and materialistic times. For decades, early in the 20th century, the couches of psychoanalysts became one of the few places where one could openly talk about nighttime visitations, which were there regarded with great interest, even love. We can all be proud that psychoanalysis performed this function as we marched into the relative soullessness of modern life. And psychoanalysis received from its devotion to dreams, a royal passage to the dynamic unconscious, a direct glimpse of our innermost psychological nature, of the shadow side of psyche. It was a most felicitous coupling; dreams and psychoanalysis in a Viennese waltz!

Not unlike the beginnings of other religious systems (e.g., Hindu, Buddhist, Christian, Moslem), we find dreams at the very foundation of our own psychoanalytic culture. Although psychoanalysis is a child of the Age of Enlightenment and of the scientific era, which has diminished religious belief, it followed the practice of religious systems by being established in part through the importance of dreams and their interpretation. Like Buddha and other great religious leaders (Young, 1999), Freud presented his dreams along with his interpretations to his followers, thus establishing his power and authority over the relation between the inner spiritual and the outer visible realms.

Self-analysis, undertaken by many in imitation of the master, was almost entirely dream analysis. One depended on the unconscious to select the material for one's own self understanding. Dreams along with free association to their images were the central tools. One did not usually spend years and years on a training analyst's couch. Dream self-analysis allowed followers a necessary independence while remaining tied to

Freud's earliest steps. As to analysis itself, it was almost impossible to conceive of conducting an analysis without dreams. This was particularly so because one of the early goals of the early analysts was simply an introduction, in one's own lived experience, to the powerful and mind-opening reality of the dynamic unconscious. Once this goal, this enlightenment, was achieved, one's eyes were opened to the true nature of things, one was changed forever, and for many the analysis was done. The patient was then free to go back into independent life with new eyes. These days, of course, we have more ambitious goals. Few of us, unfortunately, would be content with such an outcome. We find ourselves working on changing the nature of patients' relationships to all manner of persons and things, but not necessarily to their very own unconscious minds. And many of us aren't that interested in the unconscious in any event. We certainly no longer maintain the faith and the conviction that coming in contact with its ways, by itself, will lead to enlightenment and relief from mental disturbance. Merely a lived experience of the unconscious, as can issue from work with dreams, hardly seems worth the trouble.

Freud wrote that with an understanding of dream interpretation, one became a psychoanalyst. Analysts in the early decades took this most seriously. On vacations, over dinner, in conversations, on walks, in meetings, everywhere, analysts talked to each other about dreams, their own and those of their patients, family members, and friends. It was an exciting and an amazing tool for self-discovery. Psychoanalysts were on a heady voyage of discovery. On shipboard with Freud and Jung, they talked dreams, or in the Alps, or at a sidewalk cafe, or in conferences and congresses, or in an exchange of letters with a dear colleague; dreams, dreams, and more dreams. Analysts were a dreamy bunch at that time, living in a Garden of Eden of dreams.

Nowadays, most analysts do not tell each other their dreams. Perhaps we have gotten too self-conscious in our exile from Eden to show our naked minds to one another. Worries about boundaries, authority, self-disclosure, appropriateness, even liability—all this mix of modern puritan and market values have caused us shame and stilled our natural impulse to tell our dreams to one another. Our analytic ancestors were of a different inclination, a different time and place, and their intoxication with dreams flourished, but then came to slow end.

Aside from Jung's (e.g., 1974) monumental contributions to dream psychology, within the history of mainstream psychoanalysis, increasing interest in the transference and other aspects of the therapeutic relationship came to replace interest in the unconscious through dreams. Brenner (1969) and the Kris group (Waldhorn, 1967) downgraded dreams from the regal to a status equal to all other analyzable psychological phenomena. Ego psychology's interest in mental structure, object relations' interest in objects relating, and more recently, attachment theory's emphasis on all things developmental, all have contributed to the dream's being replaced from its early exalted place. Dreams, for their part are more inclusive. They can and do find room for most any point of view. Our theories and systems, however, are less generous. Further, REM research (e.g., Ellman and Antrobus, 1991) and other effective critiques of central aspects of Freud's dream theory (e.g., Grünbaum, 1984), played their role in diminishing interest in dreams in both theoretical and clinical psychoanalysis.

But there is more to our story. Within classical psychoanalysis itself, Freud's students were blinded by the master's brilliant ideas about dreams, and they followed what seemed a rote procedure in working with dreams. Because it was "known" that the disguise of the surface manifest dream would inevitably be deconstructed to reveal the gold contained in the deeper dream thoughts, the goal being the latent content that inevitably contained repressed infantile sexuality, the analyst listened to associations until they clicked with the necessary infantile wishes. Then, *voilà*, the dream was known. Such a procedure replaced mystery with certainty, ambiguity with knowingness, possibility with sureness. Freud's teaching on dreams as many layered, multidetermined, and impossible of yielding a clear and final knowing, a point of view in unacknowledged agreement with the Talmud's ancient teachings on dreams as containing many possibilities, did not disuade most analysts from transforming the rich and unknown complexities of dreams into the tight fit of Freud's own theoretical suit. Thus, the broad, happy, bustling, royal thoroughfare became transformed, through rigid ideology, to a narrow, rigid and predictable path. It is little wonder that interest waned.

Moreover, there was a certain rudeness exhibited toward dreams in the bad old days of psychoanalytic power. It was expected that dreams would be remembered. "Repression" would be the judgement if there were no dreams, "resistance" if there were too many or too long dreams. Dreams of appropriate length and in appropriate number were owed the analyst who became master of the dream. The patient supplied the dreams, the analyst, after hearing enough associations, supplied the interpretations, until the patient learned the game and could begin to do some of the work of interpretation. No wonder such an approach would eventually lead to less and less interest in dreams within psychoanalysis.

Further, beyond the clinical, in classical psychoanalytic thinking, the dream was downgraded compared to the presumed underlying theory of mind. At best, the dream was only the road to the main attraction. The interpretation therefore outweighed the dream itself in importance, again not unlike dream interpretation in religious tradition and in cultural indoctrination. The presumed latent ideas outweighed the manifest dream. The interpreter as a result was in a better position to understand the dream than the dreamer. Although seeming respectful, the associational approach could and did lead away from the dream itself and toward the ideas of the interpreter, because the interpreter did much of the weaving of the associations into the final product. Also, the dream was thought to be tricky, a disguise, an effort to "fool" dreamer and analyst through the brilliant efforts of the dream-work. In such a view, the dreamer's dreaming became antagonist to the analyst's efforts toward truth and knowledge of the unconscious.

Freud's use of associations, day residues, and other clinical material most usually led to the creation of a secondary dream alongside the original. It was to this secondary dream that attention was directed. This method may have some interesting advantages, but it also reflects a certain wariness, a distrust, even perhaps a dislike of the raw material of dreams and leads to a resulting disinclination to engage with the dreamer's own experience of the dream. Thus, dreams removed from the dreamer were placed closer to our own purposes, our theories, our designs, our needs, including of course our desire to move therapy along in good directions. Can it really be that removing dreams from the dreamer, taking possession of the dream ourselves, will advance the therapy? Only if we conceive of removing the therapy itself from the patient and bringing it closer to our own needs would it make any sense to act in the way we have toward dreams in the classical as well as in the more modern approach. Unfortunately, there is much in psychoanalytic practice old and new that seems to do just that.

## JUNG AND THE MODERN RELATIONALISTS

Jung is considered the great lover of dreams and his contributions to
our understanding of and work with dreams is monumental (Jung,
1974). It is certainly time for mainstream psychoanalysis to open to
Jungian teaching. No matter the complex reasons for the divorce from
Freud (Kerr, 1993), we are all the poorer for the relative ignorance
within psychoanalysis of Jung's ideas, especially about dreams, which
opened the mind and anticipated some of our more contemporary
views. Yet, like Freud, he developed a overarching view that molded
dreams to its grand thesis and also blinded most devoted followers to
other points of view. Jung's use of amplification of the dream's images,
like Freud's use of associations, could fit the interpreter's predilections
and needs. Both Freud and Jung, as clinicians, could be the most
sensitive of dream interpreters. But in their grand theory building
efforts, they and their followers could and did reduce the dream to fit
in with the needs of their theory. Again, as with Freud, Jung's efforts
with dreams bear similarity to the foundation of religion. In their
writings, both Freud and Jung urge openness, a capacity for surprise,
a willingness to suspend conclusion; but in the end, they can both seem
pushy and even bullying when they ultimately tell and inform a patient
about the meaning of a dream.

Dreams do not fare much better in modern interpersonal and
relational psychoanalysis. Beginning with Sullivan's (1953) own mis-
trust of dreams and of Freudian methods of interpretation, the early
interpersonalists, with the notable exception of Fromm (1951), had
difficulty with the unverifiable privacy of the products of mind in sleep.
A greater interest in relationship than mind, valuable as a correction
of the Freudian minimization of social and cultural forces in shaping
individual personality, and an emphasis on the therapeutic relationship, both led to an early devaluation of dream experience (Lippmann,
1996b). Fromm (1951), Tauber and Green (1959), Bonime (1962), Tauber
(1963), and Ullman (1978, 1988) rescued for the neoFreudian interpersonalists and culturalists the possibility of working meaningfully and
deeply with dreams. They joined Lewin (1955), Greenson (1970), and
others from the more classical approach in an effort to revive interest
in the dream. They opened technique, expanded hypotheses and
breathed new life into dream-work.

But, in general, and except for these notable exceptions, most modern interpersonalists and relationalists join the classical analysts in treating dreams poorly. We notice that dreams, partly because of their inherent ambiguity and unclarity relative to linear thought are open to meanings being read into them. Each culture in looking into dreams sees its own philosophy, its own concerns, its own needs. Like Narcissus at the pool, the dream interpreter looks into the dream and sees his own face. Each psychoanalytic point of view similarly, when looking into dreams, sees elements of its own theory of human nature. So that Freudians see repressed infantile sexual wishes; Jungians ancient archetypes; self-psychologists aspects of the self attempting cohesion; Winnicottians see play and transitional space; object relationists see objects relating; Lacanians see aspects of the real, the third, the law of the father, and so on.

Beyond theoretical specifics, most modern psychoanalysts tend to see in dreams aspects of the therapeutic relationship. In an almost exact replay of classical single-mindedness, the relationalists again and again interpret dreams to portray, to reveal, to locate, to discover aspects of the various goings-on between patient and analyst. This is not hard to do if you have a mind set in that direction. Just like it was not hard to see phallic objects, breast substitutes, symbols for sexual intercourse, and so on, in dreams, it is not too difficult to substitute or to read in the person or the spirit of the therapist for persons and objects that appear in dreams. This kind of single-mindedness, in interpretation, can reveal ideas and themes of interest. It can be therapeutically useful in the short run. But does that have anything at all to do with the dream itself? Not necessarily. It certainly has much to do with what is on the therapist's mind. And if only by suggestion, it may even eventually include what is on the patient's mind. Although what is on the interpreter's mind can, perhaps, interact in interesting ways with the dream itself to produce a discussion about deeper aspects of the patient's experience, it seems like an unnecessarily roundabout way of getting to interesting matters. The dream itself, after all, may contain information and direction that can be discovered by "staying with the dream's images" for awhile, before the potentially creative interaction between dream and interpreter takes place.

Let me be clear that a dream may well contain references to the therapist, both explicit ones, which are obvious, and implicit ones that can be fun to ferret out and discuss. I would be the first to admit that I have gone down this interpretive road more than once, and often to some profit. What I wish to question here is the modern tendency of therapists to make this virtually the sole avenue of inquiry.

The relationalists may indeed come to significant ideas about the patient's experience of the therapy, if that is what interests them, without pushing the matter quite so hard and without projecting into the dream their particular theoretic concerns. Such concerns may be more narcissistic than helpful. I know this is true with me. It may be that the history of psychoanalysis from the classical to the relational can be briefly summarized as the shift from prurience to narcissism, as we move from pushing our sexual theories to pushing our theories of the primary importance of our own role in the therapeutic relationship.

For example, a patient dreams of reading Faulkner while lying on a couch. The patient thinks of Faulkner's *As I Lay Dying*. The reporting analyst assumes that this dream contains death fears and wishes about the analyst who the day before the dream had cancelled a session because of a sore throat. The patient and analyst had a productive conversation following from this dream interpretation. Thus, the interpretation and its use in the therapy seemed to have been meaningful. But what does that have to do with the dream? We have no way of knowing. Could reading Faulkner while lying on a couch have had to do with other matters, even more salient ones? Our need to be in the middle of our patients' dreams may speak only to our own needs. Yet the repeated and tiresome injection of ourselves into our patient's dreams, until they cry "uncle" and get our drift, is entirely consistent with the psychoanalytic engagement with dreams from the beginning. Simply, we too often use them for our own purposes.

To be sure, such narcissistic engagement with dreams is not peculiar to psychoanalysis. All cultures read into dreams primarily what they need to for the purposes of the culture, which may or may not prove helpful or meaningful to the individual. But our field can do better. It promises that it is primarily concerned with the individual mind. Perhaps, we can re-engage with the dream and with a love of dreams that does not mask our own needs, that enters the dream with the patient "for the dream's sake."

At the very least, we need to acknowledge our ambivalence toward dreams, that our love is mixed with fear and hatred of dreams, of the

unknown, of the mysterious, of the unclear; in short, of the unconscious. We need to acknowledge that at times we project meanings into
dreams because we find it hard to sit with unknowingness and to submit
to our ignorance, especially at these prices. We need to acknowledge,
although trying so hard to "be better" than our patient's parents and
other victimizers that we too, often unbeknownst to ourselves, are
selfish, needful, self-involved and that often, with good intentions and
behind the manifest love of our patients, we are tending to ourselves,
our interests, our lives. This does not seem so awful or unusual, except
when we pretend to be better. Being curious about and honest about
dreams is not a bad place to start. Perhaps dreams and psychoanalysis
can come together again, but only if we regard dreams with the respect
due them and not twist them to our own purposes.

## ೞ 5 ೕ

# A NATURALIST APPROACH
# TO DREAMS

*Let us a little permit Nature to take her own way; she better understands her own affairs than we.*

—Michel de Montaigne

We have been considering dreams and psychoanalysis as two old lovers who have seen their best days together and have come to a parting of affections. Both find new partners elsewhere—dreams with as diverse a group as New Age mystics and technologically inspired neuroscientists, psychoanalysts with . . . well, with themselves, with transference and countertransference, with self-referential issues like whether to disclose or not to disclose, with whether 'tis better to hold to a one- or two-person model, and with our economic and managed care woes. Perhaps psychoanalysis was not the best kind of lover, after all; too selfish, too important, too involved with grand matters to treat dreams with the good manners, respect, and unhurried care due such an ancient creative form; perhaps, too concerned with not appearing lost at sea; perhaps intimidated by the grand and magical mantle of dream-knower;

perhaps feeling small and fraudulent in the ancient chair of dream-expert. We poor analysts are so removed from the ancient and prescientific traditions within which soul and dream were united in harmonious and cohesive systems of meaning that we had nothing else to hold onto but Freud's or Jung's grand schemes. And neither scheme left us feeling at all like dream-masters. We felt more like fakers, like a Wizard of Oz, hoping to get something right, praying not to come up empty.

I suppose from this point of view, it is just as well that psychoanalysis and dreams have gone their separate ways. Or, that dreams have had enough of our pretense, our bad manners and egocentric "love" and have gone on to other suitors. We may need to learn better how to care about dreams, for their own sake, before we become reacquainted.

In such a project of reunion, a return to history can help. There is a growing literature on ancient dreams and their interpretation. Flowing through most every age and every culture, there are old ideas, philosophies, and folklore that can illuminate aspects of the central mystery of dream consciousness. Through the prism of the diverse physical, geographic, and social worlds through which humans have traveled, dreams are revealed in all their multiplicity of colors and possibilities. Freud (1900) devoted only eight paragraphs on four pages (pp. 2–5), at the very beginning of chapter 1 of *The Interpretation of Dreams,* to a summary of the prescientific view of dreams. Freud was clearly attempting to establish his scientific credentials without an explicit mining of the rich, ancient knowledge and lore of dreams. Jung was much more respectful of the culturally derived meanings and uses of dreams through the ages. In this, we need to throw in our lot with Jung and depart from Freud. We need to immerse ourselves in the way ancient peoples viewed and lived with dreams as background and inspiraton for our own efforts. Some of this growing literature can be found in such diverse sources as Dee (1984), Krippner (1990), Rupprecht (1990), Hall (1991), Tedlock (1992), Bulkeley (1994), Stevens (1995), and Young (1999).

There is also a great deal to learn from the contemporary neuroscientists and their breathtaking brain-imaging technology. The relation between the brain's lighting-up patterns and the nightly experience of dreaming is extraordinary and can provide a harvest of ways of thinking about dreams that opens our minds beyond the narrow confines of ideas with which we have become familiar. Do silent harmonious vibrations deep in the individual brain initiate the process that becomes our remarkable nighttime journeys that can change a life or give birth to a great religion? What has all this to do with the great problem of consciousness? And what does it mean for our patients to learn from popularized REM research, if not from their analysts, that we have REM dreams for 2 hours each night but may think in REM and non-REM states all night long, that forgetting of dreams is the norm, that muscle inhibition is necessary for the sort of brain fire storms that emerge during dreaming, that most all mammals have REM states, that human neonates have REM states much of the time, and so on?

Both the mystical ancients and the electronic moderns are trying to tell us a thing or two about dreams. Our imagery about dreams can be stimulated and opened by coming in contact with Talmudic, Buddhist, Hindu, Moslem, ancient Greek, Ashanti, ancient Siberian, ancient Chinese, American Indian, ancient Egyptian as well as with fin-de-siècle Jewish-Viennese and Swiss-Christian teachings and images. And our imagery about dreams can be stimulated and opened by REM and brain studies. We are probably in an excellent position to begin to rethink and open our minds about dreams in clinical work now that Freud's dominating brilliance is open to question and has loosened its hold on our thinking. Actually, in many younger analysts and candidates in training, I find evidence of a new attitude of openmindedness, flexibility, and playfulness that can more easily accommodate an appreciaton of layered multiplicities in dreams. The old doctrinaire ways with dreams may be disappearing in our next generation.

## A Naturalist's Approach

It is an interesting moment in clinical work when dream and analyst meet. Although we have considered some aspects of the relationship from a general point of view, we have not attended to the particular and the personal. What happens when dream and analyst meet? Without the benefit of ancient traditions and beliefs within which dreams, dream experts, and dream meanings existed together in relative ease and familiarity, when we moderns listen to a dream, we often begin from a position of estrangement. This is not true for all of us. Individual differences are, as always, extremely important. Individual differences in the dream and in the analyst in relation to the dream both play an important role in determining how a dream is heard.

First, let us approach the dream. Let us see what is its variety, its range, its nature, its effect. Let us begin this more as naturalists than as analysts—because analysts, unfortunately, are hard-pressed to have to seem to know. And this trait could get in the way of a more simple mode of looking and noticing. At this point, we are on a search for the variety of kinds of dreams. The hypothesis is that we will discover that there are as many kinds of dreams as there are kinds of thought. Freud stressed wish fulfillment and repressed childhood sexual impulses, whereas Jung stressed archetypes and ancient collective images, and these theoretical constructs are advanced to organize, create coherence, and give meaning to the enormously varied experiences, contents, and types of dreams. We need to back away from such overarching schemas and take in dreams like a naturalist on a field trip. And this means, first of all, noticing, perhaps cataloguing, their great, almost infinite, variety. Outside of psychoanalysis, this effort is well underway (e.g., Hall and Van de Castle, 1966).

## DREAM LENGTH

If we look at dreams directly and not through the interpretive prism, we can make an additional number of initial observations. Some dreams are very short and some long. A dream could consist of *"a musical sound, something like a cello note, brief, deep, echoing, gone."* A dream could consist of *"he laughed,"* or *"a color, a bit of blue."* It could be *a word* or even *a single letter or number.* I know of a patient who well on her way to the safety of psychological invisibility dreamt of herself as *"a small dot on a large canvas."* Or a dream could even be *"nothing."* It is quite different to meet up with one of these as opposed to a dream that is typed, single spaced, four and one-half pages, complex, many charactered, and semi-interpreted that flows through ages and traumas and philosophies, all in intense confusion and ambiguity. Some of us would prefer the one and some the other. Some of the brief ones never leave us. Some of the long ones too. I often prefer short ones. Fragments. Pieces of a dream. I know there is a yearning to get the whole dream as dreamt, because therein dwells the full experience including, at times, a conviction of understanding and sense, and anything less renders the full meaning out. But, still I prefer the broken ones that play hide and seek. Some of it shown, some of it lost. And we are left with the broken part to see what it can show. The pleasures of archeology, I suppose. Our reactions to short dreams can be of interest. Do we feel cheated? Is something being withheld from us? Is the brokenness a sign of the condition of the patient's mind or spirit or heart or soul? Is hide and seek, showing a bit and forgetting most, the way a dream preserves its citizenship in the shadowland of unconscious thought? Is the broken dream a mirror of how the patient unconsciously experiences our participation in their lives—we hide and show? Is the small piece of a dream as much as the patient feels we can digest at once, because they may not wish to overwhelm us too soon?

The long, long ones, typed or not, slowly spoken, so that half the analytic hour is over, or breathlessly pushed out in a few minutes of cyclonic power, these long and often complex dreams sometimes do overwhelm, especially if the analyst's need is to lay bare some central meaning. Being overwhelmed by a patient's dream can be uncomfortable, like being overfed or overstimulated. The experience can easily lead to an interpretation or accusation that resistance is at work, which is to say we don't like these long and complex dreams. But, being overwhelmed need not be such a bad thing if we can notice, tolerate, and learn from the experience of overwhelmedness. Sometimes, this feeling is close to the heart of the patient's experience with us and others or with their own mind. This last possibility is especially interesting. If we can permit ourselves not to take things too personally, we sometimes realize that patients are showing, usually without awareness, how things are going between their own mind (or psyche or soul) and themselves. A long, confusing, and overwrought epic of a dream is often a signal that mind is overwrought. This is not quite the same as reaching the conclusion and then interpreting a confusing epic of a dream as "an effort to flood or confuse or defeat the therapist or the therapy." We need not automatically put ourselves in the middle of things. We can be content if the dream can show us something of what it feels like for the patient. Within the relationship, moreover, sometimes such a dream can be a great overflowing gift, sometimes a nasty challenge, sometimes like love, sometimes like feces. It is often helpful if we can allow the long dream to overflow our experience. We can submit to its ongoingness and allow it to show us whatever it will in its extensiveness—a continent of meanings. Some analysts are thin, weak, and delicate at heart and fear flooding will force their own minds away. Some are sturdier in spirit and can allow a big, complex, and difficult "Mama of a dream" to take up all the room it needs.

For the purposes of good dream conversation—my goal in all of this—it is not necessary to comment on or touch on every moment in a long dream. It is possible to take only a little piece, here or there. Or, it is possible to embrace the whole experience, as in, "My, what a big one!" Or, with wonder and even a touch of awe, as in, "Have you always dreamt like this?" Or, "Where would you care to begin? Or, "Let's take a breather for a moment. It was a marathon! Do you like these giant dreams?" Or, "I think the dream is like an odyssey. Your night of Homer. It touches on most everything we've ever talked about and more. How did you feel when you woke up, or as you were telling it?" Or simply, "What is it like to tell such a dream?"

However we begin, we end up thinking together about some piece of a great white whale of a dream. Freud's recommendation of starting at the beginning and asking for associations, piece by piece, is a good one. Then again, it is equally good if one can start anywhere and end as one will. What comes to mind as an approach to dreams is the attitude expressed by Henry Miller in the subtitle of a wonderful book on his watercolors, *Paint as You Like and Die Happy* (Young, 1960). Most often, the patient will indicate where to look and where to begin. For example, tucked away in a remote corner of a patient's immense dream was an image of a long-dead aunt who had CP. I thought briefly about these initials. I thought of the Communist Party, the CP of my youth. It is fun to think with your mouth shut and even sometimes aloud. Luckily, this time I kept my CP to myself. Because the patient lit up when she, herself, commented, "CP. Cerebral palsy. That's you." I didn't get it until she explained in peals of laughter, "You know, you Paulsy—you think too much—you're cerebral Paulsy." The immense dream was transformed by her interpretation and her commentary into her very own imitation of my occasional overcerebral offenses. We were now equally cerebral, she a bit more happily because she could at least name the thinking style. There was yet more talking to do about the connection between her view of me and her CP aunt, but mostly, the enormous dream collapsed into two initials, which then expanded into an exploration of ways of thinking, hers and mine. For a woman who had never thought her mind worth a damn, this was good news.

Short dreams or fragments have the capacity to expand enormously, and long dream epics have the capacity to contract into a single idea. This mobility, plasticity, fluidity, and flexibility of dreams as they alter within conversation mitigates against simplistically thinking their initial form or presentation is all there is. Just get going and things soon change, unless the dreamer and the analyst both require stasis. For me, the latent dream is this fluid contraction–expansion tidal experience that accompanies good dream conversation. Freud and Jung had different ways of expanding a dream and then contracting their expansion into singular and significant ideas. The concept of *condensation,* itself, consists of ideas about contraction and expansion of dream experience. Like mind itself, dreams and their consequences occupy space in interesting and mobile ways. Motion is at the center.

Thus, length of dream—short and long—is the first dimension we notice after variety. Of course, this dimension concerns dreams as remembered and reported, not necessarily as dreamt. Some researchers on dreams have made much of this significant distinction, but for now, let us be content with not worrying about this problem. Also, in discussing length of dreams in terms of extremes—shortish fragments, longish epics—I am leaving out most dreams that are middling in length. But it is fun to think about things like a long dream meets a short analyst, or a long analyst meets a short dream, and so on. I recall one very short supervisee, a bright young psychiatrist who stood well under 5 feet tall, who kept reporting on his taller female patient's very long, long dreams. When he was finally relaxed enough with his patient to mention this size issue (including his shortness, her tallness, and the dreams' length) the patient told him with relieved laughter that she didn't realize she was dreaming that way but was happy he finally "got it." And so they could finally talk together about height, which turned out to be the previously unmentionable "elephant" in the room. Patients will try in every way imaginable to bring to attention what is unmentionable. This example illustrates the way ideas that are uncomfortable and are therefore kept in the unconscious (or preconscious) realm of the relationship sometimes gain mention through dream form and structure, and not only in content. Size of dream, size of dreamer, and size of dream interpreter can interact in many ways outside of usual awareness. Years back, I worked with a starving anorectic young man who had the biggest dreams imaginable. And I recall a most overweight man who came up with teeny bits of dreams. Of course, I don't mean to suggest a necessary correlation, except in the individuals mentioned. It turned out to be enjoyable and relieving and seemed to open our minds for us to consider dream size and body size in some compensatory relationship.

Dream length or size as a focus of observation and information can also lead to considerations of patterns of dream length and size. One patient after 2 weeks of epic dreaming reported no dreams for the next month, as though she was emptied of dreams by the sheer amount of excess. This pattern was repeated for over a year; many long dreams followed by a lengthy silence. We enjoyed observing the pattern, commented on the way this pattern was similar to her sexual and work life, but never achieved a singular understanding other than a growing familiarity with her own ways, with her own mind—often a most important part of analytic therapy. In another therapy, a long period of no dream reports was followed by a tiny piece of a dream, then in the next weeks other tiny pieces, until an explosion of hugely complex dreams. Sometimes the forms can provide hypotheses (e.g., the relation between dreaming, creative bursts, activity patterns, and bowel movements), but mostly, "just" an awareness of one's own forms, one's styles, one's structures, one's ways, one's architecture of mind, is greatly beneficial to some patients. As we get older, we usually get to know ourselves and our ways better. Therapy often moves this process along and dreams can provide useful road signs along the way.

## DREAM CLARITY VERSUS CONFUSION

Let us leave dream length to consider other dimensions, still without touching too heavily on interpretation. Some dreams seem clear to dreamer and interpreter. They are straightforward and connect simply with day's events, or life's concerns, or therapy's movements. Some dreams are infinitely puzzling, confusing, ambiguous, unclear. Some clear dreams, when pursued, open into confusion. Some confusing dreams when pursued move into clarity. One's reaction (both dreamer and listener) to the dimension of clarity versus confusion is itself of interest. Further, some dreams seem open and relatively innocent of contradictions and confusions, others concealed, disguised, cooking up surprises under the surface of the story or the images. One dreamer *dreamt of riding a show horse and feeling proud, free and happy in an activity that had been a very important part of her preadolescent girlhood.* It appeared a clear dream, a clear aftereffect. But, following a consideration of the dream's pleasurable effects and its relation to newfound confidence and ability in her current life, a subsequent question about the identity of the particular horse opened onto traumatic territory—a runaway horse, a fall, terror, an injury. She was shaken by the half-forgotten, panic-filled memories. Although we considered that the dream involved some mastery efforts, her shakiness, increased by our discussion of the horse, continued for some time. Would we have done better to leave the dream alone, in its clear and innocent pleasure? We so often need to justify our efforts that it is possible to rationalize that unearthing the underlying shakiness was to the good because it called for additional work to build a more genuine confidence, but I don't really think so. I think this person, in this instance, would have been better off without an inquiry into associations, with just the simple and clear dream experience accepted and appreciated by us both.

In any event, some dreams, in their manifest form, seem clear as day, others murky, illogical, incapable of making sense. Freud (1900) attempted an explanation involving the nature and success of the censorship, of the dream work, of secondary revision to account for the lack of clarity. Hobson (1988), however, had no difficulty with this dimension and thus no need for Freud's explanation. Because the brain is operating with specific deficiencies in sleep, dreams will of necessity tend to be unclear, illogical, irrational. According to Hobson, the brain is simply trying to do the best job it can with limited capacity and limited input. But, in my opinion, differences between seemingly clear and seemingly confused dreams remain unexplained by Freud or Hobson. Bert States (1997) comes closer to a satisfactory if playful hypothesis in his reference to the old Chinese encyclopedia, in which words were catagorized by highly personal connections (e.g., canoe with Uncle Po with rainy days) such that entire systems of thought would collide in apparent zaniness but with underlying highly personal networks of meaning. Our lack of completely satisfactory explanation, however, leaves us turning our interest, for now, more to the dream's effects, mostly on the dreamer, but also on the interpreter and on their interaction. This psychological and social realm of interest does not depend on Freud or Hobson, but depends on an interest in naturalist observation and question. How do people feel about dreams that are more or less open versus disguised, clear versus confusing, simple versus complex?

Some, dreamer and interpreter alike, hate confusion in dreams and elsewhere. Some find comfort only in innocence and clarity. Others are suspicious of things that are too easily clear, and love to work their way through the difficult and the hidden, like detectives. Some interpreters are fearful of complex confusion that doesn't bend easily to an association or two. Some turn away from things that seem too obvious, some from dreams that puzzle. So dreams, in this dimension, task both dreamer and therapist. How will they react to what is clear, how will they react to what is unclear? Do dreams turn into a test for the patient? An aspect that is even more fun, although also trying is: How do ambiguous, confusing, illogically connected dreams impact on the "expert"? And what does a patient make of how the expert comports him or herself in the face of confusion? Can confusion be acknowledged, or must it be hidden? Can unknowingness survive between the two, or must it be vanquished for the sake of both? Does trust and hope in the dialogue, in our methods, in our analysis, help in the face of ignorance? And what of confusion itself? Of what does it remind both participants? When has it hurt, when helped? What does it look and feel like in oneself and others? The life of confusion, unknowingness, and ignorance, in itself, is extremely important, in my opinion, and deserves some consideration in most therapy. Isn't the idea and fact and fear of death for us living people, for example, embedded but also mercifully concealed in unknowingness? Furthermore, the experience of confusion in regard to dreams implies that a central and explanatory set of meanings is possible in order to dispell ambiguity. But what if clarity of meaning is not necessarily the point? What if there are other things to consider beside some more or less "correct" interpretation?

## DREAM'S EFFECT

For example, what is the dream's effect? This question might be as or even more important than the question of interpretation that has so bedeviled and preoccupied most dream discussion in our field. Dreams can leave the dreamer happy, sad, unmoved, profoundly puzzled, delighted, or feeling lost or found. Dreams can make people think, or lead to a vigorous rejection of thinking. Some dreams lead to action, some to an inability to get out of bed. Some dreams excite and lead to sexual activity, some lead directly to abstention from sex. For example, a man dreams of homosexual sex and for months thereafter won't initiate sex with his girlfriend for fear he will reveal the forbidden content of his dream. Or, a woman dreams of arousal with the neighbor's oldest son and turns to her husband for middle-of-the-night sex. He doesn't know what hit him, but is glad to "get lucky" any way, any time. Some dreams initiate heart attacks and other physical calamities, some instruct and lead to healthier behaviors. For example, a man who dreamed he had resumed smoking was so glad when he woke to realize he hadn't that he was fortified against the habit for the next months.

Dreams can affect one's mood and attitude for part or all of a day. Without necessarily recalling any of one's dreams, one can awaken crabby or optimistic, fearful or confident. This effect of dreams may be one of its central characteristics, but we often rush past it to the centrality of meaning. Perhaps the dream's effect is its central meaning. The effects of a dream on those told the dream, particularly the interpreter, is also of importance to us. How did the dream leave you, interpreter? Resigned? Pleased? Confused? Tested? Relieved? Sleepy? Thoughtful? In your own memories? In the memories of your patient? Hoping for the session's end? Hoping for all the time in the world? Sometimes just having the two participants converse about the dream's effect on both can be refreshing, interesting, lively, without once referring to interpretation.

## A VARIETY OF VARIETIES

Further, some dreams seem directly related to the life of the dreamer and some straight out of left field. Some have punch and some aimlessly wander about for a bit and then fade out. Some contain feelings that take hold of dreamer and listener and shake them both, or hurt them, or insult them, or shame them, or delight them, or excite them. Some leave us all alone to feel whatever we feel, including nothing at all. Some dreams seem very shy, entering the proceedings with careful tentativeness, a word or two, uncertainty, blushing, and vagueness. Some enter boldly, grabbing the spotlight, all the room, all the attention. Some are remembered with bright clarity, some run and hide from memory in the very act of being recalled. Some bring fun, play, and laughter, others misery, pain, tearfulness, anguish. Some exude anxiety through all pores, including searing nightmarishness; some feel relaxed, easygoing, tranquil.

Thus are the variety of varieties of dream as they meet up with analyst. This listing is of course only a small portion of the boundless kinds of dreams we encounter, each affecting the participants differently, each bringing a different shade to the proceedings, and these considerations bear on the varieties of dreams that are recalled, in whole or part, sufficiently to be reported to the interpreter. What of the variety of dreams that remain recalled but unreported? These are dreams and fragments that are not deemed worthy of report, or are withheld because of what they reveal in their manifest form, that is, forbidden experiences or ideas and feelings, shameful or painful for a patient to reveal about one's self. She doesn't report, "I dreamed I was a slut and showing my privates to you." Also withheld are those that may be difficult for analyst or for the patient–analyst couple to have in awareness. She also doesn't report, "And I think you were turned on." There are also those that are withheld not because of their manifest form but for their potential latent meanings, that is, because of unconscious withholding or repression. This is an old-fashioned kind of unreporting. But beyond these, what of the enormous variety of dreams, perhaps 95% of dreams, that are just not recalled at all on awakening? These are clearly the vast majority of our dreams and there may be some adaptive function in this majority occurrence. How does it affect us—dreamer and interpreter alike—that dreams are not mainly meant for the remembering, telling, and interpreting, but are mainly meant for the dreaming itself? In chapters 10, 11, and 12, the significance of this question occupies us more fully.

Is it possible that in considering the variety of dreams, we are simply asking about the varieties of thought given that dream-thinking differs from wake-thinking in that it is taking place without immediate input from the social and physical environment, without the full capacity for bodily motion, and without some feedback from orienting and reality-adaptive judgment. Instead, it is inspired by memory, connectedness, imagination, and all its other devices that light up the inner screen. We rarely inquire, nowadays, into the varieties of thinking. Perhaps we should do no better with an inquiry into the varieties of dreaming, other than to say simply that the variety is endless. Our minds come up with an infinite set of individually constructed mentation, serving countless purposes, at many levels of awareness, with many possibilities of meaning, effect, and significance whether awake or asleep. Like the heart's 24-hour beating, the mind is involved in its own 24-hour activity, in sleep called dreaming. We are still relatively early in the modern study mapping the kinds of things dreamt (Hall, 1966). The study of other aspects of the varieties of dreams (e.g., length, clarity, effect, etc.) still awaits. Our full-time pursuit of the single dimension of meaning has delayed this potentially more interesting exploration.

But as to meaning, we understand, with our postmodern colleagues, that meanings are overdetermined, multiple, never-ending, layered, or otherwise architecturally arranged. This view, derived originally from the study of texts, has been applied lately to reality in general. Students of dream-meaning were early to the understanding that interpretation is in the eyes of the beholder, and therefore many sided. With all due respect to our postmodernists and their equivocal attitude toward reality, however, it seems that dream interpretation, even more than considerations of reality, merits an entire openhandedness and should forgo notions of interpretive correctness. Dreams, even more than literary or religious texts, take us beyond reality. Dreams are themselves subjectively constructed, more so than texts, more so than are trees. However, having said that, one might still conceivably ask how they are similar. Would one ask: What is the meaning of trees or of the state of Alabama or of elephants?

The Talmud (Berakoth, 1948) speaks of the lesson of the 24 dream interpreters around the gates of 2nd century Jerusalem who were all correct in their 24 different prophetic interpretations of a single dream. Meanings, just as varieties of dreams, are endless. This is not a bad thing to think about for dreamer and interpreter. It tends to reduce the mind-numbing pressure to locate the meaning and instead inspires us to think some more, to never be sure, to keep looking, to value complexity, and to consider other aspects of dreams than meaning. These are not bad traits in an analyst. Or in a dreamer.

## ন্ধ 6 ৯৩

# ON DREAM DISGUISE

*No mask like open truth to cover lies*
*As to go naked is the best disguise.*
                                        —William Congreve

*Dream-distortion was the profoundest and most difficult problem of*
*dream life.*
                                        —Sigmund Freud

At the very beginning of the relationship between dream and psycho-analysis, the dream offered itself openly and freely. All that was required of psychoanalysis was an expression of interest, which Freud supplied in full measure. Perhaps that is all that is ever necessary with dreams—an interest in them. Dreams have been willing to show themselves freely to anyone, any method, any philosophy, any culture, or any science that shows interest. Dreams are like that. They give themselves to any and all. From dream incubation temples in ancient Greece and Egypt to the wired sleep labs of modern medical departments, it matters not to dreams; they pour out their tales with utter disregard for setting. And for the dreamer, dreams give themselves whether or not they are invited. They just offer themselves, willy-nilly, free and clear. They don't seem to mind if they are attended to or not, analyzed or not, forgotten or not. They show themselves anyhow, again and again. They are our nighttime performers, our all-night show-offs, our exhibitionists, and we dreamers are the observers, actually more the participant-observers, whereas the interpreters are later transformed into voyeurs once removed. Dreams are immoderate, easy, promiscuous, in the way they open themselves to any and all.

## THE SHYNESS OF DREAMS

At the very same time, there is a shyness to dreams, a sort of modesty. They only show up when the lights are low, when wakeful and focal attention are turned away. They hide mostly in the shadows of memory, show themselves briefly and just as quickly disappear from view. Only a very small number actually make their way through to daytime consciousness; mostly, they live in the quiet of sleep. The next day, they rarely barge into the interpreter's office unbidden. They show the good manners of shy persons and wait their turn. If ignored or, conversely, if too much is made of them, they pack up their things and leave without a fuss, to return in another form another day, or not. They rarely dominate the proceedings and are very patient while the dreamer dresses them up and while the interpreter reads into them all manner of things. One needs to slow down, like with very old people or with the very young, to make out what they are up to. Some of us have reduced our time to a 45-minute, back-to-back rush of patients and cannot possibly slow down enough to listen to the often quiet and shy dream speak its mind. The shy dream has endured 100 years of psychoanalytic interpretation, and before that of every culture translating the dream for its own purposes. And now, every New Age healer imposes the healer's need to know and heal into the shy dream; shy, but enduring.

The dreamer, in the ideal, could side with the dream and conceivably could object to all this pushiness on the part of the interpreters. But instead, the dreamers seem to abandon their very own creations and act as though they want their dreams to mean whatever the interpreters want them to mean. In this, they are like parents who give up their child to the school system at 3 or 4 or 5 years of age. Many of us know how painful this can be, like a well-rationalized betrayal of their baby, who, after all, "needs" to join the culture. And, after all, the parent now has some free time. Similarly, we give our dreams away to the interpreters from whichever culture—Ashanti to psychoanalytic—and our dreams are drawn into the culture's way of looking at things and we dreamers no longer need to be harassed by the urgings, proddings, needs, and conflicts contained in our dreams if we were to live with them a bit longer.

In this way, dreams are like our babies, and the interpreter's guiding hand is, a bit, like sending our child off to the school system. Now what does a shy creative child do in such a circumstance where the system hardly has the time or the inclination to attend to the complex nature of this particular shy dream-child? Actually, the shy child can continue to live within. The system hasn't the time to really get inside and mess things up. Just as well. The child can select and use what he or she can and for the rest, the shy creativeness goes its own way. Similarly with dreams; dreams take what is useful, disguise themselves further in the lingo of the interpreter, and go their own way. Their job is not to ruffle the system too much, not to inflame too much the school's need to "educate," and not to bring down the system's rules and regulations. Their job is to keep doing what they do—to appear in the sleeping consciouness of their hosts.

And so we observe two aspects to dreams: They can show and they can be shy. In this, they have their very own ways, their own capacities to show on their own terms and to be shy in their own ways, to conceal on occasion, to play hide and seek. And why not? Most psychological life, whether awake or asleep, has this complex and seemingly contradictory quality—to open and to close, to reveal and to hide, to make known and to make unknown, to be visible and to be invisible, all at once. The tease, the shyness, the mask, the disguise of dreams provokes in certain others—dream interpreters—a great desire to see what is going on behind the disguise. Whether or not interpretation is a worthy procedure, the interpreter is drawn, inexorably, to the scent and to the chase, by the qualities of inwardness, hiddenness, and disguise in dreams.

## FREUD AND THE DREAM WORK

The idea that the mind in sleep has the capacity to exercise distortion over its basic latent dream thoughts and wishes in order to slip past the censorship, in disguised form, and thus gain admission to dream consciousness was crucial to the entire grand edifice of Freud's theory of dreams. Distortion, concealment, artful masking, hiding through displacement and condensation, all the genius of the dream-work was invoked to account for the way the end product, the manifest dream, seemed confusing and ambiguous. This was an extraodinary idea—the dream in disguise—that gave us the push to begin the search for "the real meaning."

Earlier, I made allusion to the fancy that the ancient magical world of dreams and their interpretation required the disguise of modern science, through Freud's hands, in order to slip past the censorship of enlightenment rationality, and gain entrance through the gates of the 20th century. The parallel between Freud's theory of the individual dreaming mind and this fanciful description of the operation of large social forces is not accidental. Freud, in his dream book, had clearly made use of and had interiorized political–social forces in his description of internal goings-on. Schorske (1980) made this point most clearly. Each realm is reflected in the other. Freud, in describing the censorship as an active participant in the creation of dreams, himself was bringing the forbidden—sex, aggression, dream magic, the rag-tag army of society's hidden secrets—into modern times. Just as he described the mental distortion of forbidden wish-thoughts to slip past the forbidding censor into dream consciousness, he himself was trying to put dream interpretation on a scientific footing so that the great darkness of the unconscious could slip by the forbidding and censoring eye of enlightened, Godless, rational, modern thought. And it worked!

What he did and what the dream-work is supposed to do are identical. He was identified with Joseph and David of the Torah. But he was also identified with the essence and ingenuity of the dream-work, his favorite theoretic invention. Freud was himself the dream-work between the dark ancient forces pressing into modern times, and the very modernism he is sometimes credited with fathering. In the sense of the parallel, he reworked and revised the ingredients, and was able to lead the modern mind into thinking that his brilliant compromise theory, disguised as science, was original, could serve the spirit of the times, was not dangerous, could not disturb sleep, and should be let through. As a result, it was let through and contributed to an entire Zeitgeist that made the unconscious as familiar as soap.

We have yet to see the final flowering of Freud's compromise theory of disguise in our contemporary postmodern and electronic world. In a sense, Freud's view may have come 100 years too soon. The necessity for the private mind, in our 21st century, to disguise itself both from the social and market world and from its own inclinations, may be even more relevant than 100 years ago, when the social world was preoccupied with forbidding sexual impulses, with keeping women from economic power, and Jews, like Freud, from political power. That is, the modern world has the ability, the equipment, the need, and the will to gain entrance to our most private experience. Disguise may have once been the refuge of the underclasses, or of scoundrels, or the play of theater, or of old Vienna itself, but in today's electronic world, disguise may become an essential element of psychic survival.

## OBJECTIONS TO FREUD'S DISGUISE THEORY

Let us go back to dreams. It is not difficult to object to Freud's view. There has been much commentary and controversy on the disguise quality of dreams. From Jung (1974) to Rycroft (1979) and now to most contemporary cognitive and neuroscientists, all take issue with Freud's insistence on the disguised nature of dreams. It is not difficult to find agreement with the critics. What they are saying is that the dream as dreamt, the manifest dream, so to speak, is dream enough for them. They have plenty to engage with without positing an underdream. The idea of hiding and concealment is just not nature's way (Jung, 1974), and, further, such an idea is simply not necessary to the full engagement with and understanding of dreams (Rycroft, 1979). This point of view pretty much holds sway, though individual analytic therapists may still try to peel the dream for its inner taste. There is something pleasant and consoling about thinking that the dream is what it says it is, that distortions are not the result of deliberate disguise, that nature is not playing tricks, that we can rest from the frantic illusion of searching for hidden meanings.

And yet, there is something to this idea of disguise in dreams. I think it a mistake to rule out, on theoretic grounds, the possibility of disguise; not that all dreams are necessarily disguised. The insistence on all-or-none positions in theory building has unfortunate consequences in bullying us out of middling positions filled with "probably," "possibly," "maybe," "perhaps," and "sometimes." These tentatives are not to be mistaken for weakness, but for an awareness of subtlety, contradiction, doubt. Such a view is supported by Nietzsche, something of a bully himself, who claimed he mistrusted all systematizers and avoided them, and insisted that the will to a system is a lack of integrity. So let us dispense with the idea that all dreams are this or that. What if some dreams are more disguised than others? What if some dreams are more open than others? What if dreams and nighttime thinking are just a continuation of daytime thinking, but without any environmental feedback or need to engage with the outside world? Or, what if daytime thinking is just a continuation of nighttime thinking, but with muscles able to move and carry out intentions and with senses alert to the surround?

## DISGUISE IN AWAKE LIFE

If so, one could seek and expect to find similarities between the two—awake and dream-thinking. We would expect to find disguise in ordinary day life and disguise in night life, or lack of disguise, in both. We would agree there is plenty of disguise in regular living. Social masks, the masks of civilization, the masks of roles and of language, the disguises of respectibility, the guises of the self to others and within its self, the hidden inner self, the outer shell, both dressed in the familiar garb of convention—all disguise. Lies, white lies, large and small deceptions, hidden motives, hypocrisies, trickeries, finesse—all costumes. These characterize social living and also some of the life within the individual, despite some who in both self and social deception claim for themselves a fuller kind of sincerity, and insist on a realer kind of authenticity for others.

Civilization demands artifice. The invention of the laugh track and the deception of lip-sync are only small modern turns in the general move to greater and greater artifice and to a virtual if not virtuous life. Deception in the lived details seems to fit both capitalism and communism in practice. Both democracy and dictatorship thrive on various forms of masking. The marketing of the world is hokum on a grand scale. We have always known that the insurance industry was based on baloney. Now the industry of deception is in the middle of many of our offices and we practice hokum along with them—but, of course, for the benefit of our patients, or so we tell ourselves.

In the stories of individual lives, we are very familiar with the theme of hiding oneself, in varied and complex ways, from oneself and from others. Some disguise, it seems, is essential in life. And not only in humans but in the animal and plant worlds as well. There are fish that look like the rocks they hide under, insects that look like the plants on which they climb, harmless snakes that resemble poisonous ones, harmless berries that look like deadly ones. It is simply not true, then, that nature has no need to hide itself or to disguise. Au contraire; if anything, survival requires disguise. Then again, so is seeing the disguise for what it is. Freud's great ambition was, in part, to see beneath the disguise, to lay bare the workings and contents of the unconscious. With the success of Freud's efforts in this regard assured, we now live with a general and common recognition of the importance of unconscious and sexual life. Perhaps it is time to reverse course and begin again to appreciate the surface dimension of things, and as with Oscar Wilde, to see depth and value in the superficial, the cover, the disguise itself. The recognition and appreciation of meaning both on the surface and beneath the surface, and in complex interaction, could keep us busy for the next 100 years.

## Disguise in Night Thinking

So, if much of regular day life is in disguise, why not assume night-thinking has as much right to disguise, as well? On reflection, dreams have both less and more right to make use of disguise. Less, because the dreamer is temporarily free from external feedback. Night thinking is talking, dreaming, thinking to oneself. So, it need not disguise as much, except maybe from God—but that is a different problem, better left for now. Thus, dreams should be freer to see and say what is closer to the uncensored heart than is day thinking and day speech, on the one hand; and it often is just that—freer to see and say what is so. These are the dreams that tell analysts not only that the analyst's breasts are too big, or that he is too Jewish, or that his children are ugly, or that she is dead in spirit, but also that analysis is sometimes a scam, that it costs too much, that it doesn't work, and other calamitous appraisals. It may also tell truths of a more positive variety, but it's the terrible ones that cause analysts to blanch, take the hit, and carry on. Fromm (1951) was an early contributor to this point of view, and his clinical students were quick to recognize in dreams a capacity to see and know more than is possible in day thinking. For example, a man dreams that he is visited by his dead father who tells him to stop mistreating his own son. While analytic conversation about this dream may amplify it and reveal aspects of these three generations in more complex interaction, in essence the dream seems clear enough. No reason for a concept such as disguise.

In another example, a patient dreams of a complex and ingenious method for the murder of her aged husband. Her associations and the 2 years of our work together carry us to considerations of her identification with her murderous mother and with the patient's equally villainous daughter, her newly experienced love for her dead father, her wish to cheat on her husband, her disdain and wish for life insurance monies, her plans to build a new house using a variant of the engineering involved in the method of murder, her embarking on a piece of writing in which she makes use of a part of the dream-murder as detective subplot, and then to deep sadness at the profound sense of failure in her mother's life, her fear of following in her mother's footsteps, and her own overwhelming sense of selfishness and greed as she feels what it would be like to kill her old and faithful husband. The initial dream seemed not particularly distorted or hidden or filled with disguise. And the resulting discussion opened many feelings and experiences that were ready for harvesting. The concept of disguise is not particularly useful in this example.

On the other hand, dreams have more right to disguise because they have more uninhibited imagination at hand. There is less effort needed to rein them in, putting on whatever ingenious masks are close at hand. The world of surfaces is enormously fascinating and the imaginative mind can play with surfaces in layered and interwoven ways such that the concept of disguise might seem like a simplification. When surfaces interlace with deeper, older, or more emotionally laden, more complex ideas under the surface, there is no end to the possibilities in the texture of dreams and dream discussion.

*A woman dreams that an old girlfriend is driving a car with the dreamer in the passenger seat. The car passes scenery that is haunting and familiar and the dreamer begins to experience familiar feelings of loneliness and sadness. Suddenly, a large black bird with outspread wings crashes through the windshield and is embedded in the eye of the driver, at which point the dreamer awakens in extreme fright and misery.*

Such a dream is filled with possibilities and as we discuss it, layers upon layers pour out of the images. The girlfriend had been a beauty and the dreamer envied her in years gone by. The worry about not being beautiful enough filled her adolescent and young adult years and she sees similar worries overwhelming her 20-year-old son. The bird incident leads the dreamer to quip that "a bird in the eye is worth two in the bush" and then she continues on about Poe's raven and about American Indian lore concerning spirit animals before she returns to the horror of the scene that left her shaken and still haunts her weeks later. She assumes that the bird is her spirit animal, a great raven or crow, and that it was meant for her—to harm her, to rip open her eye, to force her to see. She recalls the metaphoric opening to the extraordinary art film, *Un Chien Andalou,* where a razor blade is shown slicing through an eye that fills the screen. The dreamer adds that she always wished to have the wisdom and insight of the blinded bisexual Tiresias. But, alas, the bird missed her and got the driver instead. "A good enough reason not ever to be a beauty or in charge in the driver's seat." Later, she attends to the image of the smashed windshield and then to the word "windshield," which occupies us for a considerable time leading to memories of living through a fierce hurricane in her childhood and to feelings about the meanings of "wind," from which she requires "shielding."

Aside from ways that dream conversation in this instance may prove meaningful to the dreamer, the idea that there exists, beneath the surface, such a world of underlying thoughts that take various guises and masks in these dream-images seems of special note. As patient and I explore the dream, this underworld of meanings and memories, feelings and deep concerns, becomes palpable and manifest. Merely the dream-image of the large black bird by itself is a treasure of meanings, memories, wishes, and fears. It condenses into its forms all manner of ideation and feeling within this dreamer. Like a large blanket, the dream-image holds and covers its diverse contents. It is, thus, a container for a world of meanings. But it also serves as disguise. Because it is, on its surface, a large black bird that crashes through a car window. Only when we take seriously its surface, its superficial, its manifest form and related meanings, can we then begin seriously to entertain accompanying ideas that the surface both reveals and conceals: an interest in Indian lore and magic, a capacity for ancient violence against competitors from earlier decades, a shunning of overt beauty and power, an interest in the idea of violent penetration, an interest in damaging something, opening a view beneath the surface of beauty, and finally, to the life of winds, shields, and smashings manifesting itself in this person.

The idea that all dreams are disguised seems as limited as the idea that all dreams show everything. Probably it could be said that some dreams do more of one than the other, that some dreamers may do more of one than the other, and that both ideas—concealment and openness—are valuable in thinking about dreams. Many persons were forced by Freud's assertion to demonstrate the correctness of his discovery; and many were later forced to demonstrate the incorrectness of his discovery. Perhaps we can now move on to viewing dreams, not so much in the cauldron of assertions and counterassertions, but for their own sake. And so we notice that dreams use disguise and we notice that dreams do not use disguise and we believe both assertions are true. But the major issue here is how both these possibilities affect the interpreter. How is one to behave if both hypotheses are valid?

The automatic request for associations in order to get to the genuine and hidden essence of the dream, although often a good idea, is not a one-size-fits-all solution, and relies too heavily on the manifest-latent dichotomy, which requires a concept of *concealment.* Probably, it is better to think up ways that don't always depend on concealment and that have less of a paranoid edge to them. One of the problems with Freud's view of distortion is that it places the dreamer and the dream in necessarily adversarial positions to the purposes of the analyst, and to the search for "truth." And many of us still turn into FBI agents when a dream is mentioned. Paranoia and suspiciousness have their place in our work, but they too often find their way into dream conversation. Dreams get very shy in front of paranoid FBI agents, because, as we all know, there is always something to hide and about which to be nervous. Why else do we get so bent out of shape when a police car shows up in our rear view mirror? Maybe not all of us. Maybe not the "sincere" and "authentic" ones among us. Perhaps the sincere and authentic ones don't assume the cops are on their trail. Actually, my guess is that a suspicious attitude, an adversarial attitude, a position that knows that the patient's dream is in disguise, is guaranteed to produce disguise, perhaps more disguise than there was to begin with.

## A PARTLY CLOSED BLOSSOM

In the absence of disagreeable suspiciousness, some dreams will open of their own accord, in conversation. The opening of a dream, in its own way, is the point; like a blossom, in its own time. A closed blossom is not a disguised flower, it is a closed blossom. The idea is to be available or even a little helpful or at least not harmful in the dream's revealing itself to dreamer and interpreter. The disappearance of a dream, the dream's shyness, and return to unconsciousness, is more the rule than the exception. Therefore, we are rowing against the tide in hoping to have a dream show more of itself than it already has in the dreaming. This will take patience, respect, manners, and a light touch. Thus, by asking about reactions to the dream, by playing with one piece, and then another, by adding your own idea if you wish, by expressing an interest in greater clarity about certain fragments, by saying nothing, by going back to last session's concerns, by all manner of methods that include one's intuitions, inclinations, and hunches, it is possible to participate in a dream's opening.

But a dream is also not a blossom. Erikson's (1954) creative teleology about the underlying purpose of the Irma dream—it was dreamt in order to become analyzed as the "specimen dream" of psychoanalysis, and thus to give birth to psychoanalysis—takes us further in this inquiry into dreams and disguise. Certainly the Irma dream, reported as the number one dream, shows a great deal more than it knows, while it also hides itself in dream, in associations, and in interpretation. Freud took up this dream, looked deeply into it, saw what he thought was its essence, which in part was his own mind in the form of his developing theory, and created an entire psychology from its study. But as for the dream itself and its deeper meanings, as we now know, as much was revealed as was concealed. His beloved and dangerous Fliess was disguised and hidden away both in the dream and in Freud's subsequent explanations and denials. The dream itself, one could say, remained somewhat hidden. Freud's theory, itself, provided an elaborate disguise for the facts behind the dream, a theory behind which the dream could remain unknown until much much later, and never

completely. The Irma dream is indeed a remarkable example of the
centrality of a dream in the origins of our religion, of our culture, and
of other cultures. Hidden and disguised in our specimen dream is not
a single set of principles, but rather the whole messy human drama of
love and betrayal, trust and dishonor, a secret confession of the worst
aspects of our method of treatment, and a need to hide our guiltiness
about our failures—all to be discovered as the century unfolded. An
unusual dream for a most unusual religion.

What is to be concluded about this dream and dreams in general?
In my opinion, a dream's wish is entirely ambivalent—just as it shows
and it hides, it wishes to be known and it wishes to remain unknown.
Freud's theory of disguise itself provided a disguise, and in so doing,
he satisfied the dream's ambivalent wish to be known and at the same
time to be left in hiding. There are three layers to Freud's engagement
with the centrality of disguise in relation to dreams. First, in his theory,
Freud viewed underlying dream-thoughts, basic wishes, as requiring
disguise to pass through the censorship into dream consciousness.
Second, in relation to his cultural role, Freud, himself, through his
theory, personified the dream-work in bringing forbidden ideas past
the censorship of Enlightenment values, into modern times in the guise
of science. Third, in his own personal life, his theory of disguise
provided a necessary disguise for some truths that were too difficult,
even dangerous, for socially shared awareness, for example that the one
man who was his dearest audience for all that became his dream book
might have been a dangerously malpracticing incompetent, sponsored
and protected (and exposed) by Freud. The theme of disguise, in
Freud's hands, runs through his personal life, finds its way into the
center of the theory, and is the means by which we can understand the
myth of the 20th century's engagement with Freud, dreams, and the
unconscious.

## A Child's Delusion of Disguise

We will return to the notion of the dream's own wish to show and hide,
to be known and remain hidden. But first, a personal excursion into an
engagement with disguise that echoes in these reflections on dreams.
Some years ago, I had the following dream:

*I was entering a large space with my son and daughter. They were small
children. I was an old man, something like my father's age when my children
were young—a grandfather, I suppose. Off to the right, a crowd of people
were forming and milling about, like going to or coming from the theater.
To the left, the actors and actresses moved about. We were in the middle,
and it got very crowded like a subway rush hour. I felt the need to protect
my children from the mob. I felt badly that we had missed the performance.
I think it was about the life of Chaliapin, the great basso. As the crowd
settled into the subway car, I found myself intently looking into the faces of
the players to see whether they had removed their makeup. Then some
shouting, screaming, yelling sounded through the subway and I awoke
feeling frightened and confused.*

The dream led me immediately to consider several experiences,
touched on in the dream. But the main association carried me back to
a time when I was about 6 years old, about the age of my son in the
dream. At that age, I had developed a frightening idea about my
parents that continued for many weeks and left me deeply shaken. I
believed that the two people who came home from work in the evening,
pretending to be my parents, were quite possibly not my parents at all.
Rather they may have been wearing perfect masks and disguises so that
they would look and sound exactly like my real parents. But they
weren't. Instead, they may have caused my parents some harm and
intended some terrible fate for me. I was terrified and felt in certain
danger for my life. My actual survival in this highly charged arena of
life and death depended on my ability to find out if these two, seemingly
loving parents, were actually my real parents or dangerous and potentially violent imposters. I set myself the task of carefully determining
the truth. In a most paranoid world, I let them embrace me, but looked
intently for tiny signs that would give away the disguise: a hair out of
place, a mark on the neck, a sudden look of strangeness, a sound that
could be fake. Seeing no obvious sign, I next took to exploring the
minds of my captors-parents. I carefully asked as many questions as I
could, without giving away my detective's purpose, questions to which
only my real parents could possibly know the answers. These would be
personal things—bits of songs, family secrets, small identifying details,
secret affectionate words in Yiddish, so particular that only my real
family could possibly know. I would have to ask these in the most

innocent seeming way not to give away my dangerous suspicions. Only when they answered these to my satisfaction and great relief, could I relax my guard and get on with the evening.

This engagement with a child's terrible suspicion and delusion was of my own creation, as far as I know, and was my personal introduction to the world of disguise, and its potential for mayhem. How did I come to such a notion? There are many routes. I may have been following the suggestion of an unremembered dream, or a radio program. I certainly came from a family where the continuous expressions of love and affection overshadowed any possibility of expressions of hatred. Hitler took care of that side of things for us. My parents, working in sweatshops, were away from home for long, long days, and often at union meetings into the night. I often looked after myself, as did many poor children, then and now. Perhaps, with a child's unconscious knowing, I couldn't imagine that my real parents could possibly love me and at the same time leave me so alone. As a "red diaper baby," I knew, understood, and appreciated as best a child could their economic struggle and was proud of their participation in the progressive labor movement. I had no complaints. I knew the score, at least consciously. But it was left to my fevered imagination to conjure up a terrible fright and accusation: "My real and loving parents could never treat me this way! You must be dangerous imposters! Have you killed my parents? Are you here to kill me?" Underlying my delusion, I believe that I was also accusing my real parents of fakery, of disguise, of aggression, of dangerous designs. But I was also giving projected voice to my own fakery, my own hiddenness, my capacity to be unreal with them, and with myself.

There was no one to tell this to. I was alone with my suspicions and my solutions. And mostly, my strategy worked. I got over it. Those terrible doubts receded into shadow. We all survived. But disguise remained a potent force in my life. As a child, I had a hard time with clowns and others in masks. Or even if there were no mask, anyone acting fake, or putting on a front, or seeming to be something other than they were, could send shivers through me. I only learned as an adult that cocktail party conversation was not an alien threat but a way that regular people got along, that a certain level of pretend and disguise was also relaxing as well as good manners.

This sensitivity to disguise was of course partly an expression of aspects of my own developing nature. I now believe I was the one in disguise, never giving hard-working, struggling, immigrant parents a moment's worry, always seeming happy and free from anything worrisome, always putting on a good front so they could be free from tragedy on the home front. Nastiness and neediness were shelved except in secret. The genuine tragedies unfolding in concentration camps in Poland, which dominated my dreams, and in my parents' sweatshops and picket lines seemed more than enough. I was not unlike many children, who took care of life's business themselves, so their parents could survive, keeping the dark side to themselves and to the streets. Despite the seemingly sympathetic concerns of the Alice Millers about unempathic, narcissistic mothers and "parentified children," there were many of us children who carried a difficult burden proudly. Some of us even became psychoanalysts because we kept doing what we learned early and well—and, I might add, to the advantage of many in our care.

But perhaps this delusional experience is merely part of what all children are capable of feeling, that parents are not always real with them; that they hide some things, that they are careful with what children are exposed to, that the cruelties of life are kept at a distance. I believe I was not particularly protected from some of life's cruelties. My parents often treated me respectfully with much of the real story of things. But, even in such an atmosphere, I felt they were hiding important truths, particularly about their own nature and intentions. Perhaps this is inevitable. After all, no matter how open and respectful or discreet and careful are the adults, a child's mind suspects and senses that it is up against mysteries that are genuinely beyond a child's comprehension; that life itself is disguised, that what is true is impossible to know, that what is false is also impossible to know. The child senses hypocrisies and notes what parents say in front of and behind other adults. The child senses false emotion and recognizes a smile that is not real, a word of affection that masks anger. All of this speaks of disguise as a major part of life. The child's delusion, therefore, may speak some truth and my dream may lead directly to the experience of that child's delusion still being worked over, mastered, lived.

The dream, then, is often—not always, but often—artful in the sense that art is the "lie" that helps us see the truth. Its creativity, its artfulness, is the very disguise that reveals what is so, on and under the surface, just as it conceals what is so, on and under the surface. The idea that the dream itself wishes to reveal and conceal at the same time is at one with Freud's notion of symptoms, which serve as artful compromises that reveal and conceal, that allow expression in disguised form. The dream's shyness, its ease of disappearance into forgetfulness, its ambiguous nature, its willingness to put up with all sorts of fanciful projections, all reflect the ambivalence in its hidden and exhibitionist nature. No wonder we have trouble with the dream. Perhaps we should just relax and let the dream be its quirky, many sided, many purposed, ambivalent self, instead of getting bent out of shape by its difficulties.

One additional note on disguise. It should be mentioned that in the encounter between dream and analyst, the dream is not the only participant that is occasionally disguised. It should be recognized that no matter the contemporary urgency to disclose, analysts are much disguised in their profession. We wear the mask of concerned therapists. We are there for the good of the patient. We don't show and tell all that is on our mind. We hide many of our own and life's secrets. The dream and the analyst together wear the necessary guises that permit us to slip quietly near one other and occasionally speak softly and deeply about some meaningful truths to one another—from the side.

# ℀ 7 ℅

# THE DREAM LISTENERS

*I believe it true that dreams are the true interpreters of our inclinations;*
*but there is an art required to sort and understand them.*
                                        —Michel de Montaigne

One is sitting quietly in one's own chair, in one's own office, minding one's own business, so to speak, and out of the corner of one's eye seeing the tree outside the window shimmer in the breeze, a squirrel perched on a limb, tail twitching, ready to spring, while at the same time one is conversing, more or less deeply, with one's patient and thinking and imagining all sorts of things, about all sorts of matters, mostly about this particular patient's particular struggles, when suddenly the patient says, "Oh, I just remembered. I had this dream I wanted to tell you." With these words, the atmosphere in the room changes. One is about to be transported to another realm. One is about to listen to a dream.

In this chapter, we turn our attention momentarily away from the dream and the dreamer and toward the dream listener, the dream expert, the paid dream authority, the dream knower, the dream analyzer, the dream interpreter. These lofty titles may bear no resemblance to how the therapist-listener actually feels. The listener may feel instantly diminished, worried, tested, sleepy, or irritated or he may feel livelier, enhanced, interested, or just plain ready and eager for some good old-fashioned "evenly hovering attention." The listener may go dead within or may get excited or agitated within. The listener may move immediately for pen and notepad, or may sink down in the chair, eyes closed, into a dreamy-headedness. The listener may want to go home to Mommy. Dreams cause all sorts of things. Who is this listener? And what is it that dream listening causes in the analytic therapist?

## A HIERARCHY OF DREAM LISTENERS

There is a hierarchy in dream listening and the analyst has to take a rightful place in the hierarchy; it is important not to assume, when a patient is telling you a dream, that you are first to listen to it. First in line is the dreamer, who gets the inaugural chance at receiving the dream. Both in initial dreaming consciousness within sleep and then in recall and response, the dreamer is the first audience. And how this first audience is affected by the dream may turn out to be the dream's primary import. There is, of course, a wide range in how the dreamer is affected and responds. The dreamer as receiver comes in all varieties ranging from dream adorer to dream despiser, from collector to destroyer, from friend to foe of dreams, from interested to bored, from playful to bothered. Some dreamers, deaf to their dreams, care little about the goings-on unless shaken by a powerful dream thrust. Their lives may be full enough without any additional concerns, or they may never have been impelled to tune in to night's mental activities. Other dreamers listen intently to their dreams, measure their messages, weigh their consequences, record their minutest activities. For these devoted dreamers, their whole life has involved great sensitivity to dreams including urgent needs to share and discuss and think about them. For these people, going to sleep and waking are merely frames for the important life, that of dreaming. Such differing styles may alternate from time to time or they may characterize the entire life of the dreamer.

I have noticed that, generally, women care more about dreams than do men, but variations in such a pattern are more interesting still. Also, I have observed that preindustrial and agrarian people give more importance to dreams than do their industrial and citified cousins. Therefore, cultural tradition as well as individual constitutional-neurological-memory styles can be relevant in determining patterns of dream significance for the dreamer. In therapy, it is most always worthwhile to inquire into the person's own way and history of attending to their dreams and to learn from the particular individual and cultural styles. Understanding the nature of one person's deafness to dreams and another's preoccupation with dreams can be meaningful, as can helping the uninterested to begin to open to dreams and the preoccupied to begin to attend to other elements of life. All in all, the analyst-dreamlistener needs to put himself or herself in back of the dreamer's own ways in attending to the dream.

Next in line of dream listening, if the dreamer is one who regularly records dreams, may be posterity or mankind or God or parents or lovers or whoever is the imagined other who will someday receive these dreams. One lonely, shy, and reserved older woman patient, quiet as a church mouse, never seen or heard from in her outer life, but a wonderful secret writer, slowly becoming quietly mad in the agreeable English style of "dotty old persons," had kept a journal of dreams since she was 9 years old. The library of volumes covered almost 60 years of recorded dreams, complete with thoughts, associations, and interpretations for each dream. From the time she was a shy, awkward, and bookish youngster, she was convinced that all humankind and God would someday gather to read her life of dreams and honor her beyond measure for her honesty and boldness. She had imagined this would occur in her senior years, when she would be elevated above all others, perhaps close to Joan of Arc or Eleanor Roosevelt. But lately, she fretted that being honored might not occur until after her death, and once she began worrying about this, her dreams had seemed rather ordinary to her. Usually her dreams seemed richly epic and instructive, guided as they were by her conviction that a deeply moved world would be gathered to read her dream record. Actually, her dreams did seem remarkable to me in their scope and wisdom. This imagined adoring and feelingful world had been her companion throughout her life. Now, it had occurred to her that she might not live to be present at the honor, and this greatly saddened her and brought her to a therapist for the first time in her long and lonely life. It turned out that I was the first person to read and discuss her dreams with her. For the year we worked together, I became an acceptable substitute, a living stand-in, for humankind and for God in receiving and prizing the evidence of an extraordinary inner life. But humankind remained her first and main dream listener. This idea was not an abstraction for her, but had specific, concrete, feelingful referents. She knew her listeners and how they would react.

Next in line of dream listening may be someone encountered earlier than the analyst. A person who shares the bed or the dwelling with the dreamer, or a relative, or a friend on the phone that morning, or a doorman or grocery store clerk or cab driver or coworker or even a beloved pet can be the first after the dreamer to listen to the dream. Sometimes patients hide and sometimes they emphasize the fact that someone other than the analyst got an earlier or later chance at the dream. If the analyst can recover from natural jealousy, it can be instructive to discover how others listen to and respond to the patient's dream. Often it is interesting to see the way the patient plays with the differences and similarities of ideas and reactions of the earlier interpreter and those of the analyst.

It should be the proper time for the analyst to attend to the dream, now that we realize we are not first or second in line. But not so fast. Transference and archetype now have their turn and the poor analyst has to wait even longer, truly at the end of the line of listeners.

### ARCHETYPE AND TRANSFERENCE IN DREAM LISTENING

When a patient tells you a dream, it may seem that the patient is telling *you* the dream. And in fact, it is probably true that the dream is being related to *you* more or less as you are. But if psychoanalysis teaches anything, it is that *you* are not always *you* in the mind of the patient, that *you* includes images, ideas, memories, generalizations of others who have mattered, consciously and unconsciously, to the patient. So when the patient is telling a dream, to whom, in this broader sense, is the patient relating the dream?

First, the archetypal transference. Although the therapist may in no way be inclined to awareness of the fact of the historical role of the dream interpreter from the beginning of recorded history through most every known culture, I believe the influence of this history is significant in the way the listener does his job. The dream listener, as suggested earlier, sits in a large and ancient chair, wearing an honored and revered mantle. The role, position, and influence of the dream interpreter from ancient days has been profound. In the birth of most every religion, one finds dreams and their interpretations. In most all methods of prescientific psychological and physical healing, the dream and its interpretations play a notable part. In magic and folklore, in prophesy and instruction, the dream interpreter regularly makes an appearance. The dream's mystery has been wrestled with in almost every philosophical system. And in all of this, the dream interpreter stands anointed, ordained, enthroned for a most special assignment. The interpreter's duty is to reveal the dream's mystery, to untangle its enigma, to lay bare its secret. In this task, systems of classification have been developed to assist the interpreter. These have included, through the ages, ideas about dreams from God and from the devil, big dreams and little dreams, conception dreams, prophetic and nonsensical dreams, dreams worth ignoring and dreams worthy of attention, dreams from various levels of the soul, dreams from various layers of the ancestral dead, with good intentions and evil intentions, sickness dreams and health dreams, and so on.

This ancient discussion of the nature and function of dreams, this ancient significance and power, this aura of magic and sorcery, of secret and profound knowledge, surrounds and infuses the modern dream interpreter, sitting in his office, minding his own business, without regard to awareness of such archetypal happenings. The dreamer, too, may be unmindful of the force of such a history. Both may exist in relative innocence, but the ancient history exerts its influence under the surface, I believe, in the deep innards of dream discussion. Small wonder many therapists feel insufficient to the task and shrink from its opportunities. Small wonder we often try to hide our inability, our ignorance, our weakness compared to what is felt to be expected of us. The patient says "I had this dream" and after telling it, sits back and waits. The patient has done his or her job. The rest is up to us. The stage is set, all await the magic of the interpreter. "Speak, great interpreter! Speak!" Sometimes the archetype forces us to a pose of knowingness. Sometimes, in contrast, we turn away from the entire engagement, rather than feel failure and shame, in response to the deeply implied expectations of our patients or our own.

Just when an open and playful mind is best, we often regress to potty-training, sphincter tightness of the mind. Like the 2-year-old uneasily perched over the large and potentially unfriendly hole, the analyst who feels unconsciously intimidated by the expectation of being an adequate knower, a genuine dream expert, tightens up when asked to let go. The mind freezing in place and refusing to move is guaranteed to make us feel small and stupid in the presence of the dream. In itself not necessarily a bad thing, it feels bad to the interpreter. It may after all lead to the dream's being left to its own devices, which can be preferable to its being pushed around.

Jungians have an entirely different set of problems. They are often too mindful of the archetypal expectation and of the profound importance of their master's dream work, and may actually "feel" the mantle and the crown. Such a view is not necessarily preferable, even if it feels better, than shrinking from the expectation and the test. If failing the test of being a dream expert makes us feel too small in relation to the dream, passing the test may make us feel too large, that is, arrogant, sure, bullying.

Freud (1900, 1911, 1923, 1925) tried to help in presenting something of a method that allowed the insecure dream analyst to approach the dream, more or less systematically, through requests for associations to progressive dream segments and to prior daytime experiences. But the general expectation that the analyst be an expert in dreams and have the "answers" to the mysteries is powerful and often stands between dream and analyst, forcing the actual analyst to the background. Although the expectation is historically powerful and interesting and even adds juice to the drama, it is only when the actual analyst, a usually unknowing, entirely fallible, and human-size partner, is able to join the proceedings that an interesting unfolding can actually take place.

But the archetypal past for the analyst listening to dreams is not the last structure that stands between dream and interpreter, that forces the analyst to wait in line. There is also transference, smaller than archetype but closer to lived experience. That is, in the actual lives of the dreamers, there are precursers and forerunners to the analyst. Just as the Torah's Joseph and our own Freud and Jung created the form of the large chair we sit in, behind our listening and reacting are the earlier listeners to our patients' dreams. These include mother mostly, but also father, siblings, other relatives, nannies, babysitters, and all manner of caretakers who might be present when the small child wakens with a dream and is eager to relate it. All participate in the early history of dream-telling and therefore in the nature of the dream-listener transference. Responses can range from avid interest to disgust to annoyance, from "It's only a dream" to "You are a terrible child for such a disgusting dream" or "How could you dare to dream that I hit you. Don't tell that to anyone. They'll think I really did" to "You made up that song in your dream? You are a little Mozart!"

Telling dreams when one is very young is for most as natural as breathing. The happenings, the adventures, the monsters, the strong feelings, all require a listener for most little children. The parents or older siblings or other caretakers are the ones who receive the breath- less, tear-filled, terrified nightmares, and who reassure the child: "No. Mommy is still here. Look. See? Here she is." Or, "There is no monster. Look, I'll turn on the light and look in the closet. See? It was only a dream." Or, "You dreamed Grandpa was dead? Omigod! Let's call him right now to see if it's true. Omigod!" Or, "Go back to bed. Can't you see I was sleeping? Stop your crying and leave me alone, you little shit." Of all these, "It was only a dream" is the most frequent response, and it helps the child distinguish, as is the custom in our culture, between dream and reality, with dream decidedly in second place.

As you can see, long before a patient says "I had this dream," there is an extensive history of dream-telling that includes various and particular patterns of listening and response to the telling of dreams. The patterns of response previously experienced and imagined by the dreamer-patient are all subtly or overtly attributed to the therapist, in transference, when a dream is told. The expectation of happy, won- drous amazement, the expectation of busy annoyance or boredom, or competitiveness, the expectation that the analyst has better things to do, is too "big" and important to deal with dream bits about "silly" things, all play through the telling of a dream to analyst and all interact with archetype and with actuality in creating a complex and varied condensation.

We have an opportunity when listening to a patient's dream to think about and inquire into the way dreams were listened to and the way the patient wished and imagined dreams would be listened to but were not. Often this dream-listener transference cannot be commented on directly, because the earlier experiences are outside awareness and not in memory. But we can sometimes learn and sense what it was like for this person to tell dreams and nightmares to early caretakers through attending to the ways they expect us to listen to and comment on their dream experiences.

These transferences can extend beyond dreams to other communicated experiences, fantasies, imaginations, creations, fabulations, stories, and other dreamy inventions. Some learn to keep these all to
themselves. Some learn that people will delight in these creations. Some
learn people will turn these private creations to their own purposes, as
in "Oh, I can't wait to show your drawing to my bridge club." Some
learn the receiver can't help but become competitive, as in "That is a
terrific joke (story, song, dream). But wait until you hear mine (or your
sister's)." A patient of mine, a wonderful dreamer and most creative
interpreter, could never tell her mother anything of delight, because
the mother needed to protect the patient's damaged younger brother,
and felt forced to derogate and disparage any of the patient's creations,
including her wonderfully rich dreams. This tragic home situation led
to our working on dreams in an atmosphere of joyous specialness and
discovery, except when elements of her brother or her mother necessarily entered aspects of our dream conversations as transference.

## FINALLY, THE ANALYST AS LISTENER AND INTERPRETER

First the dreamer is listener. Then others who might have been told the
dream join the party. Then the ancient and powerful archetype of
dream expert enters. Then earlier dream listeners take their places.
And finally, at long last, it is the turn of the analyst. Who is this person
who now enters the scene? What shapes this person's listening? What
in the personal past, or in the personal analysis, or education, or
ideology, or philosophy, or cultural background creates the way this
person attends to dreams, or the way this person reacts when hearing
"I had this dream last night. Would you be interested?"

Let us begin with the personal dimension. Each of us has had a
lifetime of dreaming. How these dreams have treated us will create, in
part, the way we feel about dreams in general and about dreams in our
work in particular. A life of being bullied by nightmares and other
unhappy dreams can cause an analyst to feel bullied yet again when
presented with dreams. In revenge or in attempts at mastery, such an
analyst can turn into the bully and the know-it-all who can wrestle and
pin down dreams without much effort. Or the analyst as dreamer may
have had prolonged experience of ignoring dreams or of disconnecting
from them. Or conversely, the analyst may have been one of those

devoted dreamers who cherish and save and study dreams. How patients' dreams are regarded will no doubt be influenced by such formative experiences. The devoted dreamer-analyst may have difficulty with the patient who doesn't give a damn about dreams. The disconnected dreamer analyst may have difficulty with the dreamer who records and prizes dreams. And both types of analyst may feel quite at home with a patient who is similarly disposed.

When exploring with patients their particular feelings about dreaming, at times I have described my own childhood disinclination to allow bad dreams into experience. Or I might describe kinds of dreams I have had and how I sometimes think about them. I have a fairly open style in general, and I like to compare ways with dreams, although I refrain from recommending such a style to others. I have found that introducing the reality of myself as dreamer often opens the range of discussion. Of course, there are patients who cannot tolerate, for a while, any information about myself, other than what they can see and imagine. With these, I tend to keep my dream existence, along with much else, to myself and in the background until, if ever, they can stand those aspects of my participation. I like to bring myself fully into the engagement and believe with some patients that it is the best way, with them, to open psychological space. But this way of being requires understanding and respect for people who don't want me too present or even present at all, who need the space more or less entirely for themselves, for as long as necessary. I think I'm probably closer to that schizoid, loner style under the surface, although I love the play and connection of a fuller engagement. Dream conversation, because it is a bit at a distance and is about imagination in sleep, can be approached a bit from the side, as opposed to the straight-on of much direct therapeutic engagement. This aspect of dream work, similar to couch analysis, allows both my more alone and my more connected sides to interweave.

The personal dimension in the way the analyst listens to and interprets dreams also includes the incorporation and identification with early dream listeners in their own lives. Without realizing it, we may treat our dreaming patients as our own dreams and other creations were treated in childhood. Perhaps of greater significance is the relation between the way dreams were handled in our own analyses and in supervision and the way we work with our patients' dreams. Greenson (1970) suggested that this factor played a role in a diminishing interest in dreams in psychoanalysis. In teaching candidates and noninstitute students about working with dreams, I have found many whose analysts and supervisors paid little or no attention to dreams. Such lack of interest is harmful both to those students whose personal style turned them away from dreams and those whose personal style is drawn to dreams. However, again it can be suggested that in those cases where dreams and their interpretation were ignored by analysts and supervisors, students still had a chance, on their own, in their own time, to warm up to dreams and to learn how best to work with them. In contrast, those analysts and supervisors who had doctrinaire certitude in their teaching, whether Freudian, Jungian, Gestalt, or whatever, often created more problems for their students who were forced to take in and imitate these approaches, before being able to work free of them, if ever, and find their own way.

In addition to personal history with dreams and professional history with dreams, another factor presents itself. Many of us learn about dreams from our patients. Their interest and enthusiasm, their patience and efforts are a significant part of the way many of us think about and work with dreams. I have been fortunate to have met up with many unusual and gifted dreamers. They have shown me more than I ever could have imagined about the world of dreams and the way that world can aid in working through difficult lives in therapy. Giving oneself over to these patients and their dreams, allowing oneself to be led through their experience, with no map of one's own, is a rare privilege and a valued education. No analyst, supervisor, or teacher could help me learn what these troubled, kind, and giving souls have helped me learn. The ones who allow me to play with them in their field of dreams have been especially helpful, not only in my learning about dreams and their use in analytic therapy, but also in helping me overcome a yearning for playmates since childhood. My best playmates have been certain patients who let me join their play. Even those who cannot or will not let me join their dream play have my deep appreciation and affection because I know how much like them I am.

The field of dream play is mostly a private affair so I can't expect or demand or need the dreamer to let me in. Whenever it is possible, whenever I prove quiet enough or worthy enough or decent enough or tough enough or dead enough or alive enough, whichever is the right key at the right time, and I am permitted to play alongside the dream-player, it is a sweet and genuine privilege. But it is not to be expected or demanded. One of the worst aspects of the bad old days when psychoanalysis was king, was that analysts claimed the royal right to enter their patients' dreams and open them for inspection, deconstruction, and interpretation. The basic privacy of mental life is such that although we may be invited in, we must not barge in. The privacy of mind is often its last refuge. Even well-meaning, well-informed dream-interpreters must be invited to the playing. We must be alert to our own authoritarian capacities for bullying. Sometimes we gain access this way, but it is never worth it, despite the bully's claims to the contrary. I recall being deeply upset when I learned that one of many associations to repeated images of Gestapo rapists, in the dreams of a patient who was the child of Holocaust survivors, was me, myself in the role of sadistic dream-listener. And I thought I was being decently respectful. The role and my interest communicated too much eagerness and was felt, by this dreamer, to be a disguise for my efforts at brutal entry into her dreams.

When dream meets up with analyst, we are in a complex field. Not only is the listener informed by a personal and professional history with dreams, he or she is also a particular kind of person, with particular ways of being in the world, being with patients, and being with dreams. For example, telling a dream to a low-key, lethargic, sleepy and depressed therapist is a different kind of experience from telling one to a high-energy, overreactive, hyperalert, manicky therapist. Just as the Talmud informs us of the same dream being presented to the 24 dream interpreters in 2nd century Jerusalem, it would be fun to present the same dream to therapists of various mood and character styles to see the effect of listener personality style on interpretation. In our next chapter we explore more fully this aspect of the analyst as dream receiver and will look at the compulsive, obsessional, hysterical, narcissistic, schizoid, depressive, paranoid, and other character and personality styles in the analyst as they impact on dream conversation.

## THE DREAM LISTENER HAS A THEORY

The dream expert, in addition to a personal and professional history with dreams, in addition to a personal character style, is "armed" with, or more kindly, lives with, a theory. This theory may be overt and consciously adhered to, or implicit and out of usual focal awareness.

Usually, orienting philosophies exist in both realms. The more general aspect of the theory concerns itself with the nature of human psychology and with the way psychotherapy is envisioned within such a view. The more specific aspect of the theory, for purposes of our discussion, is the way dreams and dream interpretation are viewed.

Freudians and Jungians have an enormous head start in this arena, because their masters were deeply invested in dreams. They worked out richly architectured visions of the meaning and uses of dreams and their interpretation. Their followers follow, because any road map is better than none at all in the off-road terrain of dream analysis. Therefore when a patient of a Freudian or Jungian analyst tells a dream, the listener is filtering the information through the theory. It is the theory that gets first crack at the dream.

In my own view, both an advantage and disadvantage travels along with a dream heard through the filter of a particular theory. It provides orientation and sometimes predictability for both participants. In the constantly shifting sands of dream work, in which enigma, ambiguity, and mystery abound, insecure analysts and patients can hold onto a point of view for a semblance of stability. As with any theory, however, it also pushes information around, highlights some aspects, ignores others. At its worst, a theory closes the mind of the expert to the dream as dreamt, and the dream becomes just another specimen, another piece of proof of the correctness of the theory. This effect robs dreams of their creative freshness and zany vitality, which is what I think happened in the classical analytic tradition as well as in the Jungian tradition.

The Gestalt therapists, Adlerians, Rankians, the existentialists, self-psychologists, object-relationalists, culturalists, Lacanians, all have had their take on dreams, and all have added a bit to the Freudian and Jungian vision. Together, these lead the individual analyst, on his or her own, to a complex, fluid, and varied view, necessary in our present state of knowledge to creative and meaningful work with dreams. The Gestaltists, for instance, in some ways precursers to the self-psychologists, suggest that we take every piece of dream image to represent a part of the self (Perls, 1969). And with their expressive bent, they further suggest that we ask the dreamer to speak from the position of that image. "What is it like to be the fire hydrant pissed on by that dog? What is it to be the dog? What is it to be the pee? Enter the being of the hydrant and tell us who you are, how you feel, and so on." Such an approach opens playful space for exploration. But some, like Hillman (1979), argued that the focus on dream images to reveal the self is mistaken. Rather than translate dreams upward to self, ego, consciousness, we need to allow the dream to take us downward, with Dante, to its natural home, to nonself, nonego, unconsciousness. Happily, we need not adhere to either point of view and can learn from both, working with some dreams upward, with some downward, with some up and downward and back again.

An adherent begins to repeat him- or herself. Therefore, a patient in therapy with a Gestaltist will soon learn what to expect. A patient with a Freudian, Jungian, or Lacanian therapist soon learns the relevant signifiers, thus, the well-known observation that Freudian patients dream Freudian dreams, and so on. The dreamer, trying hard to make sense of life, trying to deal with psychological suffering of one sort or another, aligns with the authority and often begins to dream in ways that are recognizable to the expert, such that the expert can be expert.

Of late, the relationalists are on the scene, and their point of view, balancing for earlier absences of relational emphasis, finds its expression in the way dreams are listened to. Every dream is seen as an opportunity to learn about the relationship between patient and analyst and about the various transferences and countertransferences that unfold. Often, the therapist is seen hidden away in every possible corner of a dream, and the patient is required to think, feel and talk about reactions to the therapist whenever the dream "reveals" the ghostly presence.

*I was dreaming about a train. And the conductor [= analyst?], or ticket taker [= analyst?], or engineer [= analyst?] stopped me. Someone else riding on the train [= analyst?] spoke to me and asked about my partner [= analyst?]. The tracks were taking us [= analysis?] to the city for a performance [= analysis?] of an opera [= analysis?]. The fat soprano [= analyst?] sang off key, and I left early [= analysis?].*

There is no end to this game. We can find phalluses, breasts, selves, archetypes—or analysts—wherever we look. The point is, the listener with a theory is often a listener in theory alone. Patients play with the expected responses, feed into them, chastise us for them. "Oh! I just remembered this dream. I know you'll love this one!" These are words that can make us cringe and reflect on our predictable ways.

In all this, if the dream wishes as much to be known as to remain hidden, and if such ambivalence is in the very nature of dreams, it may not be a total loss if an analyst, armed with a theory, is way off base in his or her own world of meanings. The analyst's version may reveal a great deal about the analyst, but often leaves the essence of the dream in peace. Not such a bad bargain.

## BROADER SOCIAL–ECONOMIC–CULTURAL FACTORS WITHIN THE DREAM EXPERT

The dream expert is almost in place and ready. We note a personal history with dreams, a professional history, a character style, a theory. But something is missing. The analyst does not exist in a vacuum, although it may feel that way, shuttered from the busy social and physical environment, and mostly glad for the relative peace and quiet. The times, the era, the ways of the contemporary scene all play some part in the psychology of the expert. In general, our American culture does not think much of dreams. The American dream and the dream of night's sleep are not on good terms with one another. So the expert is automatically going against the grain. Not a bad beginning, because dreams so often go against the grain of conscious living. However, the general discouragement does seep into the attitudes of our students and practitioners toward dreams and, moreover, toward the unconscious, which is after all more a European than an American invention, despite evidence to the contrary in the brilliant psychological works of fellow Berkshirites Hawthorne and Melville.

The modern rational mind is not much inclined to the underworld of dream life. After 20 or more years in schools devoted to learning the ways of the rational world, most analysts are not naturally inclined to take up with the ghosts, goblins, trolls, and other denizens of the night life that show up in the world of dreams. Analysts must gain citizenship in both worlds to be of use. It is not easy to move to dream-work from the kind of work we learn in our decades of schooling.

In addition to a general disinclination to engage with dreams in the culture and in modern times, there is a strong tide against work with dreams. The HMO takeover is a direct threat to working with dreams. We cannot, nor should we necessarily try to, prove that working with dreams is cost effective. Freud, in 1897, wrote to his dear friend, Fliess,

"It is a pity that one cannot make a living . . . on dream interpretation!" (Masson, 1985, p. 266). It remains true. Thus, dreams are left for the self-help groups, the New Age healers, the Jungians, and the neuroscientists. It is a pity, indeed, that we shrink from dreams, in part because of economic and social pressures.

The dream expert is a besieged individual. The ancient tradition, the profession's tradition, and the patient all gang up to insist that the analyst is, indeed, the dream authority. And, therefore, the dreamer should of course bring the dream to the analyst for understanding and interpretation. But the analyst, feeling underequipped by the culture, by training, and by personal qualms, shies away from the "expert" role. There can be a pretense, under the disguise of expert, that one knows what one is doing. Theory is usually of very limited benefit. And we are living in an era in which the grand old theories are being buried and the new ones have yet to take hold. The expert is no longer embedded in a coherent system of belief in the sense that religion was once able to unify individual, life and death, soul and grand designer, and that dreams and healing were seen as part of that design.

So the dream expert is, in my view, alone with the dream. That state of being, that situation, can be a bit scary. But if we cannot turn satisfactorily to received knowledge, and if we do not turn away in fear, an interesting development is possible. And I believe we are now ready for this development, particularly at a time and in a place where dreams are not warmly received in general. We have a chance, at long last, to learn about dreams as dreams.

# Ꮭ 8 Ꮭ

## WHEN THE ANALYST'S NEUROTIC STYLE MEETS THE DREAM

*O be joyful, all you patients*
*The doctor's laid in bed beside you!*
                                        —Franz Kafka

I begin this chapter with some misgivings. On the one hand, I believe too much is made, of late, of the analyst's participation in the treatment. The contemporary relational effort to achieve balance in psychoanalysis, relative to the earlier singular emphasis on the patient's intrapsychic world, demands that we enlarge the spotlight to include the analyst's experience. On the other hand, this valuable shift can sometimes go too far in reducing our interest in the primary exploration of the patient's life and mind, and engaging us in an endlessly fascinating and compelling interest in our own doings.

I believe that Freud was very shy about writing about technique for good reason. Now we have gone to the opposite extreme; we fill our journals and our debates with discussion, for example, about whether 'tis nobler to disclose or not to disclose. And so, I am hesitant to engage further in the discussion of analyst in relation to the dream. Except, I think it matters, in an upside-down sort of way. By discussing the impact of kinds of analysts on work with dreams, I am attempting to bring attention to the way analysts, by their nature and temperament, can influence dream interpretation.

Among many possibilities, there are two major ways to divide up interpreters—first, according to theory (e.g., Fosshage and Loew, 1978), and second, according to personality. Again, there are many possible ways of categorizing interpreters according to personality variables. In selecting categories usually applied to patients, I am making the obvious point, made best by Sullivan (1938) in his one-genus postulate, that we are all "in the same boat." The more usual way of linking personality with dreams is in terms of the patient's diagnosis and the kinds of dreams associated with patient diagnostic categories (e.g., Natterson, 1980). Further, I am selecting diagnostic terms derived from traditional psychoanalytic ideas advanced in the work of Rapaport, Gill, and Schafer (1945), Schafer (1948), Erikson (1950), and Shapiro (1965), but here applied to the therapist, not the patient. In using a set of terms generally and sufficiently familiar to many of us, it will not be necessary, for the purposes of this discussion, to engage in definitions. Clearly, there are other dimensions that could be usefully employed, for example, age, gender, professional affiliation, Jung's typologies, more strictly cognitive typologies, developmental typologies, and so on. It is hoped that one will not be too serious about all this and will not be put off by this effort to talk about the therapist in ways usually reserved for our patients.

The analyst personality styles considered will be the compulsive, obsessional, hysteric, narcissistic, schizoid, depressive, and paranoid. If I have left anyone out, please forgive. I would add that, to the best of my knowledge, all of us live with bits and pieces of all of these defensive styles. That is, there are times, events, and conditions that will bring each of these character styles to the fore. I think that is partly why we can work with a range of such individuals; none is completely alien to us.

## THE COMPULSIVE ANALYST MEETS THE DREAM

Dreams and compulsivity in the interpreter are usually the result of a "marriage made in hell." Dreams are often lightness itself, spontaneous, without will, metaphoric, creative, unclear, of no useful purpose, at times deranged. In complete contrast, compulsive individuals are often heavy spirited, rigid, will personified, concrete, orderly, functional, controlling, and rational to a fault. So when an ambiguous dream is told to an analyst with a decidedly compulsive bent, we are in the presence of two conflicting weather fronts and fog is the result. Extremely compulsive analysts can get quite worried about dreams because the analyst's essential nature is being questioned, even mocked, by the very nature of the dream. Many compulsive people hate being mocked, but are used to it. As children, they were often ridiculed for their lack of childishness, for their rigidities, for their inability to play.

Remember, this particular personality style (or social character, in Fromm's sense) was made by and for the machine age: perfectionistic, rigid, orderly, unspontaneous, careful, soulless. This diagnostic category had in it, until recently, more males than females, because males at one time were more likely to be shaped to serve as fodder for the machine or for administration, women more for the home and children. Little boys in training, thus, were like little machines—rigid, lifeless, feelings turned to dust, rules ruling the heart. Imagine these overcontrolled, somewhat lifeless little children, now in the analyst's chair, listening to a dream. "Well, first, one should insist on the details; one requires clarity and order. How can one discuss the dream if it is unclear? How do we even know the dream reported is the same as the one dreamt?" One of Freud's suggestions, to go step by step through the images obtaining asssociations, was perfect for our grown-up compulsive, a wonderful way to bind the anxiety of uncertainty. Jung's unruly ways were more dangerous, more like the devil for a seriously compulsive person. But any rules are better than no rules at all.

A compulsive style in the dream listener can accompany a dogged tracking down of details, a way of making sure there are no loose ends that bespeak an irritability with the vagaries of dream ambiguity, a need to clean things up, a pressure to record each minute detail. Writing down the dream accurately becomes more important than anything in the dream. Or if the reaction formations are not in good shape, or have "been analyzed out," the dream might meet up with a messiness, a sloppiness in approach, a great interest in messy and anal details. But more usually, the dream will meet with a stern and rigid rectitude, especially in the face of the often immoral and unethical wishes played with in dreams. The dream-listener becomes something like the film maker Ingmar Bergman's depiction of his male Lutheran pastor ancestors.

Such an approach could leave the dreamer feeling quite ignored and pushed around or, conversely, deeply reassured that the therapist cares greatly about one's tiniest particulars. The therapist's reliance on will and order can be lifesaving or enraging. Ultimately, however, through trying to pin the dream down in the manner of a butterfly collector, the compulsive interpreter will insistently miss the living, beating heart within the dream. The dream and the compulsive analyst will, ultimately, each go their own lonely way. Sometimes a dream will take pity on the poor machine man and turn out a dream that speaks machine talk: orderly, neat, packaged. But dreams cannot stay that way for too long and will eventually "bust out." On occasion, the compulsive analyst and the dream become warm partners. The interpreter may need the spontaneity of the dream to spark some life; and the dream may welcome being approached by a shy and rigid soul who has lost the capacity to play. In this way, a shy compulsive may be worth a lot more than a compulsive bully—except for dreams that speak in terms of bondage, domination, and submission. On occasion, the compulsive interpreter and the dream may become engaged in sadistic warfare, each torturing the other, each enjoying the misery of the other, each vying for control.

Here is an example of the latter situation: a dream in which there is the portrayal of the essence of uncertainty: *"I saw the sea, or a river, or was it the sky, I wasn't sure, or was it a grassy area? Maybe it was the sea and I was on it, or maybe it was my brother, and we were on a boat or maybe we weren't."* The dream is told to a compulsively organized interpreter. Naturally, he or she insists on some clear formulation. In time, dream and interpreter can drive each other nuts. But the dream will always win in the end. It will not be boxed forever. The powerful emphasis on will and autonomy of the compulsive person when it meets up with the seemingly unwilled freedom of dreams will eventually falter—if the analyst does not go "native" in the meantime. I think some compulsive analysts come to envy the freedom of dreams. I think some compulsive analysts seek the elimination of such freedom. To capture and to jail a dream's uncertainties are ways to reduce one's envy of freedom.

It must be a major human achievement to live with uncertainty and doubt. Dreams and dreamers require the space and time to breathe until meaning shows itself, more from within the dream's own story than from without. The capacity to live with uncertainty can be a major advantage in this project. Unfortunately, a compulsive personality style has a most difficult time with this particular virtue.

### THE OBSESSIONAL ANALYST MEETS THE DREAM

Usually, and for good reasons, compulsive and obsessional traits are put together, as in the term *obsessive-compulsive*. I would like to separate them for now, however, to see what differences can be observed (and also to cast a vote against the simplistic ideas associated with the newly popular OCD diagnosis). A mainly obsessional style in the therapist, when conversing about dreams, could lead to an overvaluation of abstraction and conceptualization. Philosophy about experience will outdistance the more raw feel of experience. The obsessional analyst, and this includes most of us who, by definition, have spent decades in books and in schools, will be more comfortable with ideas about ideas than with images. One will observe an interest in associations that weave far from the dream's main images and themes. At home in words and their interweavings, there results a relative disinterest in feeling, action, and impulse. At times, obsessed with a particular interpretive approach, the analyst will have a hard time with the ambiguities, the zany shiftiness of dreams. Ideas and theoretic conceptions about the dream will dominate over other possibilities in dream conversation, and a dry, pedantic crust can envelop the proceedings.

As a young man, I discontinued therapy with a fine analyst over his overly pedantic, although possibly "correct," interpretation of a panicky dream of mine. I felt that his refinement and intellectualism would not allow him to get more fully into the messy and confusing violence that was then plaguing me and pushing its way into my frightened awareness. Such a style can seem too careful and distancing when a more robust response is necessary. The "correctness" of an interpretation, the obsessional's goal, is often in direct contrast with what is necessary, that is, a spirit of collaboration, a willingness to enter the dream's mystery together without premature knowingness, an ability to put shoulder to the wheel, to share the burden. In other circumstances, however, the obsessional approach can calm and reassure disorganized persons who need a bit of distance from the raw stuff and for whom knowingness, no matter its defensiveness, is welcome.

An intellectual-obsessional style meeting up with a dream is of particular relevance because the interplay between secondary and primary process thinking, thought to be characteristic of the inner workings of dreaming, is played out between interpreter and dream. How these two styles of thinking interact is of enduring interest. It is when an obsessional interpreter needs to assert ideational authority, control, and domination over a patient's dream that trouble begins.

The thoughtfulness, the slight distancing, and the capacity for doubt afforded by the sort of reliance on ideation characteristic of some obsessional analysts can represent a cautious, soothing, and unthreatening manner to some overheated patients. Some dreams may enjoy being thought about, philosophized, and theorized over. But then again, dreams seem to be able to put up with most any style. Unless they are severely mistreated, they keep showing up and offering themselves to all listeners. The obsessive and compulsive interpreter is often being given a gift—the gift of creative thought and feeling at the center of a patient's dream—as an opportunity over and over to open one's mind and one's feelings. Our patients' dreams themselves give us a chance to relax our defensive intellectual style and to join the play. If we miss out, they'll come again and again. "Can Johnny come out and play?" The right dream at the right time, thus, can help cut through the neurotic style of excessive ideation on the part of an interpreter and move the heart. Such a dream is worth its weight in gold.

## THE ANALYST AS HYSTERIC MEETS THE DREAM

The most fun of all is in the interaction of the hysteric and the dream. Just as the obsessive-compulsive used to be more male than female, the hysteric used to be more female than male. If the male had to be emptied of feeling to fit the world of the industrial machine, the female had to be emptied of thought and authority in order to comply with her role in that world. Sexualization as competition, seduction as disguised control, hidden power, heightened imaginativeness, boundary confusion, fluidity and impressionism in thinking, a reliance on intuition and feelingfulness, such characteristics of an hysterical personality style are made to order for much good dream conversation. These interpreters often can see themselves reflected in the very nature of dreams. Thus, they can feel at home in listening to and talking about many dreams with their patients. They just sit back and let themselves go in simply being themselves. They can feel their way into, empathically and intuitively connect with, and allow themselves to relax within the dream's mysteries. The torture of unclarity for an obsessive and compulsive is transformed within hysterics into an opportunity for fun and play. "What, me worry?" The unknown can give shivers of pleasure instead of an urgency for control. The unconscious, after all, was the realm made known in Freud's work with his hysterical Viennese women patients. And, truth be told, Freud's own hysterical neurosis was made to order for associational work with dreams in his self-analysis.

It is sometimes fun to find a three-layer cake in supervision: a mysterious dream told to an analyst with a prominent hysterical style related to an obsessive-compulsive supervisor. The hysterical analyst, at home with the unclarity and ambiguity of the dream, just can't understand why the supervisor is so insistent on clarification and details and feels a bit stupid in the face of the supervisor's irritation. Alternatively, an obsessional analyst may present a patient's dream to an hysterical supervisor who keeps insisting the analyst learn to relax and play, advice that is guaranteed to tighten things up even more. I have often found, however, that it is the most obsessive and compulsively organized therapists and supervisors who grimly insist on "playfulness" in their patients and students. The dynamics of patient, dream, analyst, and supervisor are often mind boggling in their complexity. Could it be that the term *parallel process* is both useful and a grievous oversimplification? I wonder at the kind of clarity about these matters often reported in books, papers, and meetings.

However, anxiety is a problem for hysterics as is the capacity for repression, disorganization, splitting, dissociation, and avoidance, the price paid for feelingfulness. In its worst form, anxiety, fear, or panic can disable the interpreter and make listening, taking in, thinking, and talking difficult. If a particular dream touches on concerns, worries, or fantasies that provoke anxiety, the interpreter can go blank or disconnect from the proceedings. The empathic strength of such persons can, however, lead to making some use of their anxious periods; their episodic anxiety may occasionally correlate with anxieties and hidden disruptions in the dream itself. Hysteria, thus coupled with some obsessive-compulsive traits, can be an excellent combination. I think this combination coexisted in both Freud and Jung. Feelingfulness joined with reflectiveness often leads to the right mixture, particularly in creating the conditions for good dream discussion in clinical work. The mixed neurotic, an hysterical style mixed with an obsessive-compulsive style, is therefore in a fine position to work well with dreams. Or, it could also be said that *anima* mixed with *animus*, or female mixed with male personality traits, is a good idea.

The relationship between an hysteric's style and the powerful themes of sex and aggression, along with issues of dependence and independence, has been the subject of an enormous amount of speculation. For our purposes, it suffices to suggest curiosity about the ways an hysterical interpreter meets up with hidden and overt sexuality, hidden and overt aggression, and various shadings of dependence and independence. These themes will show themselves in dreams and if avoided or overemphasized, the dream can "toy" with the interpreter. For example, says the dream: "Oh. You don't like me to mention sex? Well how about this version, or that version, or still a third and fourth version? Or what if I spell it out for you: S-E-X?" Similarly with aggression and dependence and with any of the important themes depicted and elaborated in dreams; either turning away or focusing an excessive spotlight can cause the dream to engage in commentary on the interpreter's ways.

For example, an analyst with a markedly hysterical style including an aversion to real talk about real sex consistently turned a blind eye to dreams in which specific and graphic sexual activity was described, preferring instead to emphasize the dependent relational aspects. Finally, as if in exasperation, a dream was told in which appeared characters from the play "The Miracle Worker" by William Gibson, seen by the patient on television two nights previous. *In the dream, the patient angrily confronted Helen Keller: "Look! Open your eyes, dummy!"* The analyst, and Helen Keller's teacher, and the actress playing the teacher all shared the same first name: Anne. *In the next dream scene, the patient looked over at Annie Sullivan, the teacher, and said: "You're the real dummy. Why are you so blind?" as she witnesses Helen Keller and her teacher touch each other's hands and intertwine fingers in sexual play.* There are many ways to think about this dream, but *"Open your eyes, dummy!"* deserves to be heard as a direct communication both to the nonobserving self and to the nonobserving analyst, not only to see but to speak as well about the sexual aspects of the relationship, and not just about the relational aspects of the sexuality.

## THE NARCISSISTIC ANALYST MEETS THE DREAM

One of the most dramatic relationships is that between narcissistic interpreter and dream. Such a relationship must be seen against the general background of the evident, though often disguised, narcissism of many in our profession. I suppose the new requirement, seemingly central in much contemporary psychotherapy, that we be "more finely empathically attuned" and somehow "better" and "more loving" than our patients' narcissistic mothers, forces the healer's plentiful narcissism more into shadowland, where it can be even more potent.

In relation to the dream, I focus on a single aspect of this meeting between two self-absorbed forces. The question is: Can the interpreter open his or her eyes and mind sufficiently to see what might actually exist in the dream apart from the interpreter's own needs? I believe this to be the central question in dream interpretation inasmuch as psychoanalysis itself can be thought of as exceptionally self-absorbed and self-interested when it comes to dreams. Psychoanalysis, within every school, has looked into dreams and seen its own face, has seen its own theories reflected in the dreamer's dream. Beyond psychoanalysis, every culture sees in dreams the culture's own version of life (Lippmann, 1998).

But beyond theory and culture, each individual dream listener has the tendency to pour his or her notions into the other's dream. The dream, like the pool for Narcissus, offers a surface onto which it is possible to project one's innermost needs, fears, and preoccupations. The narcissistic projection of one's deepest concerns into the dream of the other is such a ubiquitous event that it can be regarded as somewhat natural, inevitable, and even necessary by virtue of the ambiguous nature of dreams. To the extent that dreams are a mystery, the interpreter enters the proceedings to bring some consensual social agreement to the mystery, in contrast to the disarray ushered in by the dream's deeply private and irrational nature. Naturally, this means bringing in the self of the interpreter.

This natural tendency, however, is exaggerated in the case of the narcissistic character style. Such an interpreter must have things his or her own way. Patients do a variety of things with the narcissism of their analysts, from protection to war, and dreams follow suit. Dreams can play with the self-esteem of the listener. They can inflate and deflate.

They can enhance and undermine. They can fill the analyst with pride and with shame. They can lead to an analyst feeling wonderful and to feeling terrible about self and work. They can help an analyst hide deficiencies and they can expose with brutal frankness. Thus, they can evolve into one of the major ways a patient plays with an analyst's narcissism.

The engagement of narcissistic analyst with dream is particularly interesting if one views the dream as an entirely self-absorbed product of mind. Alone in the privacy of sleep, shut away from the need to interact and live out one's social concerns, the dream, initiated in deeply private instigation of still unknown origin, is created and lives of its own accord, for its own reasons, in its own ways, for its own purposes. It does what it does without a thought to the other. The very few that are remembered into day and the fewer still that are communicated to another make up but a tiny fraction of dreams dreamt. To think that dreaming is communication from self to other, from patient to analyst, seems untrue on the face of it, despite our narcissistic needs to be included in the privacy of our patient's thoughts. There may well be some small communicative function, but the vast majority of dreaming does not involve any need to take the "other" into serious account. The other exists in our dreams, perhaps as subject matter for reverie, but not for the sake of the other, but for our own sake. The dream, in its way, is almost a perfect narcissist.

This narcissistic core of dreaming is sometimes experienced as offensive by narcissistic interpreters who have a hard time with anything that lives for its own sake and not with interpreter in mind. The relational emphasis on the omnipresence of the analyst and of the analytic relationship in dreams is, thus, perfectly suited to the needs of the narcissistic dream expert. "Where am I in my patient's dream?" is the motto, which inadvertently reveals the narcissist's central doubt about his or her very own reality in existence.

There is an inevitable competition between self-created and self-absorbed dream, on the one hand, and narcissistic interpreter, on the other hand. The winner is the one who cares less about the other while forcing the other to care. The interpreter wins by insisting the dream is about him or her and madly projects himself or herself into the dream's content. "You're so vain, you think this dream is about you." The dream wins by going its own way, by not really giving a damn. The dreamer may care about these goings on, but the dream, entirely insulated from external and social needs, could care less. There is no way the narcissistic interpreter can win in this competition. The narcissist most usually does care beneath layers of contempt and disdain for others. The dream doesn't. The narcissistic interpreter could learn a thing or two from the dream about genuine narcissism, namely that needing the approval of the other, needing the validation of the other, needing to be made real by the other, is a losing proposition. Maintaining mystery and unclarity about the self is the way to go. Some narcissistic analysts know this very well and follow the path of the enigmatic. Supported by the myth of the virtue of anonymity, such analysts often create an aura around themselves of the secret, the unknown, the hidden, the strange, all tell-tale signs of a narcissist at work.

## THE SCHIZOID ANALYST MEETS THE DREAM

The competitive narcissisms of dream and interpreter can lead to conflict and mutual claims for the preferred position, whereas the schizoid analyst and the dream seem to me to be on the same side of things right from the outset. Just as the schizoid character style is born of the need to retreat from the social, to find a home in the private domain, to commune within one's own mind, to find one's best friend in interior conversation, to look at the world more as observer than as participant, to be consistently misunderstood, to have one's silence filled with the projections of others—all of this is close kin to the dream.

The shy, strange, aloof schizoid person and the dream are made of similar stuff and can reside in a room together without doing harm to one another. I am making the assumption that the schizoid analyst—and we can agree that the schizoid aspect of our personalities is partly what has drawn us away from the fray and into the inner sanctum of psychological analysis—has a natural affinity for the experience of dreams. The more outgoing, expressive, extroverted, expansive interpreter, however, may have an easier time with the second phase, that is, with therapeutic conversations about dreams.

But given the relative safety of our offices, along with the many gratifications afforded by the fact that persons are coming to us for our company and knowledge, and also by the fact that many of our basic needs are being taken care of by our being paid by these persons, allows even the most schizoid of us to feel some security sufficient to enable us to open up just enough to talk with our patients and to meet with their dreams without our dissolving in shyness. Loneliness is a killer for most schizoid persons. Our patients help with that one. Insecurity and social shyness are awful for schizoid people. Our patients help with that one, too. We are wanted, needed, made to feel important, and can stay "at home." That is terrific for us schizoids. And, we are paid, to boot. What a wonderful world for the schizoid analyst. No wonder we can give it our best. Small wonder we can be our best and most loving selves in our work.

In teaching dream work to student analysts and therapists, I am convinced that the more strange, shy, introverted, private, diffident—schizoid—the dream listener, the more able he or she is to tune in on the life of the dream. Again, conversing about it with the patient is another matter; but most find the way. Shyness is in the essence of dreams, I believe, and dreams show themselves best to shy listeners. They are least offended by unusual, original, private thinking. And on the other side, schizoid analysts are best able to enjoy the zany antics of some dreams. Because working with dreams is all "from the side," and not usually a frontal contact sport, schizoid interpreters are able, in their way, to relax enough to come very close to the dream's heart.

Freud's ways—obtain associations until the hidden dream shows itself—seem better suited to the schizoid interpreter than to today's more heated relational and interactional approaches that, in some hands, come closer to a frontal contact sport. If they adopt such an approach, schizoid individuals need to pretend to a certain connectiveness they may not feel. And they need to pretend to a certain ability to mix it up, of which they may not actually be capable. Do the relationalists allow the sort of "from the side" approach that was once possible for the Freudians? Today, however, even the Freudians are becoming more "genuine" and interactive. Pity.

An appreciation for the realm of the private, the dignity of the secluded, the importance of the unsocialized inner being is part of the inheritance of Freud. But so is the analyst's interest in penetrating such realms and in turning id to ego, in socializing the primitive. We live within and between these two dialectically opposed forces. The schizoid analyst has a headstart on the first pole and can use some help in relation to the second.

Many overly socialized and extroverted persons who find themselves as analysts and interpreters listening to dreams have a difficult time understanding the central aspect of dreams that speaks from the inner self to the remainder of the self. I suspect that schizoid analysts have a better time recognizing the many rooms within the inner sanctum. They have an easier time knowing that dreams can be about conscience speaking to impulse and vice versa, or about unconscious speaking to consciousness and vice versa, or about an older self speaking with a younger self and vice versa, about all the extraordinary internal conversations that make up so much of mental life. Dreams seem to me, more than most psychological phenomena, often to reflect the stuff of deepest internal conversation. Dreams give us a royal opportunity to listen in on these dialogues within mind. It seems a shame to turn dreams into mere reflections of social living. Schizoid analysts, even if they are poor at cocktail conversation, often really "get it" when it comes to the world of dreams.

### THE DEPRESSIVE ANALYST MEETS THE DREAM

Depression in the analyst is a big problem. If there is a vocational hazard, it can be seen in the dual possibilities of narcissistic inflation and depression, the first by virtue of our exalted position, especially in the young, the second by virtue of emotional exhaustion, especially in the old. The general problem of depression in the analyst overshadows the particular problem of a depressed interpreter looking into a particular dream. The various aspects of a depressed experience—lack of interest, fatigue, low energy, sleepiness, falling back on the familiar, fear of novelty, bitterness, pessimism, a sense of failure, a disappointment in life's promise, a colorlessness, an absence in the flow of creative juices—all of these can make listening to and working with dreams arduous, draining, even painful. Dreams are always an invitation to play. There are times when this invitation can help a depressed analyst regain a sense of interest, a bit of liveliness. But there are times when "I had a dream last night," leads to fatigue, guiltiness, irritation, and a wish for it all to go away.

For some, the ancient idea that dreams and death are related can help the depressed interpreter feel more at home and less estranged by the invitation to play and explore. For some, Hillman's (1979) optimistic idea that sleepiness in the analyst can be a call from the unconscious "to go deeper" can be a stimulating and arousing possibility that adds a moment of liveliness to "dead" feelings. We exist in a field of work that can find usefulness for some of our worst vulnerabilities and weaknesses, thank God. For a depressed interpreter to imagine that one's inner feelings of sadness or deadness can connect meaningfully with the very ground, underground, underworld, from which dreams spring is a most helpful possibility. To have the idea that life in the shadows, within a depression, is twin to the shadow life of dreams is to gain a foothold for meaningful work in the midst of feeling helpless and hopeless. Thus dreams and their interpretation, as advertised from ancient times, can assist in psychological healing, not only for the dreamer but, in this instance, for the dream interpreter. Many have always known that the dream listener, the expert of dreams, is the one most helped by working with dreams and no one more so than the depressed analyst. I strongly recommend that depressed therapists familiarize themselves with the literature on ancient dream interpretation that integrates death, sleep, and dreams in most creative ways. There is more promise in such an approach, in my opinion, than in our own culture's soulless solutions—antidepressant chemicals.

## THE PARANOID ANALYST MEETS THE DREAM

Freud was greatly helpful to the paranoid style as it meets up with the dream. The notion of the dream in disguise, of the hidden nature of the latent dream, of the falseness of the manifest, of the need for the "real dream" to slip past a censorship, of the necessity to revise the final story to make it more plausible to the self-audience—all this is entirely familiar to the paranoid mind. The paranoid analyst is unable to trust what is put before him. He must deconstruct according to his suspicions. And a dream—that ambiguous, mysterious, unclear bundle of irrational confusions—is just the right stimulation to force the paranoid interpreter to spring into action. "What does this mean? And that? And that? How shall we make patterns? How shall we discover the hidden and secret meanings? How shall we create meanings where there may be none?" Not knowing is a huge problem for paranoid individuals.

Not being clear, not being able to make out the plot, not being "in the know"—are all awful sources of insecurity and anxiety for the paranoid therapist. The detective in us, the seeker after hidden meanings, the dogged determination to find what is so, the certainty that resistance is at work to keep us from the truth—these are all the hallmarks of paranoid styles of thinking in our work with patients. But also is the need for the single, all-embracing explanation that can have a grandiose side to it (akin to an overuse of the "W" in Rorschach scoring terminology). In working with dreams, we see paranoid sides of ourselves showing up, the more the dream seems to play hide and seek, as it so often does.

The paranoid dream interpreter sits in disguise, hiding his hidden suspicions, and is, thus, equal to the dream, which also may sit in disguise. The task for the interpreter vis-à-vis the dream is to unmask the dream and to reveal its real, usually unsavory, innards. But so often, it works both ways, and the interpreter is unmasked in the effort to unmask. Sitting in dream workshops and listening to therapist-participants respond to a patient's dream as best they can, one listens to repetitive themes coming from certain participants, no matter what the dream. One devoutly heterosexual fellow keeps hearing anal homosexual wishes. One young analyst repeatedly alludes to the inauthenticity of the dreamers. Another worries again and again about disorganization and incipient schizophrenia. Another is convinced every dream is a sexual seduction, or that hidden sadistic aggression is the issue, or that death lurks in every dream.

The point is that in our thoughts about a dream, and in our interventions, we reveal ourselves the way a paranoid person often reveals what is hidden, without realizing it, by the nature of his or her projections. So much of dream interpretation is projection—a field day for that quintessential paranoid defense. If dreams, by their nature, invite the paranoid, projecting side of ourselves out into the open, is there some purpose in it? Is it not just Freud's view, but in the nature of dreams, themselves, that a paranoid response is called out in the listener? Is it possible that in night- and sleep-thinking, when there is less feedback from the external world, when there is no light of day to correct our misperceptions and misapprehensions, when we rely more entirely on our own internal world of shadow, memory, reflection, and creation—that in such a circumstance, visions are created that arouse suspicion in the daytime listener? The interpreter, after all, is living within the rules of day thought, of more or less secondary process thinking. Is it not understandable that among the various responses would be doubt, suspicion as to origin, worry about unclarity and confusion, along with a corrective effort to read some of one's own sense into things? Making the unfamiliar familiar, making sense, creating rational connections is part of the work of the day mind as it reacts to the night mind. The day mind, concerned about basic survival and devoted to keeping one's eyes open to dangers, views the dream, product of the night mind, as something of a stranger; it comes from the self, probably, but it is not necessarily entirely of the self, at least not of a self about which one is conscious.

The dilemma of dream consciousness is one of the major philosophical and scientific problems from the beginning of time. A paranoid approach to dreams, although constricting in a therapeutic sense, makes good sense especially in our times, within which there is no embracing philosophy or religion that connects dreams, soul, healing, nature, and God and that can allow us to think that dreams are an intimate part of all of living. Freud's "paranoid" system seems ideal for a day mind, in modern times, that remains suspicious of the outpourings of the night mind, of the creative, irrational, drive related realm of forbidden and free thoughts. The order above keeps a suspicious eye on the anarchy below. It is something like the old-timers, the first pioneers, viewing the immigrants with suspicion; if you take them into your home and heart without suspicion, who knows what illness, crime, danger, lowering of standards, is possible.

So the paranoid interpreter is not an aberration, at least not in modern times. Yet the analytic project sets before us the task of attempting to integrate, in the absence of an all-embracing religion, the night dream with the day mind. And so, the paranoid suspiciousness within the interpreter may be a necessary starting point, but it doesn't carry us far enough into the world of integration. Our patients and their symptoms come to us as symptoms of modern times, divided, estranged from self, family, and community. They dream and their dreams may feel alien to many, as well as to us. Our task is to bring the alien, dream and patient alike, to a place of recognition, to a place where there is sufficient room to know oneself, including the fact of one's unknown life. Our task is to speak with the alien dream, perhaps to learn something of its native language, and to invite it to join us for a short while, to engage in good conversation with it and about it, and to part on better terms—at least in mutual recognition of our having shared a part of life for a bit.

It should be clear by now, that the analyst's ability to engage in all of these defensive styles at different times, under differing circumstances, is not only necessary and desirable for analytic work with patients, but especially for analytic work with dreams. Each personality style—compulsive, obsessional, hysteric, narcissistic, schizoid, depressive, paranoid—brings with it an aspect of dreaming itself. For example, the paranoid capacity for projection is related to the dream's projection of needs and wishes onto the inner screen; the obsessional interest in ideational associational networks is related to the dream's use of wide-ranging connections; the schizoid's apartness and the dream's separation from social living is related. Each style, and all of them together, reflect the ways of the dreaming mind and can be most useful in entering the patient's world in good dream conversation.

In his paper on dreams, Freud (1911) posed the issue "at what stage in the treatment and how rapidly should the analyst introduce the patient to the knowledge of what lies veiled in his mind." Clearly Freud had in mind "the patient's mind." However, there is an alternative reading. Dreams, for better or worse, offer ways of introducing the patient to what lies veiled in the analyst's mind, as well.

# ෬ 9 ෨

## A Child's Question
### "Where Do Dreams Come From?"

*Backward, turn backward, O Time, in thy flight.*
*Make me a child again, just for tonight.*
—Elizabeth Akers Allen

She used to wake up slowly when she was little. It was about 7 o'clock one spring morning, many years ago. My daughter was 5 years old. I remember the birds had been singing loudly for the past hour or so, whole operas outside the window. Probably lots of early worms. Lots to sing about. I had made coffee and was sitting on the rug in her small bedroom, reading I don't remember what, waiting for her to waken and begin the day for us both. She opened her eyes, one eye at a time, smiled when she saw me sitting on the rug, began a slow stretch, and said, "Daddy? Where do dreams come from?"

From the point of view of being a young psychologist and psychoanalyst, the experience of daily living with small children is an extraordinary learning adventure, over and above the universal joys and pains of parenting. No amount of graduate and postgraduate schooling, no amount of experience with research subjects or patients can equal the deep and wide range of learning made possible from being close to a young child from the very beginning. As for me, things I used to think I knew evaporated daily in the bright light of the reality of being with my real children. From the inside, becoming a father, day by day, was the most powerful experience of my life—as it continues to be.

I had known from earliest childhood, and had rehearsed in my imagination, my wish to be a father, although I think it was only after I found out I couldn't be a mother that I had gone on to the next best. Yet despite this lifelong ambition, the reality left me to understand that I had been totally unprepared for the fact of it. In the modern world, we are left on our own to improvise our most important roles in life.

Those who spend time with a baby and a young child come closest to knowing the secret harvest of an evolving and growing mind. For a psychologist, there is no surer way to understanding than to take part in the actual birth and growth of an actual psyche. This is not the "psyche" and "mind" described by the theorists. The hypothetical reconstructions of the baby's mind by Freud or Klein or Kohut belong to the business of system building, and have precious little to do with the day-by-day development of an actual mind. Although so much is going on under the surface and is not subject to direct observation, being with a child in intimate daily and nightly contact gives one immediate access to crucial aspects of the development of the child's mind. Accordingly, mothers have always been the most knowing about the "ins and outs" of the infant's and child's mental evolution. Nowadays, some young psychologists who are also fathers of young children are sharing more of the hours and the details of childcare than did many of us older father-psychologists and have more of an opportunity to learn what mothers have been in the position to learn from the beginning. Babies show much of what is going on within, but you have to be there with them to see it. Freud and Jung learned deeply from their adult patients and from their introspective selves and their friends and colleagues, but chances are they did not learn much about the growth of the psyche from the best place to learn, from the daily, moment-to-moment lives of their many children.

Even though my colleague-wife and I had moved to rural country so that we could share more evenly in making a living and in childcare, we quickly became a traditional family. Our own natures and the times conspired to have me, the father, need to make more of a living and she, the mother, to spend more time with the children. I am reminded of two friends, a homosexual couple, thoroughly committed to role equality, who recently adopted a baby boy. One of them soon became the mommy with the baby, the major caretaker, feeder, washer-upper, insider, and the other soon became the daddy, the major earner, reader of newspapers, outsider. Is it the baby who requires and therefore creates these divergent roles? Does the baby beget and call into existence the one who sits on the floor with baby, bottle, bib, and toys, and the other who talks politics with the company? In all our conversations about genes, the construction of gender, and cultural influences, we rarely consider the power and influence of the baby in all this. The baby may have more to contribute to who we become with them than we usually realize. But this idea might begin to erode our culture's and our profession's self-serving myth of the needful, dependent, helpless infant and the unempathic parents who drive them (luckily) to our doors and our couches.

For my wife and me, reading Erik Erikson's (1950) *Childhood and Society* helped a lot, as did Doctor Spock's *Baby and Child Care* (1957) and Selma Fraiberg's *The Magic Years* (1959). Erikson, especially, helped us feel that special, moving, and deeply pleasurable synthesis of parent and psychologist going about the remarkable adventure of having and raising children, as all our "mutual life-cycles" were "cogwheeling" at the same time as we were being mindful of a mind in growth.

But still, I missed a lot. And so when she asked, "Daddy? Where do dreams come from?" I knew I was at one of those moments.

The birds sang more loudly. I was almost about to answer, "From the unconscious, dear," but thought better of it, and instead asked her where she thought they came from—an old psychologist's trick. She pointed to her eyelids, but then said, "I think sometimes they come in the window." One bird singing louder than the others may have been calling out the answer, but I couldn't make it out. Our dog ambled up the stairs and into the room, but kept the answer to herself. My daughter went on to tell me her dream, and never asked me again.

It was a good question. I've been thinking about it since. And I'm not at all sure I have an answer still. My daughter now has a daughter of her own, who at age 2 is beginning to tell her dreams in the morning. Maybe I'll have an answer ready if I'm lucky enough to be at the right place at the right time and my granddaughter happens to ask me. It is more likely that my daughter will be the one to be there if and when the question is asked, and perhaps she will say, "Let's ask Grandpa."

Or because she's more imaginative than I, perhaps she will simply say, "From the dream-fairy."

When I was a child, I thought my dreams came from Europe. Because they were so often about the horrors of Nazi brutality in the concentration camps, I thought my dreams came straight from Auschwitz and Treblinka, places I knew well in my mind, places burned into my fevered imagination and associated with family in Europe. I was hardly in a position to say, in response to my child's question, "From the dream-fairy." But, I could hardly say "From hell," where I actually thought, as a child, they were cooked up, so instead, I came up with the unspoken, "From the unconscious, dear."

Of course, my daughter's question is a question that philosophers, scientists, psychologists, psychoanalysts, anthropologists, mystics, theologists, healers, and others interested in the origins of dreams have contemplated from the beginning of time.

Do dreams originate outside the person and find their way inside? Do they originate from nature—like wind, storm, and moon? Are they carried by singing birds? Do they originate from gods who place them within to teach, or frighten, or pleasure? Do they originate from one's body, from intestines, heart, or brain? Do they originate from one's social group, from culture, from its history and its needs and experiences, from its collective memory? Do they originate from one's infancy, from wishes and traumas and individual memory? Do they come from the future with messages of prophesy? Do they come from the dead, from the other side, from the world of souls and spirits? Are they emanations and communications from other persons? Are they the images and voices of the unconscious?

The child is pretty sure dreams come from outside and points to window or ceiling or wallpaper pattern or closet. The child also thinks the dreams are real, that during a dream he or she is experiencing real events in the real world, that the tiger is a real tiger in the bedroom, that the monster is really there when eyes are closed. Yet the dreamer is in there, too, engaged in the action, feeling the feelings, living the life within the dream. So the dream is from outside, but the dreamer is inside it, or better, the dreamer's insides are involved. The child can become so afraid of the outside power of dreams that sleep itself becomes undesirable, a state to be avoided as if one's very life were at stake, as though the dream were something from outside that can sweep you up into it. From early in life, the issue of the location and origin of the dream's images is of importance.

The idea that dreams originate from outside the sleeper has been a consistent view in different times and cultures. Dreams have been thought to have originated in spirits and gods and God, in dead relatives, or in souls waiting to be born, in persons dead or alive trying to communicate with the dreamer. They have been thought to have their origin in the collective spirit of the people, in forces of nature, in history, in the future, in the stars, in the whole booming cacophony of life itself. Each of these beliefs has blossomed into an entire realm of explanations.

As for the dreamer, all one needs to do is to sleep and receive what is being sent from outside to one's own mind. One is not necessarily personally responsible for any of it. The dream is seen, not had, in such a view (Young, 1999). The individual dreamer can be more or less receptive; certain people can be more open to certain outside dream forces—shamans, psychics, holy persons—and sometimes innocents can be particularly prone to receptivity, and thus develop a certain facility, even a familiarity. For them, the dream's images can seem to come as much from within as from without. But on the whole, the dreamer is visited.

Related to, but different from, the view of the external origin of dreams, is the view that dreams are the actual living-sleeping experiences of the psyche or the soul or the mind, departed from the sleeper's body and traveling through differing dimensions, places, times, and adventures, visiting here and there, and returning to the sleeper's body by night's end. This view is an experience-near view of dreams, and is admirable on that account, even though science teaches otherwise. It was further thought that it was most unwise to awaken a person before the traveling soul could return to its home. Imagine the danger both to the soul locked out of its body and to the body awakening without its soul. Some mornings, it actually feels that way. It can take hours before one feels whole again, sometimes only when a piece of dream is remembered, or when some other life experience—sex, work, brushing the teeth, or the next night's dreams—helps mind and body rejoin.

Whether from the gods or from the experience of soul travel, the dreamer, in such belief systems, exists in close proximity to the origin of dreams. Gods speak with them; souls travel within them or they travel outward to other souls; animals, trees, monsters, friends, all the flora and fauna of dream life come from near and far to visit the dreamer. Or else the dreamer exits the bedroom and travels to meet up with all the familiar and the strange of nightlife in an experience of direct engagement. When an 11-year-old Catholic child dreams of consoling Mary, it *is* Mary in the dream. And the child is in direct engagement, an intimate, immediate connection. When the young neophyte warrior dreams of the soaring hawk looking him straight in the eye, it is not a mediated experience, it *is* the hawk with which the warrior engages. When the Chasid dreams that the Baal Shem Tov sings a dream-created song to him, the Chasid will take the dream and its song seriously as a direct communication from the Baal Shem Tov. In days gone by and in most all cultures, people lived on intimate terms with their dreams, more intimate than is true for us.

These varied ideas about the origins of dreams are the fruit of imagination. Once upon a time, we looked into the sky and saw hunters, dippers, faces, animals, where "in reality" there was nothing but planets, stars, and galaxies. Imagination plays with reality, amplifies it, extends it, fits it to our own nature and needs for coherence, and thereby creates a personal and collective universe within which one can feel at home. This is no small matter. States of alienation and estrangement, the inability to feel at home in one's body, in one's mind, in one's society, in one's universe, are powerful by-products of modern living.

This process of imaginative elaboration of the origin and nature of dreams is particularly interesting because such elaboration is made of the same stuff as are dreams themselves. Even if we adopt Hobson's (1988) reductive explanations, we see that the dream begins in random firings but is soon seized upon by the mind's capacity and need for meaningfulness in which imaginative connections of sets of memory fragments leads to a better or worse sense of coherence, to wholeness, a patterned gestalt, a story, a narrative, a dream. The move from chaos to pattern, from unknowing to knowing, from randomness to order seems to be a requirement of our own minds. This same process is duplicated in our prescientific ideas about the origins of dreams and their interpretation. Imagination fills our explanations—both within the dream and later about the dream. It brings ideas and facts together with needs and wishes in a rich "soup" of understanding (Casey, 1976). The very nature of dreams together with explanations about them exist side by side in the realm of imagination.

But as we control nature more, we seem to become more estranged from nature. Our relationship with mystery seems closer than is our relationship with mystery laid bare. Are we closer in our spirit, for example, to the butterfly in free disarrayed flight, or to the pinned, dissected, categorized, DNA-identified, "known" butterfly? Are we closer to the moon since we set foot on its surface than we were to the moon as object of mystery, adoration, fear, curiosity, imagination? Are we closer to the spirit, the feel, the power of the unconscious since we began its more or less scientific study? I am not suggesting that ignorance is a superior state of mind. I do believe that laying bare many of the mysteries of the cell, for example, opens the possibility of profound engagement with reality up close. And in such engagement, the possibilities of enriched discovery and imagination multiply with our further dissections.

But still there may be a price we pay for scientific knowing, and for the intellectual and physical control of nature that follows such knowing. We may lose the integrative capacity of imagination. And with it, we may lose some essential soul connection, some experience of the world that is more fullhearted, more direct. Some think of this as a child's naive experience. In our modern culture, approaches such as Zen Buddhism are attractive precisely because they attempt to restore the experience of direct engagement lost to the knowing, evaluating, judging, conceptualizing mind.

Reared as we are in the enlightenment traditions of Western scientific rational thought, we experience the dream in a way that is decidedly different from the way our ancestors did and as people in preindustrial cultures continue to experience it today. Scientific closeness has replaced imaginative coherence. In particular, the dream's origin is viewed as located within the person, within the mind. Freud's great contribution brought into this century the dream as an object worthy of serious study. Once and for all, the origin of dreams was the dreamer. The dreamer's wishes, conflicts, memories, the dreamer's own and unique mind, psyche, unconscious were the source. Now, of course, we locate the dream's origins in the brain and more specifically in the firing and activation of pontine, geniculate, occipital neurons. We've almost got it nailed, like the pinned butterfly. Thus, the dream is no longer thought to originate outside the dreamer, whether from God or gods, nature, spirits, or culture, but from within, from one's own mind, one's own psychology, one's own nature, one's own history, one's own brain, one's own personality, one's own inner self. This significant change in ideas on origination has profoundly affected our view of dreams and our relationship with them.

It should seem that we would feel more connected to our dreams knowing as we do that they originate from within our very own minds, that they are made of the stuff of our own individual lives. And now with REM studies combined with brain imaging techniques, we can almost watch a dream through its pathways, lighting up parts of the brain, and we can awaken a dreamer in the midst of a dream for its immediate report. But rather than feel closer to our dreams, the opposite seems to be the case. We seem less connected to our dreams, involve ourselves less with their messages and meanings, give them far less import than was once true. Our culture can be thought of as dream unfriendly for many reasons, not the least of which is our obsession with the material realm. But the idea of personal authorship has had a peculiar side effect. The modern citizen seems somewhat shy and hesitant in relation to dreams. The knowledge that dreams come from within seems to increase one's alienation from them. With personal authorship comes increased personal responsibility and occasional guiltiness or even shame whether in the dream's images or in interpretation. A more imaginative, mystical, religious point of view about the origins of dreams may have permitted a greater feeling of familiarity and closeness with one's own nightly mental productions, as though one could feel closer with less personal ownership. Herein is a paradox that marks the modern engagement with dreams: the closer we get to its origins, the further we feel from its power. Imagination has been stifled.

What will be the effect of the further erosion of the imaginative capacity brought about by the increasing importance of the external screen in filling our need for stories? If Hollywood is the dream factory, if DreamWorks is only the latest in the business of image manufacturing, what will become of the mind's own internal screen on which our own stories are nightly portrayed? That is, how does the "dream factory" impact on our own imaginations? What is the difference between being read to, reading, listening to stories on the radio, and watching stories on the external screen in relation to our own imagining minds? If a future child asks, "Where do dreams come from?," will we be inclined to point to the computer?

In my opinion, psychoanalysis plays an important role in assisting the modern mind to rediscover the miracle of dream life, especially in its remarkable capacity for play and creative imagination. The scientific discoveries of the origin and nature of dreams can increase our wonder at and appreciation of the remarkable and infinitely complex night world of memory and imagination. But in order to assist in this rediscovery, psychoanalysis must be open to ancient as well as modern ideas about dreams and it must not be too quick or too sure when it approaches a dream's mystery.

A child's question, "Where do dreams come from?" A good question still.

# ०४ 10 ४०

## Apple Tree Dreams
### On the Ecology of Unremembered Dreams

*Keep me as the apple of the eye; hide me under the shadow of thy wings.*

—Psalms 17:8

Dream science has demonstrated that we dream all night long in both REM and nonREM states. Like the heart and lungs that never stop working, the brain and mind also take no time off. REM dreams are those dreamy dreams that are metaphoric, symbolic, strange, complex, feelingful. NonREM dreams are more like daytime thinking although somewhat freer, loops of concerned worry, obsessional checking, going over details from the days before or the days to come. Both activities proceed at intervals all the night through.

### The Vast Majority of Dreams Are Forgotten

But most important for this discussion, in all this dream activity, only an exceedingly small portion of all dreams are remembered into the

next day. Let's say 5% to 10% of dreams are remembered. Of the ten or
so REM dreams each night (or 70 a week), only about three a week are
remembered, which leaves close to 95% of all dreams unremembered.
A very large number of dream experiences, thus, briefly rise to awareness within sleep and then quickly fall back to that vast realm of
unawareness. It seems like an enormous amount of mental energy and
activity that ends up unremembered. Not that unremembered mental
life is unusual or unimportant. Studies of implicit mental processes and
thinking outside of awareness demonstrate the wide range and significance of such cognitive activities. We clearly are fortunate not to have
to be aware or consciously thinking about everything. But what is
different about dreams is that we are, in sleep, conscious of the dream
experience during dreaming. But then, most all such dream-conscious
experience is soon and completely forgotten. Because in psychoanalysis
we have focused only on remembered dreams, unremembered dreams
have been of little interest, except in their being mistakenly interpreted
as the result of repression and resistance. But now we have mostly
recovered from that unfortunate theory-driven error and can begin to
recognize that forgotten dreams are the natural right of mind in that
they comprise the vast majority of all dreaming experience.

   To think about forgotten dreams is not a particularly ordinary thing
to do in psychoanalysis. Why is all this dreaming so quickly, easily, and
completely forgotten? What for? Could there be some function, an
evolutionary design to this continuous repetition of such an on–off
experience? Here today. Gone tomorrow. Certainly, so many experiences, often vivid ones, feelingful ones, tragic ones, enraged ones,
stupid ones, sexy ones, relational ones—so many experiences and then
gone! Goodby! Finished! Forgotten! What for? For just keeping the
mind going during sleep? For emptying out excess information like
garbage, like defecation? For showing us how little we know of our own
mental life? For teaching us in little bits and pieces something essential
about life, and about death? Out, brief candle.

   But this questioning of the meaning of such massive forgetting could
instead be framed as "why ever is any dream remembered?" With what
purpose? According to what evolutionary design? For the sake of
analysis? Probably not. For one's own mind's sake? More likely. Also,
in order to have the opportunity to reflect on dream life oneself or to
communicate to another, to the tribe, to the social order about what
has taken place in dreams? Perhaps. And also to invite the day mind

of the self, and the other, the tribe and the social order to join in commentary on the dream? To put the personal and usually private dream into the day world of self and others and also to take into the private dream, the thinking, the judgment, the imagination, the needs, the projections, the interpretations of the day mind and of the world of others? Not a bad possibility. Later we consider more fully this hypothesized social aspect of dreams.

Actually both questions are of interest. Why are so few dreams remembered? And why is so vast a majority of dreams forgotten? Difficulty in remembering dreams has long been recognized, long before Freud. But Freud (1900) also added: "we are so familiar with the fact of dreams being liable to be forgotten, that we see no absurdity in the possibility of someone having had a dream in the night and of his not being aware in the morning either of what he has dreamt or even of the fact that he has dreamt at all" (p. 43). The repression and resistance hypotheses, however, dominated over common observation. Yet there is something difficult about this subcontinent of forgotten dreams, this other side of the moon that shows itself in sleep but soon turns dark; this massive elusiveness. Repression or resistance to analysis seems like small potatoes. Something bigger is probably at stake.

## VARIETIES OF UNREMEMBERED DREAMS

Unremembered dreams, we will therefore agree, are a strange and interesting piece of mental life. How often do we wake just on the edge of a piece of dream life and, "poof," gone, just as we move an arm or open an eye? If only we could recapture the dream that was so vivid just a moment ago. Perhaps if we moved our arm back to its original position or if we closed our eyes again, we could reenter the dream or at least recover its memory. What was it that was so gripping just a second ago? Or "I knew it was a remarkable night; I was all over the world. I was exhausted. What a night. But I don't remember a single thing, just that I wore funny clothes and you were in it, too." Perhaps pieces of the dream come back hours later, or two days later at the movies, or ten years later through another dream, or never at all. And there are parts of dreams, fragments, moments that are remembered but not other moments. Sometimes there is a feeling that an entire saga pertaining to life's great mysteries or pertaining to one's entire development or concerning the essential meaning of the symptom for which one came to analysis has been revealed in the night's dreams. But only a small piece is recalled, the rest an unrecoverable Atlantis lying vast but unseen at the bottom of the sea. Surely, catching a brief glimpse but then losing such adventures, such understandings, such experiences has some effect on the dreamer.

A patient reported a dream in which

> *her long-dead parents were standing at the bedroom door, watching her have intercourse with her husband. She smiled over to them as if to show them how it was done. She knew they would learn from her example, make love themselves, join sperm to egg, and then she, the patient, could at long last be born again. Her own dead soul could enter the proceedings just at the very instant that the parents' egg and seed would combine when they had dream sex, and she could then finally become alive.*

She felt she had waited for this moment forever, lost hope when her parents died, but maintained the unconscious process in her world of unremembered dreams. As she related this extraordinary dream, she recalled suddenly an entire series of previously unremembered dreams over the last several decades. She had been totally unaware of these other dreams until this very moment of reporting last night's install-ment. This interconnected program of dreams consisted of *her parents, at first at opposite ends of the universe, slowly, over the years, and in different dreams, coming closer and closer in each dream, continent by continent, country by country, until this last one when they finally stood together receiving instruction.* She had been working on this unconscious project for most of her life, requiring and leading her parents to make love again so that she could be born. It is, of course, possible that she confabulated or imagined the idea of the past program of dreams. But I think not. Her report of the content of the past dreams was too vivid and specific. I have collected considerable evidence of the existence of dream themes, of various kinds, developing over years, sometimes partly remembered, usually not, until a dream or other experience causes the memory of the dream program to present itself. Persons like this patient actually do hope and intend to heal themselves—in this case, to be rid of a sense of a dead soul—in the most remarkable, ingenious, magical, extraordinary ways, often through dreams. And often through dreams that never reach the light of day. It may even be true that we are doing this sort of healing–thinking all the time without ever realizing it. This vast sub-continent of forgotten dreams may hold many of our most precious secrets.

Is there meaning in this wholesale forgetting, some adaptation, some survival advantage that accrues to the fact of first experiencing but then rapidly forgetting and losing memory of dreams? For example, Crick and Mitchison's (1983) "garbage" hypothesis would consider the forgetting of dreams to be the "getting rid of" psychic waste stuff so that new material can be assimilated. But they seem uninterested in the possibility that waste can be recycled and reassimilated and that waste can be a rich source of nutriment to subsequent growth. Whichever way one looks at it, the experiencing and subsequent forgetting of dreams is the normal mode. We are so constituted as to forget most all our dreams. We probably have more than enough to think about in ordinary living without having to remember and ruminate on all we have dreamt. And yet we dream and dream, and rarely remember. Like fish in the sea, we might catch a few, but millions remain in their own realm. However, modern technology may be changing this fact of fish life. Can it also change the fact of dream life?

There is an entire gradation in relation to memory of dreams. There are some dreams that are remembered vividly for one's entire life. There are others that are remembered for just part of a day. There are dreams that are experienced and forgotten immediately, or forgotten gradually through the night, or carried in memory into awake consciousness briefly or longer, and some that are unable to survive the change in state that comes with awakening. There are undoubtedly some dream memories that exist only within the realm of dreams themselves. Some dreams, like the ones unremembered by my patient, connect with each other, build on each other, comment on each other, refer to and cross-reference each other, without once entering awake consciousness. Others leapfrog in and out of consciousness through the years. Some dreams are only remembered if told to oneself or another once awake, or if recorded. Some dreams remain only in someone else's memory and not the dreamer's. I have had the experience of reading a dream back to a patient that was originally reported a week or two earlier, only to find that the patient has no memory whatsoever of the dream itself, but perhaps some partial memory of the implications of our discussion. Interpretation and dream conversation sometimes out-live the dream itself; sometimes the dream outlives any subsequent discussion; sometimes both fade into oblivion.

Each of these kinds of remembering and forgetting of dreams, I suppose, has its own value: dream experience forgotten immediately in sleep, dream experience forgotten before morning, dream experi-ence partly remembered a bit into daytime, dream experience well remembered into daytime, dream experience remembered sometime during the subsequent days or remembered not until weeks, months, or years later.

Memory of a dream is probably a complicated matter, certainly as, perhaps more, complicated than memory of an experience in daytime living. There is undoubtedly short- and long-term memory storage, and some in between. And memory, like perception, is probably distributed widely in part memories for color, design, form, recognizability, name, meaning. This process may be similar to the construction of dreams out of varied bits and pieces of consciously or unconsciously remem-bered perceptions and experiences. Dreams are possibly assembled of various parts; dreams are possibly disassembled into various parts.

As to the assembly and construction of dreams: percepts, images, pieces of memory, ideas are assembled, disassembled, reassembled, connected, disconnected, reconnected, ordered, disordered, reordered, "membered," remembered, dismembered, shifted, changed, held onto and let go of. Ideas, idea fragments, images, components of images, memories, bits of memories, themes, and subthemes are woven and unwoven and rewoven into fabrics of experiences and are lit up on sleep's internal screen. However they may originate, whether in the collective unconscious, in infantile wishes, or in random subcortical vibrations, by the time they become dreams, they have been processed, reprocessed, and rendered as creations of a multitude of varieties. Why all this ordering and reordering, connecting and disconnecting of bits and pieces of mental life into such a rich variety of mental experiences? And then in their forgetting, is all of this construction simply reversed in a complex deconstruction back into the bits and pieces of mental life disassembled, disconnected, let go of, into various bins of memory or discharged entirely from the system without a trace?

There is also the complex issue of the potential for interconnections between memory of daytime events and memory of dream experience. One example might be the déjà vu phenomenon in which one feels a certain vague familiarity in a circumstance that in all respects is unfamiliar. The thousands of unremembered dreams one has in a single year could well serve as background and basis for a sense of "having been there before." The universe of unremembered dreams, I believe, serves as background for hosts of experiences of small and large magnitude. We may have not the slightest idea in consciousness, but there may well be plentiful unremembered dream experiences, rehearsals, prophesies, reconstructions, soothings, warnings, experiments, new ideas, breakdowns, pleasures, that shape life as we know it. Rarely mentioned as a cause of things, unremembered dreams may play a large share in coloring mood, in creating background for decisions, in our hunches and intuitions, in our daytime moves.

## ANCESTORS AND DESCENDANTS

Alongside the observation that most dreams are unremembered is the important conclusion that we exist within the experience of an entire universe outside our usual awareness—the universe of dream experience. The lack of memory is sometimes taken to represent a void, but it is an interesting kind of void, one in which an experience, the dream, has taken place, but without subsequent memory in conscious awareness. What is the psychological effect on the mind of the dreamer of this repeated experience? What might be the metaphoric or symbolic or psychological meanings of the phenomenon of forgotten dreams?

There are many ways to approach this question. First, the class of dreams that are unremembered belongs to the larger class of life outside of awareness. Because such dreams are not in waking awareness, they belong to the vast category of internal events that "exist" outside of consciousness, that is, "in the unconscious." In short, such dreams, in their being lost to remembered awareness, become part of unconscious life, although they were briefly once conscious, in sleeping dreams. This brings us briefly to a division in the unconscious between that which was once experienced, was once in awareness—the forgotten—and that which was never in awareness, which existed beyond our capacity for awareness, such as the silent psychological impact of genetic information, or of ancient cultural patterns. Although unremembered dreams belong to the former category, both aspects of unconscious life can be considered together for our present purposes.

This background of unremembered dreams can be compared, for example, with ancestors one never knew or only rarely heard about, yet who exert strong influence under the surface of conscious life. For example, I never knew three of my four grandparents. I never met them, or they me. They never saw me, or I them. All three died long before I was born, far away on another continent, in another era, long before my parents met and married. If at all, I existed for them as a distant wish, a dream, a hope or a fear, only in imagination, an idea. I may have "existed" for them as my own dreamed-up grandchildren or great-grandchildren exist for me—a wish, an idea, a dream of the future.

This ideational reaching across generations, I believe, is an important part of life. With the present as anchor, we reach back to our ancestors—unseen and unknown—and forward to our descendants—unseen and unknown. We create linkages of various kinds, in imagination, weaving together what bits and pieces we may know or dream up. From the point of view of our ancestors, looking forward means dreaming and imagining us, our lives, our experience. Did they imagine us as I imagine the lives, problems, opportunities, and travails of my imagined grandchildren? From the point of view of our descendants, looking back means their dreaming and imagining us, our lives, our experience. Will they imagine us as I imagine my grandparents? This idea of communication across the generations, between persons literally unknown to one another, is just one small piece of the way unknown life can be of influence. Of course, the generations affect each other in many ways, material as well as spiritual. The choices and experiences of our ancestors provide the groundwork for our psychological and material lives. Jung's idea of the collective unconscious is only one version of this understanding of the effect on the present of what came before, whether we know it or not. The effect of past experience on the psychological present is vast, whereas what we may know, in consciousness, of that effect may be miniscule.

We lost our first child just before birth. The baby died in the eighth month of pregnancy. We never met the baby, yet the unborn child lived on in memory, mostly unconsciously, as time went on. It affected the way we experienced subsequent pregnancies and even the way we experienced our subsequent live children, as well as affecting many aspects of the way all of life was viewed. Like a dream, briefly experienced and forgotten, our unborn child touched all of our subsequent life in profound ways.

What becomes of all those dreams unremembered—thousands of dreams in a year's time? Where do they go? How do they affect subsequent dreams? How do they affect subsequent waking psychology? Is it possible that these forgotten dreams—like my unknown grandparents and unknown grandchildren, like our unborn child—have an influence on life?

## An Apple Tree

Sometimes questions can be approached through an image. Just as in a dream, wherein a single image is often a rich condensation of many thoughts, images, and meanings, I once came upon a scene that expresses some of the ideas in this chapter. In the middle of a bright late autumn day, while driving from Great Barrington to Stockbridge, I saw an apple tree in an open field. Beneath the tree lay its fallen apples turned golden and brown, heaped in a thick circle around the trunk. The tree's gold and brown leaves had also fallen and now mingled with the apples on the ground. It looked as though the tree's branches had in a single moment dropped their treasure. Because the tree stood in a large country field, it was likely that no one would remove the fallen leaves and apples. They would simply lie there during the following months, season after season, slowly transformed by various organisms and microorganisms, bugs and worms and what have you, all engaged in ecological decay and salvage. As time passed, the apples and leaves would slowly become once again part of the soil that would nourish the tree in its future growth and its future flowering and fruiting; that is, the tree's fallen apples and leaves would slowly become fertilizer and nourishment for the tree's future life.

I believe this image can be considered as a metaphor for the phenomena of unremembered dreams. Let us suppose the tree represents individual mental life. The apples and leaves, then, are overt expressions of that mental life. Some few of the apples, perhaps, are picked, tasted, eaten, and digested. These become part of the being of the apple eater. These few picked and tasted apples are like dreams that are remembered. They are noticed, thought about, analyzed, and are occasionally, deeply transformative. Picked, eaten, digested, they become part of the person. Some picked and eaten apples can be sour, some wormy. Some remembered dreams can be sour and certainly they

can be "wormy." Sometimes they can upset the stomach. Some are
nightmares. Eaten apples, then, like remembered dreams, can range
from the delightful to the awful. And occasionally, to continue the
analogy, some dreams, like some apples, can change the course of
history. Eve's apple was the first. Newton's apple another. The role of
Buddha's mother's dream and subsequently the role of Buddha's
dreams in the development of Buddhism and of Mohammed's dreams
in the founding of Islam, Paul's and Peter's dreams in the development
of Christianity are but a few of the many examples of the enormous
power dreams have had through history, maybe even more than apples.

But what about the unpicked apples, fallen to ground, becoming part
of earth? Certainly most all the apples of this one tree were unpicked,
like most dreams are "unpicked" by subsequent consciousness and
memory and analysis. These dreams are alive for an instant, experienced as dream, but then left alone, no longer in awareness, unremembered. I believe these unpicked dream-apples slowly decompose naturally,
and become nourishment for the mind and its emotional life—from
below, from the soil of unconscious mental life. Our entire conscious
mental life like the visible tree and its expression in leaves and fruit, is
nourished, I believe, by the entirety of mental life outside of awareness,
by all of unconscious thought and imagery. The thoughts, images,
activated and reassembled memories and associated feelings expressed
in dreams, then immediately forgotten or unremembered, become the
soil and the nourishment, all outside of awareness, for subsequent
mental life and, more broadly, for the adaptive survival of the person.

The creative ordering and reordering found in dreams have their
own value. So much of its being forgotten brings us to the conclusion
that this forgetting also has its value. I suggest that, in being forgotten,
attention is withdrawn and the bits and pieces that went into the dream
are now free to exist within the mental system without much energy
expended. There is also the possibility of still additional transformation
taking place of the once again unconscious material. This continuous
surfacing and disappearing and resurfacing of unconscious material
can be seen as analogous to turning the earth over again and again,
exposing the earth's bits to the nutrients within air and returning them
to the soil's deeper nutrients. The nature and quality of the soil will
determine the nature and quality of the tree and its apples. In an
analogous way, the bits and pieces of forgotten dream stuff, once
again unconscious, colors, affects, influences, shapes, and nourishes

subsequent conscious mental life. This influence can operate in small and large ways. The point is that the continuous dreaming and forgetting serves, in mental ecology, continuously to nourish and freshen, order and reorder, express and submerge pieces of mental life; from the stored unconscious depths to the light of awareness in dreams and back again. Again and again, this continuous turning of mental soil serves as a backdrop for all mental life. My son, an organic farmer here in western New England, assures me that soil requires continuing nourishment. If overused, soil cannot grow good organic crops. The soil has to be treated, fed, rested, used. I think the mind may not be so different. At least, I prefer analogies that compare mind to aspects of the world closer to nature rather than to aspects of our own tools, like computers, electricity, plumbing. Thus, dreaming and forgetting can be compared to an apple tree along with the turning of soil. Continuing in this vein of comparisons within nature, the mind can be compared to a sea anemone or a sea fan, which opens and closes depending on the relative state of safety and need for nutriment. The use of analogies and metaphors from nature for psychological and mental life makes good sense to me.

Unremembered dreams, therefore, can be seen as the ground from which other dreams, including remembered ones, grow. But they are more than that. The universe of unremembered dreams is doing all the things dreams are thought to be doing: these unremembered dreams solve problems; they search and scan for examples and categories; they deal with integration within the self; they attempt to master trauma; they compensate and balance for conscious life; they allow the shadow side its moment onstage; they gratify infantile and adult wishes; they discharge and rid the system of unuseful information; they allow the psyche briefly to embody and picture itself; they are a deeply private set of internal experiences taking place in asocial sleep; they are the voice of the culture circulating in individual minds in sleep; they are a basic expression of the mind's own natural self-healing capacity.

Indeed, remembering the dream seems an unusual circumstance, perhaps even an aberration, perhaps something gone wrong with the process. Freud postulated that a dream that wakes the sleeper is a failed dream. What if a dream that is remembered in the morning is also a failed dream, its original but unattained goal having been to be dreamt and then forgotten? What if psychoanalysis has been sponsoring an aberrant, even a potentially harmful and unnatural event—the remembering and then pouring over of dreams, which were "meant" to have been gotten rid of, not thought about, erased? And further, what if psychoanalysis then goes on to judge, criticize, interpret, and "punish" the poor patient who quite naturally is doing his or her best to forget. In short, what if the dream is meant to be forgotten?

Perhaps most of what a dream is doing can be accomplished in its unremembered form, in any event. The question again is not why are dreams forgotten, it is why are they remembered at all? What particular aspect of mental life necessitates the remembering of dreams because they seem to do quite well in their usually unremembered form? Could there be some sort of need to see, graphically portray, and then hold onto what is going on within one's own active, sleeping, conceptual, and associational mind; or some social need that lifts the dream to regions of the mind that enable their memory and eventual communication to others? Memory of dreams, I suggest, may be related to social need, and opens the way to a consideration of the brain's own linkage to communication and ultimately to the subsequent art of dream interpretation.

Whatever its occasional use in remembered form, the ancient mind in REM sleep does whatever it needs to do, prior to or even in the absence of any considerations of memory or subsequent communication. The dream itself is the main attraction. This brief flash of interwoven events and meanings, lighting up the mind like the aurora borealis, *is* the show. And, I suggest, it becomes the soil and the nourishment for subsequent mental life. Apple-tree dreams.

## THE USES OF FORGETTING

Freud's forceful and repeated insistence on the role of resistance in the forgetting of dreams (Freud, 1900) has cast a deep shadow on the clinical analytic attitude toward unremembered dreams to the present day. He considered the lowering of mental resistance during sleep to be the reason for the occurrence of dreams. The increase in resistance on awakening, then, results in the forgetting of parts or the whole of dreams. When added to this hypothesis is the dictum that "whatever interrupts the progress of analysis is resistance" (Freud, 1900, p. 555), we are well prepared and disposed to take a most dim view of the patient's inability to remember dreams. For the analyst, a "successful" completion of the night's work results in a remembered dream, no matter how fragmentary. According to Anzieu (1989), "If everything goes well, we can on waking develop the film (dream), view it, re-edit it or even project it in the form of a narrative told to another person" (p. 211). What, then, of the findings of REM science that instruct us that most all dreams are quite naturally unremembered? How might this influence our clinical stance?

First, we could no longer assume that resistance is at work in all dream forgetting. Freud's argument about resistance might still hold for a small portion of wholly or partially forgotten dreams but the argument would not apply to the vast number of dreams experienced but unremembered. This consideration would lead to a less suspicious and negative attitude toward the dreamer's lack of dream report. Second, we would no longer assume that dreams "belong" to the analysis and that they are being withheld, even unconsciously, from the analysis. Rather, dreams belong to the dreamer, and most of them to the dreamer's unconscious. A more respectful attitude toward the dreamer's night life is required. The vast majority of dreams do their "work" in the absence of subsequent memory, consciousness, communication, and analysis. We are not necessary in this process. Although we might yet have a role in helping think about them.

Whether dreams are messages from God or the gods, whether they are thought of as prophesies or as hallucinatory wish fulfillments (Freud, 1900), whether they are seen as "reverse learning" to remove overloads of "neural garbage" (Crick and Mitchison, 1983), or as rehearsals for complex motor programs and behaviors (Jouvet, 1980), it is clear that most of this activity goes on in the absence of memory and subsequent waking consciousness. In short, it is no sin to forget dreams. It may even be natural to forget dreams. It may even be beneficial to forget dreams, for example, in certain mental states like depression in which the remembering of dreams can add to the problem (Cartwright, 1986).

Cartwright's work on dreams and depression is most instructive. If depressed persons spend their days in self-judgment and self-accusation for their failures and faults, one would hope that sleep and dreams could bring relief, or as Jung would have it, compensation, balance, healing. However, in depression, the usual rules seem not to apply and the disorder can be thought of as something of a perversion of the expected and usual life force, up to and including a wish to die because of unbearable psychological pain. Dreams may bring more pain than relief for depressed persons. Dreams of the depressed often continue and amplify, into night, the bad self-feelings of the day; more accusations, more judgments, more self-criticism, more release of self-hatred. By morning's time, the depressed person has often been badly pummeled by dreams. No wonder the poor and interrupted sleep of many depressed persons can be hypothesized as an effort by the beleaguered self to interrupt or stop these nightly self-punishments. In research that limits or eliminates REM dreams, depressed patients get better. Now, this is most surprising. Dreams have long been thought of as a way of self-healing, a creative effort to make life better. Well, it's not necessarily so. Therefore, the forgetting of dreams can be most salutary, a blessing. This idea can lead us to a more helpful approach to depression, a disorder which so easily angers the frustrated therapist, thus adding to the patient's already brimming self-hatred and despair.

Most patients however, even some depressed ones, can find encouragement in the idea that, in their own sleeping minds, and all night long, they are creating, connecting, unconnecting, reconnecting, and weaving layers and worlds of meaning for their own mind's benefit. They can sometimes feel a bit of hope in the idea that their own natural mind, even without psychotherapy, can be attempting, at the deepest levels, to put things together in interesting and adaptive ways. When the occasional dream shows itself and allows us together to see its ways, we are privileged to catch a glimpse of what the natural mind, in nightly sleep, is constantly engaged in—a window into the mind's nightly prowling. This constant activity of REM behavior, from its origins in the mammalian brain and in individual uterine existence, until death, is every person's heritage and legacy. The remembered dream is an exception. The rule is the dreaming unremembered.

For the patient who feels an inner void, such an idea is a challenge for us to explore the difference between the nightly, nourishing, dreaming mind and the experience of conscious emptiness. For the one who has always felt uncreative, the discovery of the reality of one's own continuous stream of nightly creations, mostly forgotten, can be most instructive and helpful. For constricted persons, to discover the shadow side of awake life adds dimension and breath. Communicated dreams open the door to working with patients on every level, in subtle and complex ways. But beyond the glimpses we are afforded of dream life in ourselves and in our patients, there is this remarkable universe of dream life. The patient's mind is a miracle of activity and adaptation. We are at the service of the dream, not the other way around.

## DREAMS AND DEATH

The experience of forgetting most all dreams, as briefly indicated, has in it a number of psychological ramifications. What is it one learns through such nightly tidal activity, such nightly presences and absences, such appearances and disappearances? Perhaps the dreamer comes unconsciously to recognize that nothing is forever, nothing is certain, nothing lasts, that precious and meaningful experience can be lost in an instant, that holding on is impossible. This Buddhist version of life may be in the essence of the nightly forgetting of dreams. Perhaps that is one reason the Buddhist study of mind has illusion and impermanence at its center. Further and at deeper levels of possible meaning is the relation between dreaming and death and, more specifically, between dream forgetting and death. Each night there is a direct experience of brief theater followed by forgetfulness and silence. We are informed again and again, without our even being aware of it, circuited in the very middle of our minds, that a brief illumination, a brief life, is followed by an absence, a death within the mind. This repeated activity may, as a side effect, or in its central meaning, be teaching us, slowly and quietly reminding us, or alluding to, or giving us a taste of, the fact of the inevitable, inescapable, predestined ending to come. Most of us live with the knowledge of inevitable death in a hide-and-seek way. We know it but we don't really know it, can't really stand to know it. How could we believe such an ending because we have no experience of it. Well, perhaps there is a slow, barely noticeable warming up to the terrible and inevitable experience of it both in sleep and in the forgetting of dreams. The dream forgotten brings to mind Shakespeare's Macbeth: "Out, out, brief candle! / Life's but a walking shadow, a poor player / That struts and frets his hour upon the stage, / and then is heard no more."

One dream about death, although not a forgotten one. *Not long ago, I dreamed of an esteemed professor of clinical psychology with whom I had had an ambivalent relationship and who had died many years earlier. In the dream, he was clearly returning for a visit from the beyond and after some preliminaries, I began to relate to him some of the recent events in our field and in the lives of his family members that had transpired since his death. I told him about the admission of psychologists into the American Psychoanalytic Association. I told him how his widow, a painter of considerable talent, had gone on to many successes. I gave him the good news that his daughter had just given birth to his only grandchild. While telling him of these events to his evident pleasure, I wondered, in the dream, whether or not in informing him of these events since his death, I was perhaps transgressing some eternal law, some essential barrier between the living and the dead, which required that the dead not know about events following their death. As a child, death meant for me no longer being able to know what was going on. A terrible tragedy in my young mind. So, I decided, in the dream, that the risk was worth taking and continued informing my old teacher about life following the end of his life. While still in the dream, I strongly wished that someone, after my own death, even some ambivalent student, might return the favor and fill me in on events in our field, in the world, in the lives of my family members, on what had happened following my death.* A dream's wish awaiting fulfillment in the next life. It wouldn't matter if it were remembered or not. The mere dream of it would be sufficient for me.

# ෬ II ෨

## On the Private Nature Of Dreams

*A privacy, an obscure nook for me.*
*I want to be forgotten even by God.*
                                        —Robert Browning

As we described in "Apple Tree Dreams" in chapter 10, few dreams survive to fully awake consciousness, let alone to dream journals or to communication to others. Therefore, even before morning's arousal, there are many dreams and fragments, whole adventures, scenes, memories and cogitations, whole universes, that are private even to the dreamer, that rise from and quickly fall back to the unconscious. The dream, therefore, is usually a most private event. It is so private it is most often completely unremembered and, hence, invisible to the conscious mind. Disappeared. Imagine, a psychological event that is so thoroughly tucked and hidden away, from self and certainly from the prying eyes of others, in an extreme of privacy. Dreams are among the most private of human experiences.

And all of this is going on while we are in sleep, out of touch, away from life's activities and others, wrapped in ourselves, dead to the world. And all is going on in pictures and stories in the mind, no one watching, no one hearing except perhaps a REM researcher (Dement, 1978), but even then it's just squiggles and MRI impressions, not the "real McCoy," not the experience itself. That remains private. Furthermore, either through involuntary forgetting or by choosing not to report the dream to another, the dream is kept private. The analyst is in a unique position. By virtue of strict confidentiality, dreams can be told to the analyst and yet remain relatively private. I believe this aspect of dreams to be of considerable interest and importance. Dreams are of the essence of the privacy of mind.

## THE PRIVATE MIND ENDANGERED

Private experience, especially of the sort that includes the self communicating with, to, and for the self, or of the mind engaging in its own sort of activities for its own sort of purposes, seems to generate diminishing interest in contemporary psychotherapies as well as in the general culture. How could that be? There seems to me nothing more interesting or significant in relation to large-scale, contemporary, social trends than the mind's effort to maintain a private domain. To be sure, even the private nature of dreams is socially shaped in its basic vocabulary as well as in much of its content. Still, it remains in the realm of private experience. Even though we are all socially constructed, and even though some think we are simply narratives, good or poor stories about ourselves, we have this private side nonetheless. We still live deep within ourselves, whether the other knows it or not, whether we ourselves know it or not. This private side is not only under assault in the social world, it is also under assault even within our own concepts. Modern psychoanalysis seems to lose interest in the centrality of the private dimensions of life and of mind; a betrayal of sorts, an abandonment of the private just when it is most endangered.

Now it should be added, in all fairness, that we ourselves have played a part in the reduction of the private. Our Freud, our movement, our method played a central role in opening things up, in unrepressing, in freely associating, in showing the nature and content of the unconscious; and then labeling, diagnosing, treating, interpreting, advocating a relationship with the hidden ways of the unconscious. The talking cure. Nabokov, Lolita's brilliant creator, had only contempt for this aspect of psychoanalysis, that what is usually kept secret needs to be revealed and worked through. Even when psychoanalysis responded with, "But we mean only when there is psychological sickness, is such a method recommended," Nabokov saw through this ruse. He realized we therapists would define what was sickness until all fell under our purview and until there was nothing that could be kept to oneself or between oneself and one's God, or between oneself and one's secret love. Of course anyone objecting to the scrutiny of our psychoanalytic insights were suspect. And Nabokov as "pedophile" was perfectly suspect. A great many cultured and complex minds were offended by our arrogance and by our intrusion into the private domain. So there is an important contradiction in our devotion to the private and in our destruction of the private, as seen in our relation to dreams. It is possible to reconnect with the essentially private nature of mind. But we must first disabuse ourselves of some of our cherished ideas.

For example, what does it mean to suggest the possibility that dreams take place for their own purpose? Although they may be brought to our offices for mutual consideration in privacy, they are dreamt for reasons still unknown, not necessarily for our purposes, more likely to satisfy their own requirements. We may try to make use of them. Some may even have been dreamt for the purposes of our work together, but most come around because they come around, it seems to me. We can detect certain trends here and there: for example, no dreams for a while and then a torrent of them, or vice versa. Or confused dreams followed by a period of clear, simple dreams. Or sexual dreams followed by dreams of death. Or a period of high mood followed by dreams of falling apart. Or more and more anger revealed slowly in dreams. We try to make sense of these patterns. But mostly dreams come and go of their own design, for their own reasons, often impossible to know.

## The Dream Exists for Its Own Sake

Let us hypothesize that dream images engage with, connect with, and play with each other just for their own reasons. In a lovely collection of short writings on his experiences as a physician, William Carlos

Williams, in *The Doctor Stories* (1984), writes, "Everything that varies a hair's breadth from another is an invitation to the dance. Either dance or annihilation. There can be only the dance or ONE" (p. 90). That is, any hair's breadth variation in two or more images invites movement between and within them, for their own sake. And Bert States, in his latest illuminating work on dreams, *Seeing in the Dark* (1997), gives a Darwinian twist to the competition between dream images for consciousness, that is, for survival and domination. All this is within the inner world of dream images. Not for our purposes, as far as we can tell, but for their own. This view echos James Hillman's (1979). When added to Hobson's (1988) contributions, and to ideas about PGO (pontine-geniculate-occipital) activation alongside of REM events, we begin to think of dreams as existing, at first, within and for themselves; only later, in our cerebral connecting, does the meaning-making mind-brain join the party. Thus, there are many levels to the basic privacy of dreams. In my view, this basic privacy is not on friendly terms with much of contemporary psychotherapy or with much of the cultural context.

We live in a confessional era, in part because of a transformation of cultural values brought about, in no small measure, by the impact of our own profession. The entirely private experience, moment, reaction, or thought is rather unwelcome in this climate, is even conceived of as somewhat subversive. Also, we live at a time in which the electronic revolution is quietly and efficiently contributing to the erosion of the once proud realm of privacy, of private information, as well as of private time. And, further, the sheer increase in numbers of our species may contribute to privacy becoming a more unusual, even an endangered, experience.

The deep privacy, which still prevails at the center of dream experience, is, therefore, of special interest, as it provides continuous and direct evidence of an inner world still, more or less, of one's own. Dreams have always held the possibility of an addition to, an alternative to, perhaps a compensation for, the requirements of public living, in the same way that social life and communication hold the possibility of alternatives to inner life. Obviously, these two realms balance, interact with, enrich, and require each other in complex ways that are part of our human evolution. The essential privacy of dreams is, therefore, seen as one part of an interactive system including our deeply social nature.

As to its private nature, no matter the conditions of one's external life, it is almost guaranteed that in sleep the mind will travel nightly on its own course, in its own way, in an exercise of its own personal freedom of thought. No king or god, no boss or general, no lover or enemy can have access to a dream without the internal consent of its dreamer. No matter the manifest power structure, the dream will have its own version, its own mind. There is something in this unrestrained exercise of free mind that can provide a necessary balance for the inevitable constraints of social living. While the content of dreams can certainly be affected by elements of the social system, still the mind has its own way in the end. In dreams, the free man can be slave and the slave free. In dreams, the last shall be first. In dreams, a bitter life can be momentarily sweetened, a sweet life momentarily soured. Jung considered this property an example of the dream's important compensatory function. Freud considered this an example of wish-life.

In passing, mention should be made that the particular view of dreams just expressed is itself not free from significant cultural influence. The idea of the dream's inherent freedom, an idea not familiar in many older cultures' views of the nature of dreams, is partly generated by complex ambivalence in our own culture's views on autonomy and independence. Freedom can be given conceptual status as a characteristic of sleep-thinking, in part because we are enamored with the idea of private freedom as well as suspicious of it, and partly because, in dreaming, action is inhibited and no social disarray can result. Is this "freedom of thought" an actual characteristic of dreaming or is it a social construction about dreaming? In an older view of dreams (e.g., Stevens, 1995), the soul is conceived as being nightly carried by the gods to far reaches for various forms of edification. Freedom is not an issue in such a view of dreaming; rather we find duty or community responsibility or justice or spiritual enlightenment. I mention this to suggest that views of the basic nature of dreams are packed with cultural meaning, and incidentally, can inform us about themes in the general culture, just as dream interpretation tells us something about themes and preoccupations in the mind of the interpreter. So, it is not lost on me that my own ideas about freedom and the "private mind" within dreams are undoubtedly culturally derived and expressed in a particular cultural period.

To continue in our context, dreams in their private dimension have always had a crucial role in human life. They have the capacity to provide immediate and direct benefit, on their own, and without the intercession of interpretation. As persons engaged in the social "business" of psychotherapy, we need to be reminded, from time to time, that the brain and mind, even in deranged individuals, have evolved remarkably complex ways of supporting survival. We sometimes make the narcissistic assumption that without our various intercessions, there might be no healing. The phenomena of dreaming and dreams argue most forcibly and convincingly for a contrary point of view. Such a view includes the observation that many forms of psychological healing, psychoanalysis included, can be seen as socially constructed elaborations of the basic, inborn, and private aspect of the dream's many capacities, including the tendency to effect a wide range of mental and emotional connections within the safety of sleep imagination (Hartmann, 1995), the capacity to play (Sanville, 1991), more fancifully, the creativity that permits the soul to "see itself" (Hillman, 1979), and in general, the continuous tendency to portray and explore, in private, and outside of waking awareness, the vast range and rich intricacies of the innermost experience of life (Lippmann, 1997).

## THE DREAM AS TEACHER

Such a point of view invites us to replace an unfortunate tendency for psychoanalytic arrogance in the practice of dream interpretation, including the ubiquitous manner in which we crowd dreams into our interpretive architectures, with a quieter and more respectful attention to what dream life may have to teach us. The private mind is an extraordinary part of nature, a great teacher, as well as an occasional menace. And the dream provides a glimpse, for the sleeping mind, into its own inner sanctum. When we, dream receivers, are in the privileged position of listening to and are invited into working with another's dreams, we are being given a glimpse of this private realm, which has worked its way from neuronal activation and memory sorting to its cerebral development into sleeping awareness of a dream, to waking awareness, to memory, and ultimately, perhaps to communication. This amazing emanation from the private workings of brain and mind can be appreciated and valued for what it teaches and shows, and not narrowly pressed into the service of our particular theories and philosophies.

In ancient times, dreams illuminated the dark night from within and gave nightly flight to the imagination of early humans. It stretched the limits of inner thought and thereby provided an important self-generated experience that could be an alternative to the struggles, survival functionings, and conscious problem solvings of waking thinking and action. Dreams reflected the mind's capacity for its most extraordinary adventures in imagination (Casey, 1976), which was once, and is still, that faculty of mind so powerful in creating, elaborating, and playing with meaning, and in trying to understand, define, and explore the nature and limits of the known world. Imagination, coupled with observation, was a great teacher, and nighttime imagination, in its associational free-style logic and fluid imagery, provided an immense harvest for early life.

Dreams may well have been the first storyteller, the first art form, the first sign of evidence of life after death and of the spirit world. Dreams may have provided the first "direct" experience of the personification of forces beyond our control, that is, of gods. It certainly provided plentiful "presences in the night," both benevolent and malevolent, such that there was much company from within during the darkness of night and the aloneness of sleep. These reflections join the modern discoveries of neurological and cognitive advantages of dream thinking to provide a convincing argument that dreams, of and by themselves, even when forgotten, even without the intercession of interpretation, and as an entirely private experience, are a most significant feature of human evolution and adaptation.

Finally, I believe we are entering a new cultural era in which dreams may come to serve as a necessary private hiding place for the postmodern dreamer. Dreams have always served as a more or less safe hiding place for unwelcome or forbidden experiences. Aspects of Freud's (1900) dream theory are an elaborate commentary on this theme. The dreaming mind, in the face of social and self-generated prohibition, is free to go its own way in the expression of deep internal opposition or, for that matter, in mocking acquiescence, through the whole imageful vocabulary of "no." Dreams will not be controlled from without, nor even from within. They remain, perhaps, that function of mind that cannot betray itself even under extreme pressure and duress. The dreamer, thus, if only for an instant, escapes the torturer, escapes life's conditions, oppressive and otherwise, and may even, in fluid flights of imagination, escape such omnipresent forces as gravity or the global market.

This aspect of dreams may become more evident and significant as modern technological and related socioeconomic political events push the individual more and more into a corner for the experience and expression of individuality within the private sphere of psychological living. That is, this more contemporary significance of the intrinsic privacy of dreams lies precisely in its relation to the increasing contemporary erosion of privacy. The modern world has the technology, apparently the need, and certainly the will, to keep tabs on all its growing population. From insurance data to social security records, from taxes to credit ratings, from phone records and school history to purchasing patterns, the computer permits our system to keep an eye on nearly everyone. In addition, our new technology—cellular phones, e-mail, faxes, beepers, and so on—points in the direction of instantaneous contact around the world, and creates conditions in which it becomes increasingly unlikely that one can, even for an instant, "disconnect" from the blitz of information and immediate connection.

The private moment and the experience of solitude are rapidly disappearing. The market and its police will make their claim. The world awake is at the ready. The world asleep may provide the only peace, and within that world, the dreaming mind may represent a last frontier for private experience and for the increasingly rare opportunity for moments of uninterrupted internal reflection. But, even this last refuge is under serious attack, far beyond the gentle voyeurism of the REM scientists, as the ancient internal screen and its creations are increasingly dwarfed by the enormity of a competing industry that has externalized and now manufactures our dreams, within a social context, and sells an endless variety of potent images, stories, products on the external screen. The private mind is besieged.

## THE SOCIAL NATURE OF THE PRIVATE DREAM

But it is also true that dreams, themselves, have never been completely separated from the social dimension. There is some preliminary research (Zborowski and McNamara, 1998), which suggests that REM dreams play a role in earliest bonding, in helping regulate and coordinate mental functioning within the mother–child relationship, beginning in utero. And throughout life, the creation and construction of dreams from bits of memory to the artful weaving of story and adventure carry with them the imprint of shared social meaning. This is not a new idea, especially within the interpersonal perspective, which from its beginnings has insisted that there is no percept, image, memory, or idea, private or otherwise, that has not been shaped by our nature as social beings. A dream of teeth falling out, of a walk through the woods, of driving a car, of a fight with a neighbor, of sexual intrigue—all are infused in their essence with the origins of the shared meanings of percepts and with the acquisition of language. This observation, from an entirely different social context, is most clearly made in Young's (1999) scholarly report on ancient dreams within the Buddhist tradition, within which the very dream images and stories (before interpretation) are directly reflective of the images and stories of the surrounding world of myth and belief.

The sleeping individual, alone in dream mentation, is at the same time deeply and unconsciously embedded in the psychologic habits of the human community, including the habits of sleep and dreaming, and is making use of the way this community shapes the very bits and pieces of mental life. One's upbringing, one's cultural heritage, one's language and styles of thought and emotion, one's family and social class, one's ancestors and their history—all find their way into the ABCs of a dream. The biology of dreaming in no way contradicts the omnipresence of the social world in the construction, experience, and memory of a dream. Our biology and our social nature are intimate partners at every level of experience. The individual dreamer weaves these partners together and gives it all a creative, personal and unique twist.

Even Freud's theory of the construction of dreams, embedded in intrapsychic concepts and concerning itself entirely with the interior workings of mind, is rooted in an unacknowledged and latent world of social meanings. *Repressed infantile sexual impulses,* presumed to serve as the dream's originator, are rooted in the object-related and interpersonal realities, experiences, desires, urges, and wishes of early development. One's complex positive and negative reactions to one's earliest wish life are thoroughly shaped by culture and family. Defenses against the experience and expression of early wishes, similarly are shaped. The concept of *censorship,* central in Freud's hypothesis, takes on meaning within the background of internalizations of communal ideas of what is possible or not possible to think, imagine, and remember. The concept of *day residue* refers to experiences of the recent past, experiences that are often, although not always, embedded in one's life with others. The concept of *secondary elaboration,* leading to the final remembered version of a dream, is filled with ideas of the ways stories are constructed in one's social context, the ways ideas are judged sane or insane, coherent or incoherent, worthy or unworthy. Thus, far beyond Freud's use of the "capitalist" and "entrepreneur" analogy, and even beyond the Talmudic lore that, while unacknowledged, fills his conceptions, his intrapsychic view of the dream is replete with its social nature.

It could therefore be said that cultural patterns, social influence, and, to use Fromm's concept, "social character" (Cortina and Maccoby, 1996), reside in every dream. They shape the memories, guide meanings, and give meaning to the dream's combinations. An elaboration of Hall's (1966) fruitful content studies could explore the cultural hypothesis: do dreams in their manifest form and content, from within a particular culture, and without interpretation, show demonstrable similarity? Do dreams show similarities within a particular century, or in a particular climate or geography, or within particular kinds of defining life experiences such as stage of life, class, occupation, across differing cultures? In short, to what extent and in what way do dreams reflect shared conditions of life within their private boundaries?

In addition to the hypothesis that dreams carry the nuances and styles of social influence (e.g., Adler, 1936; Fromm, 1951; Erikson, 1954; Ullman, 1988), dreams, in turn, can be thought of as contributing to the development and maintenance of social life and social character. The varied experiences in dreams may be thought of as continuously exploring, portraying, rehearsing, commenting on, criticizing, adding to, varying, and improvising aspects of the socially shared characteristics of a people. That is, I am suggesting that in the deepest privacy of dreaming, the culture's ways are being developed, tested, explored, and sometimes reinforced. As Stevens (1995) summarized: "Anthropologists are in no doubt about the contribution that dreaming makes to cultural stability and innovation" (p. 12).

The way the phenomenon of dreams is regarded, the way dreaming and dreams themselves are viewed, is developed early in life and is thoroughly shaped by the culture's attitudes toward dreams. Hunting, agricultural, and preindustrial cultures rely more on dreams for information, social cohesion, and the transmission of the culture's values than do modern industrial societies. In the contemporary world, certain societies are more likely to be dream-friendly and others dream-distant. This difference is correlated, to some extent, with degree of industrialization. For example, rural populations, whether in Mexico or China, are more likely to discuss, draw meaning from, pay attention to, and value dreams than are the populations, say, of urban England or Japan. The more that people are separated from nature, from the productive use of their own labor, from shared customs and religious beliefs, the less significance are they likely to attribute to their dreams. The linkage between dreams and nature, elaborated in recent works in the field of ecopsychology, is entirely relevant.

## The Politics of Dreams

Within our own culture, dreams have never been particularly highly regarded. From pioneer beginnings, through our nation-building phases, to our current position of international power, the heralding of the American Dream has never particularly included interest in the night-time variety. Quite the contrary. The greater the emphasis on material progress, the less the interest in inner life and its various modes of expression. In such a cultural climate, dreams are waste. Daytime life becomes the only show in town, daytime struggles the main attraction. Dreams may become the object of scientific investigation, but have little value in their own right. They no longer teach. They no longer engage with the essential mysteries. In this regard, it should be mentioned that psychoanalysis, although displaying unacknowledged ambivalence toward dreams, is one of the very few activities in our culture in which dreams are regarded as having potential significance. For the most part, we have become alienated from our own dreams. The recent New Age interest in dreams and things mystical appears on the edges of the social system, and we have yet to learn whether this phenomenon represents a necessary cultural balance and correction or is just another marketable commodity for a soul-hungry population.

Again, we observe the way cultural values influence the popularity of scientific findings. Both Crick and Mitchison (1983) and Hobson (1988) presented views that are consistent with a social, economic and political climate that shows less and less respect for inner psychological life. The popularity of their views has less to do with the actual merits and validity of their respective arguments, I believe, than with the way "objective" science is utilized by the culture for its own complex purposes. At the opposite end, the increasing popularity of a view of dreams that stresses its layered complexity and its multiplicity of meanings and uses (e.g., Hunt, 1989) fits rather well with a culture increasingly interested in its own diversity as well as in the marketability of multiple sides of the self.

Dreams and their study have always existed in an interesting relationship with the social and political world. Freud's work with dreams, itself, was in part a response to the social and political world of fin-de-siècle Vienna (Schorske, 1980). Unable to enter or affect the political world above, Freud turned to the world below for the power to overtake the material world. In general, however, earlier in the 20th century psychoanalysis and its emphasis on the interior study of the world of dreams were seen by those attempting social change to be a diversion, a distraction, just another form of opiate for the masses, a self-centered retreat from engagement in polis. More recently, some social and political thinkers see in dreams—the private imaginary—and in psychoanalysis an antithesis to the dominating and erosive influences of the world market. From revolutionary to antirevolutionary and back again, dreams can be used to suit most any philosophy so long as the dream itself is a springboard rather than the subject.

A recent experience with a colleague, whose therapy work we discuss together, brought to light the way in which political attitudes shape one's approach to dreams. Feeling uninspired and deadened in her approach to her patients' dreams for quite a while, she recognized, at one point, that her early upbringing in a prominent and active radical political family meant that dreams were considered, as it was by the entire radical left, a low order of mental life, suspect, a waste of one's energy, a thorn in the side of socialist realism. To "play" with dreams, to devote one's work time and energies to talking about dreams was, more or less, reactionary. It was just not the kind of activity a serious Marxist should undertake. Fromm was an exception, but then again, he was also suspect as a reformist by the radical Left. She recalled that "dreams" were mentioned, in her culture, in two songs, significant for their propaganda and "correct" social meaning: *"Last night I had the strangest dream, I'd never dreamed before. I dreamed the world had all agreed to put an end to war. I dreamed I saw a mighty room, the room was full of men, and the paper they were signing said they'd never fight again.*" She also remembered "*I dreamed I saw Joe Hill last night.*" Obviously dreams were not left to more frivolous purposes, like "*I dreamed I wanted Mommy last night.*" I remembered that from the proletarian poetry of Moishe Rosenfeld, set to song, there was also *the little boy who awakens from a dream in which he is asking when will he see his dear Poppa. Standing over his bed is his tearful sweatshop-overworked father who laments how he is never able to see his dear child when awake.* Serious stuff. No simple wish-fulfillment here. Beneath the social character of a radical, however, my colleague had a poet's heart and, in secret, valued dreams and the inner world so much that, without realizing it, she was keeping her distance from her patients' dreams, "so they could breathe their own air."

It could be a therapist's greatest gift to a patient to permit dreams to remain somewhat unknown, puzzling, private. The interpreter, in an ancient and powerful chair, has the capacity, through suggestion, to affect the way a person regards his or her very own dreams. A respectful lightness of touch is called for, more an invitation to explore and to play than to interpret, more an effort at good conversation about a dream than an effort to "pin it down." In our contemporary situation, the growing power and reach of the market, and its ability to shape affect, thought, and motivation, calls on us quietly to respect and appreciate the private creative powers of the individual mind in sleep. It calls on us to be mindful of the capacity we have, unconsciously, to further the market's social agenda or our own political agenda, or our therapeutic or personal agenda, in the way we respond to the incredible lightness of the poetry of nighttime.

# ൫ 12 ൽ

# ON THE FATE OF REMEMBERED
# DREAMS

*I shall remember while the light lives yet,*
*And in the night-time I shall not forget.*
　　　　　　　　—Algernon Charles Swinburne

As we have seen, the vast majority of dreams are forgotten. I have
suggested that this forgetting is not the end of the story. Rather, the
wholesale removal of dreams from awareness is part of the mind's
ability to redigest and reabsorb forgotten dream material, and from
such material nourishment—fertilizer—is created for subsequent day-
thinking and night-dreaming. Thus, dreaming, forgetting, dreaming,
forgetting is seen as the mind's organic capacity to recirculate and make
use of its contents and qualities.

　　Some few dreams, probably fewer than 5% of all dreams, do not fall
to the ground to be reabsorbed. Some are remembered in bits and
pieces or in their entirety, more now than later, some in their original
imaginal form, and some in words, some in a wisp of a mood or attitude.
Most of these few remembered dreams are soon forgotten as well, to

join their compatriots in the nourishment of the undersoil. Some are remembered for a lifetime. These various kinds of remembered dreams are, again in our analogy, the apples for eating.

Although this version of the analogy seems to take us inward to the experiences and processes of tasting, eating, and digesting, actually I want to use the apple-eating analogy to take us in two directions—inward to the person's experience of remembered dreams along with their reflections, interpretations, and the aftereffects of such dreams, and outward to communication and interaction in the social world. Let us remember, while we travel these two directions with remembered dreams, we are speaking of a very small minority of dreams. These few dreams that are remembered in part or whole, are a very special subgroup of dreams. Everything ever written about the interpretation of dreams and most written about dreams themselves refers to this small special subgroup. So they seem very important, out of all proportion to their numbers, to their minority status.

## SOME ASPECTS OF REMEMBERED DREAMS

There must be something of parallel importance that accounts for the most unusual survival of these few dreams into memory and subsequent awareness. What could be so special about them? It has been reported that REM dreams become more symbolic, more dreamlike as they evolve through the night and that those closer to waking, therefore, are most dreamy, and most past oriented. It has been reported that dreams occurring later in the night, closer to morning's awakening, have a better chance of being remembered than the earlier ones. Also, some dreams containing strong emotions are more likely to be remembered, like nightmares, or like some wet dreams in adolescent boys. Some of these are so strong in affect and effect that they waken the dreamer and are thus more likely still to be remembered.

Also, some dreams, during their dreaming, have in them various small reminders to be remembered. One patient reported thinking "You need to remember this" while dreaming an important discussion with her grown-up son that seemed to clarify problems they had. She remembered only a small part of the dream discussion, but it was enough to open an entire side of her experience with him, in therapy and then in life. Another patient recalled hearing over and over, as background for a dream scene, the opening line from the song "As Time Goes By." He kept hearing the music, not the words, of the line, "You must remember this . . . ," and took it as a direction to recall the dream. These small tags are interesting. Often, in dreams, there are messages and instructions, signals and communications, sent directly to the person to remember when awake: "Listen to this!" or "Pay attention," just as, at times, there are messages sent to the underworld of the dreamer during waking life. One patient instructs himself, before going to sleep, that he would like to dream on a particular problem. Sometimes, he does, or at least he thinks he does. This is a modern version of the events surrounding the important use of dream incubation temples in ancient Egypt and Greece. People in need of psychological healing would travel to a dream temple, prepare and purify themselves, and ask the gods for assistance through their dreams, which would then be interpreted by dream priests. Efforts at communication from the dream to wakefulness and vice versa, then, are often direct and reflect an ancient wisdom that day-thinking and night-thinking can talk to one another, in fact, must talk to one another.

To return, remembering dreams is not the usual aftereffect of dreams. Its relative unusualness causes us to think there might be some reason, some purpose, some design in their being remembered, because their usual night work seems quite sufficient. There may be some necessity built into our brains and minds for being able to hold onto, remember, and think about some small number of dreams. Although I don't know why this should be so, on the level of experience, it seems a small way that we have of knowing that we dream at all, and that we are capable of such strange, fanciful, imagistic thinking while asleep.

Memory therefore assists the dreamer, not only to know that dreaming took place, but provides the dreamer with a puzzle, with a kind of question, with the beginnings of an internal conversation about the dream: "What on earth or in heaven was that about?" We provide ourselves with entertainment, with information, with puzzles, with questions—all within our own minds. Thus, in our social species, if alone, or if needing to rely on oneself for conversation, stimulation, engagement, we are so constructed that we will occasionally think over our own dreams and thoughts. That is, the absence of others need not do us in; we have ourselves to be with—and not just in an abstract sense, but concretely in being provided some of our remembered dreams as starting point for internal dialogue. Tasting and eating the apples of mind can sustain and nourish.

Further, memory of and reflection about one's own dreams can help in knowing and becoming familiar with aspects of one's own being, often hidden from view. Patient's have reported dreams in which unexpected hatreds, loves, abilities, lost years, lost memories, lost persons, talents, interests, attitudes all relatively unknown to the dreamer, show themselves and lend themselves to an expanded and fuller sense of mind and self.

While for many, dreams hold little interest, for some, dream memory and the resulting capacity for dream reflection are a central aspect of their lives. Whether they believe dreams were sent by God or by a collective or personal unconscious, they could not function as well without being instructed by them or thinking about them. Some dreamers therefore attempt to enhance dream memory by recording them or by instructing themselves to remember or in other ways guarantee that as many as possible will emerge from the more usual forgetfulness.

## ON LETTING DREAMS COME AND GO

I myself enjoy dreams coming and going as they will. I enjoy knowing that they live beneath the surface and, therefore I tend not to focus on trying to remember more of them. Also, I am not a fan of the lucid dreaming movement, in which dreamers try to enlarge their spheres of awareness, intention, and willed action within dreams—like some yogas are reported to be able to do. This approach seems to be helpful to some children in an effort to become active and master scary nightmares. One patient remembers her mother telling her when she was about 4 years old, "You will turn around when the monster runs after you, trying to frighten you. You will face the monster, look it right in the eye, and invite it to tea in your most mannerly fashion. Maybe the monster is grumpy because it's lonely." This patient remembers trying it and it worked here and there, but not always. She told this to her own 4-year-old daughter, 30 years later, who burst into tears, crying, "You're a stupid Mommy! You don't know anything!" Her child apparently required her simply to say, "It's not real. It's only a dream." She didn't want anyone to try to tell her what to do in her dreams, an intervention that made the dream too real for her.

For myself, I don't like forcing consciousness into dreams. We are too busy controlling everything. We can allow dreams their own ways, even if scary. They really don't need us taking over their territory with what we think they should be. But the lucid dream movement is on the march. Bookstores sell more and more on this topic. I guess there is a need. I guess we can't trust our own dreams to watch over things; we need to get in there and mess around. I urge against it. Young (1999) argued convincingly against such Western efforts to borrow superficially from significant and ancient Hindu and Buddhist dream traditions.

But then again, I also think it's often a poor idea to know the sex of a baby before it's born. I figure the psychological and social bisexuality that accrues to not knowing if it's a boy or if it's a girl is an advantage. As soon as the baby is born and the sex known, the other side, the other sex, sinks into the unconscious where it can take up residence and do what it needs to, in the world of shadow. That other sex is prepared for in the 9-month prebirth experience of not knowing. Some men hope for girls, some women for boys, precisely in order to be able to love—on the outside, in consciousness—the hidden opposite sex they once were half the time while in utero, at least in the minds of their parents and others.

But, who knows? Maybe the new world will require that bisexuality not be an unconscious affair, that dreams not be an unwilled, unconscious business. In such an event, I am more and more of a conservative, more and more in favor of the old ways, as oppositional. I suppose this old-fashioned way is made up, in part, of a kind of respect for unconscious mental life and a fear that this hidden side of life is being eroded, removed, diminished, taken away from us in part by our own profession, in part by our own need to know and control, in part by the needs of our modern culture and our global economy. Although it is likely that the hidden sides will just sink deeper into hiding as they are ferreted out. Memory for dreams is occasionally lovely because it is occasional and leaves most dreams alone, and because it is a reminder of that dark continent within, an endlessly abundant and fruitful side of our own nature. I worry that the modern electronic world may find ways, eventually, of strip-mining that continent for control and profit. I hope this anxious prophesy is more paranoid than accurate.

## DREAMS AND SOCIAL RESPONSE

Remembered dreams are not only for self-reflection, not only for inward communication, they also are communicated outwardly to others. And here we enter our more usual concerns: the dream in psychoanalysis and, I would add, the dream in social living. Thus, remembering opens dreams to the possibility of outside influence, of social reaction, commentary, and interpretation. This consideration leads to the question: Is there built in, within brain and mind, the capacity to bring these nightly creations into memory and waking thought, in part, in order to bring them to social response?

There does seem some mechanism in us that compels the telling of dreams. From earliest childhood, we feel the impulse to report our nightly adventures, horrors, pleasures, discoveries, and strange experiences. This dream expressiveness may be connected to the need to bring at least an occasional dream and its puzzling nature to the attention of others. Of course, there are also remembered dreams that are kept to oneself in order to avoid shame, embarrassment, or discovery.

One cannot be sure ahead of time what kind of response a dream will get. Each culture and each family has a different way of engaging with dreams. For the young child learning the ways of dream communication, each family plays a role in shaping the particular mode of communication as well as the style of evaluative judgment of the importance and worth of dreams. The earliest dreams openly communicated by a child, prior to the acquisition of verbal speech, are most often the ones that disturb sleep. These are often dreams of an unsettling and frightening variety and often lead the child-dreamer to cry out in the night. The parents' or caretakers' characteristic reactions to being awakened by a child's dream-cry become an early part of the child's experience of dreaming.

When sleep is at a premium for the parents, especially during the child's early months, being awakened in the middle of the night by a baby's cry of distress is rarely a pleasure. The differences between a child awakening because of problems with respiration, with temperature regulation, with hunger or other aspects of digestion, with elimination, or with emotional distress stemming from being alone in the dark, or from the aftereffects of frightening dreams, are at first difficult to distinguish. Differential parental responses become gradually attuned to these different experiences in correlation with the child slowly learning to communicate differentially. Eventually, a bad dream awakening is communicated to the parents who then, in our culture, will traditionally convey and communicate to the child that "it's only a dream," thus helping the child to differentiate internal from external sources of danger and also to reduce the potential importance of dreams. Parents and caretakers who are always angry at being awakened by a child frightened by "only a dream" soon convey to the child to keep dream distress private.

In short, one's own feeling about communicating dreams is shaped early in childhood, differently in different families and cultures. Such early learning—loving and hating to tell dreams, being loved and hated for their telling—can be thought of as an early background for attitudes and feelings, in general, about dreams, and about the inner world, nighttime experiences, communication of emotional distress, and communication of private life. Because attitudes toward the inner world are an important aspect of social learning, the way in which dream-experience and dream-reporting are learned in different circumstances is a potentially rich source of investigation.

In a narrower sense, such experiences serve as historical background for feelings about telling dreams to one's therapist. If the therapist, like the sleep-deprived parent, hates to be "awakened" in the middle of his or her work by the way a dream often dramatically changes the topic, or needs to reduce the perplexing dream to some predictable formula, or immediately translates the experiences of the underworld to the language of daytime control or some aspect of the therapeutic relationship, or rather enjoys hearing the imaginative creations of his or her patient and takes time with the patient to appreciate and wonder about them—each of these responses will resonate with childhood experiences of dream-telling and with the culture's prevailing attitudes toward the world of dreams.

I hope that more therapists will take the time to explore the range and variety of their patients' early experiences in dream telling. In addition to providing a context for work with dreams, such information could yield a fuller understanding of the early development and shaping of aspects of social character. The early dream listener, as representative of the culture, provides a context and a set of orienting ideas for some of the most private experiences imaginable. In this way does the social world enter and shape the innermost sanctum of the human heart. The dream interpreter continues this process through the life cycle.

The effect on the listener of a reported dream is also of interest. Dreams are not only delusively "real" to the dreamer, they also take on reality to those dreamt about, when told the dream. When someone tells you a dream in which you or a close facsimile are present, is it not usual for you to react as though the events reported are actually or objectively about you? "You kissed me, or insulted me, or beat me, or helped me, in my dream last night" brings to the listener the experience of having in fact kissed, insulted, beaten, or helped the dreamer, and with this reaction come associated feelings, including feelings of responsibility, guilt, shame, or pride. There is in this a most subtle level of interpersonal discourse and experience allowing persons to interact from the side, so to speak. The effects of dream telling on dreamer and listener are an area calling for study.

The ancient idea that the dreamer's soul is traveling about and interacting with the souls of others is of relevance here, not as an old foolish idea of the prescientific era, but rather as a way of talking about the actual effects dreams have on people, both the dreamer and the dreamed about (e.g., the dramatic and desired effect on Tevyeh's wife of his made-up dream in *Fiddler on the Roof*). In this sense, there are multiple effects of a dream and its telling that truly reside in an interpersonal world.

### The Power of the Dream Interpreter

Of course, the social world has its own ways of defending against the impact of a dream. The main one is interpretation. From the earliest recorded history, dreams and their interpretations moved hand in hand. The dream interpreter, whether medicine man or shaman, priest or village elder, or psychoanalyst, has taken the dream's images and stories and woven into them the beliefs, customs, values, purposes, wishes, goals, and philosophies of the culture. If the dream itself reflects, in part, the underlying motifs of the community, the dream interpreter applies the coups de grâce, the finishing touches. The dream's inherent ambiguity calls for an attempt at coherent understanding, explanation, interpretation. And it is thus highly vulnerable to the ideas read into it. The interpreter is able to suggest to the dreamer what the dreamer, in his or her deepest and most private imaginings, was "really" thinking about, that is, what the interpreter thinks the dreamer was "really" thinking about. Prophetic interpretation, for example, could "come true," so to speak, through the power of the interpreter's suggestion in the psychology of the more submissive dreamer.

Dream interpreters were thus persons of considerable influence and power. In the ancient Middle East, in ancient China, India, and Japan, in the dream incubation temples of Egypt and Greece, in the Jewish Biblical, but less in its Talmudic, traditions, in early Moslem teachings, in native and shamanic healing practices, throughout the world, the dream interpreter looked into the dreams of pharaohs, kings, princes, chiefs, and common men and women and brought to bear on the "innocent" dream all the weight of the traditions of social custom and belief. The dream's images were transformed into messages from God and the gods, into instructions on hunting and planting, into prophesies, warnings, and omens, into decisions about war and peace, into decisions about the best time and manner to conduct the affairs of state or of an individual's life.

There are many ways that dream interpreters gained power in traditional cultures. Young's (1999) is the most recent documentation of the complexities of the dream interpreter's capabilities and charisma, including the interpreter's ability to move freely between the worlds of reality and dream and to be knowing in both realms. Also, the ability to prophesy correctly, to heal, to be able to interpret one's own dreams, and to connect deeply and personally with both dreamer and social context are considered significant aspects of the dream interpreter's power.

In early social organization, a commonality in life's patterns and problems enabled a dream interpreter to read the images as symbols. Dream books in which meanings are ascribed to particular images, and which may seem foolish to us, contain common understandings and shared experiences within the context of a homogeneous society. Our modern psychotherapeutic tradition requires that we request the dreamer's own associations before the work of interpretation. Although this practice seems respectful, it also reflects our modern lack of common experience and our alienation, one from another, and one generation from another. Depending on the cultural history of a particular community, a dream of running water, or fire, or a black bird, or a tree, or two people having sex, could be interpreted to contain certain specific meanings because the community out of which both

the dream and interpreter arose held common assumptions and experiences evolved from centuries of repeated and predictable life events.
Freud, Fromm, and, to a greater extent, Jung, relied on such understandings in their work with dream symbols.

It is in the nature of dreams that when a dream interpreter looks
into a dream, like Narcissus peering into the pool, the interpreter's own
face will be seen. We cannot help but see our own deepest concerns in
the dreams of others. It may be in the nature of human dreams to invite
the other and the community into one's most private musings. Therefore, the deeply private nature of dreams takes on social meaning, not
only in the way its specific vocabulary of imagery and story is shaped
by cultural patterns, but, as soon as another looks into the dream for
its meanings, the entire cultural heritage of the interpreter enters the
proceedings. It would be instructive to take a single dream idea—a
dream of flying, for example—and subject it to the ideas of varying
cultures or varying psychoanalytic or other interpretive perspectives,
as did Shafton (1995) who stopped at 24 different and potentially valid
interpretations of the dream of flying, paralleling the Talmudic story
of the 24 dream interpreters giving 24 correct interpretations of a single
dream (Frieden, 1990).

Further, in the telling of a dream to oneself or to another, that is, in
the translation of a dream into its verbal form, the social nature of
language makes its appearance. The intimate interaction of the private
and the social is seen in the way the dream's inner thought expressed
in imagery combines, at times in the dream and always in its telling,
with verbal language. Sanville (1991) wrote:

> I propose that (1) dream imagery is uniquely suitable for commu-
> nication of the self with the self, while speech, derived from
> language proper, is necessary for interpersonal discourse and
> even for supplementing the image both in the dream state and in
> the waking life, that (2) there is ideally a continuous interplay
> between these two modes out of which each is enriched, and that
> (3) these considerations are important for clinical theory and
> method [p. 179].

Elsewhere, I (1996c) have discussed the way in which Freud, in his view
of dreams, expressed the Jewish religious tradition of focus on the
latent meaning, that is, on word and concept hidden in Torah and not

on image; and the way in which Jung in his view of mind and dream drew on the Christian tradition of focus on image. Both together, of course, are necessary for the full story.

I suggest that the inherent ambiguity and the resulting puzzling nature of dreams, on the one hand, and the tendency to read one's own interests and concerns into the ambiguous dream, on the other, join to create the dream as an ideal vehicle for social learning and indoctrination. From the earliest times to contemporary psychotherapy practice, I believe, dreams have been turned to the purposes of the culture and the social system. The dream itself remains a mystery. It comes and goes its own way. But a huge number and variety of meanings have been piled onto the dream. These attributed meanings, consistent with the values and interests of the particular social system, shape the dream to its own purposes and designs. Thus, the dream-interpreter is a most powerful agent for the transmission and maintenance of social learning and social character. The dream-interpreter may be entirely unconscious of this function and role and most often thinks that what he or she sees in the dream is actually in the dream itself. But this is self deception.

At best, in an effort to bring coherence to a dream, the dream, together with the meanings attributed to it by dreamer or other interpreter, enter a conversation, a dialogue, a dance, in which both play their part in an often highly creative activity. This ancient dance between dream and interpretation probably serves many functions. Among these may be:

1. The transformation of the deeply private and idiosyncratic into the social, or the return to daytime communal ways of thinking of the interior nighttime domain.
2. The transformation of the irrational into the rational.
3. The reduction of fearful and inchoate experience and its replacement by coherent meanings.
4. The control of nature as in the conceptual ordering of spontaneous mental life.
5. The introduction of socially approved patterns of thought and judgment.
6. The use of dream imagery to aid in psychological healing.
7. The use of dream imagery to help understand one's past, one's circumstances, one's future, one's place in the social and physical universe.

8. The deeper understanding of one's relationship to others.
9. The expansion of spiritual understanding.
10. The anticipation of death and an opening in one's relationship to ancestors and to the future.

In all of this, it is proposed that the brain and mind's capacity to make new connections and to create meanings within a dream are matched by the introduction of afterthought (interpretation), which continues the process of creating meanings and forging new connections. Surrounding and infusing the dream, therefore, is the action of the creation of meanings from every imaginable level of inquiry. In a recent paper, Goldstein (1997) argued that although dreams may well arise from random neuronal activation, as Hobson (1988) advocated, coupled with random day experience, the "self-organizing properties of the mind" are seen in the way the "random events have the potential for perturbing the psyche to a higher synthesis," which is then further developed and organized through the social nature of interpretation.

Thus, let us consider that from the deepest stirrings of brain within the solitude of sleep, that is, from the nightly dance of atoms and molecules within neuronal activation, there eventually result the private images and stories of dreamlife. These contain in their patterns not only one's personal elaborations but also elements of social meaning seen, for instance, in their metaphoric construction. But then, further, in their interpretation, the entirety of cultural emphasis finds its way into the dream. In this way do neurons and culture meet and intermingle in the dream and in its meanings, each informing and shaping the other. Dreams have had their documented effect on culture and culture its evident effect on dreams. There is thus, in this view, an intimate bond connecting elemental events in neurophysiology, through the privacy of dreams, to the highest reaches of complex social and cultural attainment. If the scientist and the religious mystic meet in the poetic idea that subatomic life and the structure of the galaxies are linked, then in a similar way, the dream's nature shows architectural linkage between tiny brain events, private meanings, and large cultural patterns.

INTERPRETATION IN THERAPY

The clinical implications of the social universe entering the private domain of dreams are many, complex, and potentially both positive and negative. Dreams not only lend themselves to the projections and importations from the interpreter's agenda, they also begin to speak in the idiom of the interpreter. It has been widely reported, thus, that Freudian patients have Freudian dreams, Jungian patients have Jungian dreams, Kleinian and Lacanian patients have Kleinian and Lacanian dreams, and so on. After a period of interpretive indoctrination, the dreams will begin to speak, at least superficially, in ways that are useful to the interpreter. In this way do dreams and dreamers come to line themselves up, on the surface, with the values, ideas, and prejudices of the interpreter. In an urgent, at times desperate, wish to be loved and helped, people will think, feel, and behave, consciously and unconsciously, in ways they believe are required, needed, and expected of them. It is not only cult members who yield their outer and inner lives to domination and subjugation. Dependency and the capacity for submission go deep in the human heart, where imagined love and belief—as in transference—remain a potent aspect of the healer's art. The piles of crutches left in some churches due to the great power of imagined love by an imagined Mary are potent evidence of the importance of belief in healing. Thus, patients will bend their dreams to fit the needs of their analysts, who may be bending their minds to fit the needs of their particular analytic systems. In this way does the analytic enterprise create, develop, mold, and maintain the social character, in a narrower sense, of both its practitioners and their patients. It is the activity of our "enlightenment religion."

Recently, there has been a striking increase in the way relationally inspired transference and countertransference interpretations are used in dream interpretation. This use can create an atmosphere of constriction and airlessness in the therapy, a lack of range, a lack of depth, in the treatment of individuals already suffering from feelings of emptiness, alienation, and meaninglessness. In such a context, dreams are often used for the relief of insecurity and the gratification of unacknowledged narcissism in the therapist. No matter what the actual content of the dream, the therapist, as interpreter, is free to read into dream after dream, not infantile sexual wishes, which while often a fiction were at least fictions about the patient, but ideas, attitudes, worries, wishes, theories about the therapist. That is, under the surface, in the latent world, which becomes the domain of the interpreter's interests, the interpreter often sees reflections of ideas about himself or herself. In an excellent interpersonal psychoanalytic contribution on dreams

and countertransference, for example, Blechner (1995), while joining
Levenson in warning against arbitrary latent interpretations, wrote:

> In the interpretation of most dreams, the analyst should consider
> how the characters in the dream might refer to the patient and
> himself. . . . When the analyst fails to perceive any correspon-
> dences between the dream and the analyst-patient dyad, some
> problematic countertransference may be at work. . . . There is no
> limit to the range of features of the analyst that can be included
> in the patient's dream, and the analyst should always be ready to
> discover new ones [pp. 9–10].

I agree that such a focus can give rise to very interesting possibilities
about the complex interplay between the participants, and, when used
with subtlety, can expand the range of expressible ideas and feelings.
Also, some patients can only find the courage to say things about the
therapist or the proceedings through dreams. But the automatic search
for transference in much contemporary work with dreams seems
unnecessarily reductive and is eventually as limiting as any arbitrary
latent interpretations. It is more likely that a single dream image will
reflect a host of interrelated meanings that may well include, but are
not restricted to, ideas about the therapeutic interaction.

There seems to be a relentless force that compels a therapist to see
his or her own face in patients' dreams, to see little but aspects of the
therapeutic relationship, and to reduce any and all dream content to
ideas about the therapist, then reduced to some other figure from the
patient's past. It is a shifty process in which the interpreter holds the
cards until the patient learns to think like the therapist and also reads
the therapist into all dream material. Thus, nowadays, trained, rather
than free, associations continue to echo psychotherapy's preoccupations, but instead of "phallic objects" they refer to "the therapist." Now
it is certainly possible, even likely, that dreams, in their potential for
multiple meanings and complex layerings, will occasionally refer, on
or under the surface, to aspects of the therapeutic engagement. They
often can be about other matters, however; yet therapists are increasingly conditioned to impose ideas about the relationship onto dreams.
To reduce the dream's kaleidoscopic range to the goings on of the
therapy is akin to caging an animal from the wild in a zoo for our
entertainment and edification. The adventure of following a dream's

own paths of meaning, wherever they may lead (Lippmann, 1996a), is closer to the adventure of natural observation.

One example is a therapist's report of her patient's dream in a dream seminar: *"The patient is on a train. It is dark, crowded, noisy. There are lots of people. Teenagers, using drugs. It is wild and crazy. She is with her sister who is high on drugs. Her sister kisses her, a tongue kiss. It was a good kiss not like they ever did."* The therapist and her colleagues in the dream seminar associate the train to the therapy—as in a journey—the "high" sister to the lively therapist, and the kiss to oral communication—as in interpretations.

As I listen to the group of bright young analysts-in-training, I am made aware of the way dream interpretation is increasingly practiced as an automatic translation of the bits and pieces of dream imagery into bits and pieces of the therapeutic relationship. In the old days, at a Freudian institute, the dream might be thought of as reflecting the surfacing of repressed homosexual impulses, once superego constraints are reduced. But in either case, what of the dream itself? Does it matter that the uninterpreted dream is a creation that stands on its own? It is, on its own terms, neither about the therapist nor about repressed homosexuality. It is about what it is about and might perhaps benefit from some inquiry, expansion, amplification. It may or may not have a thing to say about therapy. Both dreamer and therapist may wish to explore the therapy superimposed on the dream, or for that matter superimposed on anything they wish, but that is not the same as thinking this particular dream is about this therapy. The existentialist analyst writers make this point, but inevitably introduce their own philosophic agenda. Using dreams to make a point in the attempt to move the therapy along seems a bit like cheating "for the good of the patient." But then again, this same sort of rationale has been used by dream interpreters since the beginning of time.

My own view is that, in general, we have much overdone a preoccupation with meanings and interpretations of dreams. REM research has demonstrated that forgotten and uninterpreted dreams are a significant feature of mental life. Long before we turn to the thorny question of the potential meanings of remembered dreams, we and our patients have enormous potential range for inquiry and discussion. For example, we could pay attention to the phenomenological experience of the dream itself, to how dreamers feel about their dreams, to how people generally view their dream life, to one's history and habits of dreaming, to the experience of waking to forgotten dreams, to the family's and the culture's traditions with dreams, to the emotional and cognitive aftereffects of both remembered and forgotten dreams, that is, their effect on the subsequent day's emotional tone, to the events surrounding the communication of one's dreams, that is, to whom does one tell one's dreams and why and with what result, to the experience of being told that one is present in someone else's dream. In addition, the surrounding context of night life and the physical, social, and psychological experiences of sleep merit our attention.

These projects have been relatively ignored in psychoanalysis as we rush passionately, and quite naturally, but I believe, prematurely, to considerations of dream meaning. We and our brains seem "meaning addled," "meaning addicted." We cannot seem to help ourselves. Although it is in this meaning realm that we are most playful and creative, we are also often most self-absorbed, most wrongheaded, and arrogant. Not knowing too quickly is a difficult strength (Franklin, 1992). How to not know and, at the same time, to explore manifold possibilities takes practice and experience. Our species' powerful and wonderful yet dangerous and deadly drive to dominate and control nature and the unknown is reflected in our approach to dream life. It has always been thus. Interpretation as indoctrination has a long and (dis)honorable history. But perhaps, in our efforts to understand our patients, we can do better than interpret. Perhaps we can learn to appreciate.

# ❧ 13 ❧

## Waking and Sleeping

*Life is a dream ... we sleeping wake and waking sleep.*
— Michel de Montaigne

*Blest be the man who first invented sleep—a cloak to cover all human imaginings.*
— Miguel de Cervantes

One morning this past winter, I woke from a retreating dream that contained *several many-leveled elevators, some happy apartment hunting in New York City, and two children, previously unknown to me, pulling or pushing two large, dead, yellow-green alligators, down a swollen river.* I lay still for a while, hoping the dream would remain in mind until I could think a bit more about it. The images and their connections slowly disappeared although the alligators remained clearly in mind. But our dog, Odessa, wanted to get outside and the day called. I was to meet my first patient in 2 hours and had lots to do before driving down the road to my office in town. I found myself thinking again that morning about the many and diverse ways there are of waking up: perhaps, a dream retreating;

173

finding oneself in the middle of a dream; no dream; an emptiness; feelings of agitation and worry; feelings of happiness and contentment, even bliss and eager anticipation; or confusion; not immediately knowing the date, or my age, or the place; obsessive worrying, self-blaming and list-making; lazy lolling about; body pain and discomfort; sexual interest; wishing to return to sleep; hating the day; loving the day; beginning a conversation with my wife; enfolding within myself; and on and on. So many different ways of waking in the morning.

It seems like the kind of experience that might interest psychoanalysts. How does the day begin? What are the moods? What is the content of mind? How does the person greet the day? Just as it is of interest to consider the way a person goes to sleep—in what habits of bodily position or thought or behavior, in what kinds of rituals to prepare for or to bring about sleep? In what kind of mood or anticipation or dread of the sleep experience ahead? Going into and emerging from night and sleep is an adventure in change, in threshold life, in life on the edge, in the experience of life between two worlds. And it is precisely this latter aspect that could be of particular interest to the psychoanalyst, who also lives between two worlds—the realms of the conscious and the unconscious portions of mind. How does one move from one to the other? What occurs in the transition?

## BETWEEN TWO WORLDS

*Between Two Worlds (Tvishn Tsvai Velt)* was the original title of S. Ansky's brilliant, dark Yiddish drama, popularly known as *The Dybbuk,* in which he explored the poignant and dangerous relationship between the world of the dead and the world of the living, of the painful efforts of the souls of two star-crossed Jewish lovers, one alive in death and one dead in living, to reunite. In this work, enduring because of its power to evoke many layers of meaning, Ansky captures, in our own particular realm of interest, the essence of the mysterious relationship between conscious and unconscious forces, between substance and shadow, between dream and reality, between waking and sleeping.

Last week, I awoke into a puzzlement about my age. Was I 35 or 65? It took only a moment to remember, a bit sorrowfully, that I was 65, not 35. I know what I would have wished. What was it that made me think I was still in my thirties, besides the obvious? I didn't recall emerging from a dream or any kind of preawake (hypnopompic) reverie or fantasy. And so I awoke with a bit of wry disappointment in my getting old, although with some internal reverberation between where I was at 35 and where I seem to be at 65—a dose of reality at the outset of this particular day. I am reminded of a patient who reported that he woke from a dream in which he was again single, lonely, and in need of searching for and finding a woman. He woke feeling poorly about this until he recalled fully that lying next to him was his dear wife, whose presence in his life had ended his loneliness. He felt enormous gratitude for the reality of his life as his day began, and the feeling was still with him when he embraced his wife warmly before dinner. Or consider the dream of an ex-smoker who had desperately struggled to give up the habit, and had finally been victorious, only to dream, after years of abstinence, of one more pleasure-filled cigarette. This dream-event was followed by a subsequent awakening filled, of course, with a sense of failure and horror that the valiant effort was all for naught. The recognition that "it was only a dream," brought great relief and pleas-ure as the day began, along with a new resolve to maintain abstinence.

The early moods and underlying attitudes of the day can be formed in sleep and dreams without any awareness on our part. Waking with some kind of confusion, for example, followed by the slow dawning of reality through the filling in of the necessary bits and pieces of the fabric of memory, is an occasional and interesting experience of waking. Such waking disorientation and confusion may increase during daytime naps or when one is traveling, and they seem to come and go for most people at different times in their lives and are not necessarily correlated with daytime experiences of confusion or dislocation. Where did we go and what happened to us that we could lose the threads of the various facts of our identities and our actual lives? Some contemporary views of the self, along with ancient Buddhist ideas, hold that the "self" is an illusion or a social construction; here there is no difficulty with the way self experience can occasionally deconstruct in sleep. But from the point of view of the experiencing self, it seems jolting to wake into a confusion resulting from memory loss or gaps and spaces in one's hold on the facts of one's own actual existence. In sleep, the mind seems to disconnect from these facts. As it turns inward, away from external sources of sensory information, it seems also, at times, to turn away from memory of our place in the external world: name, address, age, kind of work, family membership, geographic location, familiar attitudes, and so on. At times, it feels like early Alzheimer's, or a late infancy, or an amnesia in that, for a moment, we are adrift without those customary longitudes and latitudes that help us fix our particular place in the huge cosmos. For a moment, we are identityless, as sleep leaves us on the shores of consciousness, without knowing who we are or where we have been.

The disconnection in sleep is hardly universal or complete. The slightest sounds of a baby stirring in a nearby room can waken a sleeping parent. External sounds and light patterns can enter the sleeper's awareness, sometimes finding their way into an ongoing dream that, as Freud observed, allows the dreamer to remain asleep. Some persons can awaken precisely at a particular time as though an internal clock had been programmed. Some persons awaken immediately and completely and move instantly to the task at hand. And so there are many ways of waking and many variations in how the day's moods can be shaped. But I find myself drawn to the way and the extent to which the mind seems to disconnect from the "facts" of one's life and history as it turns inward to its nighttime activities.

What are these nighttime activities that require such disconnection? Neuroscientists as well as the archetypal psychologist Hillman (1979) and others suggest that sleep is given over to the digestion of daytime's activities and to turning the facts of day life into the internal "stuff" of memory, unconscious thought, and dream imagery. Others suggest that for the soul to wander about in sleep, it is necessary for it to disconnect and to temporarily sever its ties to the body and to the particular facts of its daytime existence. Still others suggest that in turning away from the identity of day life, one is able to open the identity of one's night life. Or, it can be hypothesized that the energy required for nighttime's excursions and adventures in dream imagination require that energy be decathected from the usual sources of daytime memory. No single generalization, however, seems to fit the diversity of experiences. For example, at times, on awakening, memory for one's surroundings seems momentarily disorganized and fragmentary. Yet, in dreams, one can experience a heightened sharpening of memory for particular pieces of life—the face, dress, and manner of a 6-year-old chum from 50 years ago, or the exact notes of a piece of music heard several days before. Or one can awaken with the specifics of some unfinished task vividly in mind.

It is difficult to generalize about the kind and degree of disconnection in sleep or with the nature of reconnection in the return to waking life. I envision a disconnection in sleep that can at times be quite profound and at other times quite superficial. In either case, nighttime and sleep are accompanied by a turn away from daytime's overt pursuits and identities, such that the mind can "take a break" from the day-to-day survival and adaptational interests that customarily occupy and preoccupy it. Without external sources of sensation and perception, and without the feedback-checking mechanisms allowed by our perceptual apparatuses, and without social contact to frame and affect our thinking, and without the body's musculature ready to carry out our intentions, the mind is "finally" free to enter "its own realm" in which memory and imagination rule, or at least in which the nature and requirements of the world without are no longer the only master.

## TWO MODES OF THOUGHT

Freud wrote that the primary process dominated the goings on in the inner world. Thus, a different kind of structure, logic, and language was hypothesized for the realm of sleep-thinking, whereas the secondary process was proposed for most of the activities of awake-thinking. The mind awake, it was proposed, is required by the experiences of life in the world as it is given, to function according to the reality principle, in linear logic, in the syntactic mode (Sullivan, 1953), in which time, for example, proceeds from past to future, and in which there is an inherent stability in forms. The mind asleep, it was proposed, is freed from the usual rules of logic, consistency, and coherence and can range between ideas and images with greater freedom and without as much regard for the constraints of time, logical cohesiveness, or "the known and acceptable ways of regarding the world." The ways of the dream work, including picture-thinking, condensation, displacement, and symbolization, were suggested by Freud to describe the way primary-process thinking operated.

Let us consider condensation, the concept that seems most important to nighttime thinking. In the greater freedom and fluidity of dream-thinking, ideas and parts of ideas can join together, it is proposed, and thus can cohere in new combinations. A mother's face, or at least her eyebrows, plus a daughter's voice, plus the dreamer's own clothes, plus a stranger's gait and manner, can come together in a single dream figure. Similarly, ideas, attitudes, philosophies, and other organized mental contents can come apart and rearrange in unusual ways. Perhaps condensation requires an accompanying concept, such as dissemination or separation or division or disconnection, to convey the "cutting and pasting" that allows images and ideas to be taken apart and reassembled in new and unusual ways. Perhaps daytime thinking, as coherent as it tries to be, requires a significant degree of loosening in the night to retain its coherence. Perhaps nighttime thinking, as playful, idiosyncratic, and illogical as it sometimes seems to be, requires a significant degree of tightening in the day for it to retain its freedom. Flaubert advised artists to think like a demigod but live like a bourgeois. Perhaps the bourgeois and the artist require each other. Perhaps they even cross over at times, such that the bourgeois sometimes goes out at night to play, and the artist at times tends to necessary household chores. That is, what of the creativity of daytime thinking and the occasional "housekeeping" of nighttime thinking? Or what of the mundane and the logical (and the secondary process) in our dreams and the creative and playful (and the primary process) in our waking thinking?

These considerations lead to the idea that confusion and disorientation on awakening may be only one side of the story. There is also the counterpart observation that in fully awake thinking, we may at times be disoriented and lost in relation to our nighttime identities. Although in sleep and on awakening we may lose our names for a moment, it is equally possible that in being wide awake, we may lose a sense of our inner nature. Many persons seem to lose a feeling of connection with their inner universe in their conscious lives. I have worked with patients who are determined to forget their dream lives, as though these inner lives are a threat to their highly organized and controlled existence.

Psychoanalysis, from its beginnings, has sought to reconnect these two realms and to remind us that both the unconscious and the conscious minds require each other for survival, and they are both part of a single, unified mind. In a version of the ancient Greek prescription for the good life as a balance between a sound mind and a sound body, we recommend the good life as consisting of a balance between the conscious and unconscious mind, between awake-thinking and sleep-thinking. For many patients, particularly those overconnected to the control and organization often necessary for successful material life, an important task is to help them recognize the essential role of nighttime thinking, or of primary-process thinking, or of imagination, or of creativity, or of a less organized, more playful, even zany mode of thinking and experience. Similarly, it is important for some patients to be helped to consider the importance of logical, coherent, secondary-process thinking if their ordinary experience is dominated by dreamlike experience.

### THE WORLD OF SLEEPING

The renewed interest in sleep and dreams, initiated by the remarkable discoveries of Aserinsky and Kleitman (1953), leads to a general consideration of sleep more as a biological and physiological phenomenon than a psychological experience. Psychoanalysis has relatively little to say about sleep per say or about the transitions between sleep and waking. Sullivan (1953) is a noticeable exception. He discusses sleep as "a phase of living which is very important indeed, in that . . . it is the part of life in which we are almost by definition relieved from the necessity of maintaining security . . . free from dangers to one's self-esteem" (p. 329). It is as though, except for dreaming (REM) and other associated night time mentation (nonREM), we have no interest in the vast domain of sleep unconsciousness. This is particularly unfortunate because psychoanalysis, with its broad interest in the psychological meanings of things, can easily extend its interest to include even the meanings of nothingness, let alone the meanings of sleep. Lewin (1954), especially, explored the relationship between psychoanalysis and sleep in his observation that the use of the couch equals sleep for many patients and the reliance on free association equals dreams in the clinical psychoanalytic evocation of our night life. I believe there is much to recommend an extended inquiry, with our patients, into the nature of their sleep experiences as well as into the nature of the transitions between wakefulness and sleep, before, during, and after one's usual night of sleep.

Unless directed to such an inquiry by complaints of a noticeable sleep disturbance, most of us steer clear of the world of sleep, except perhaps for interest in an occasional remembered dream. There is something about a therapy hour early in the morning that can invite an inquiry into patterns of sleeping and awakening. My patient and I were meeting early one morning, not long after we both emerged from our respective sleep realms. It seemed a good time to inquire into the world of sleep and waking. She is a youthful, zestful, and handsome woman, a teacher who had been depressed on and off for several years. I began by asking her about her experience of going to sleep the night before and waking up this morning. She began to describe her night-time preparations, and at my requests for details, she gradually revealed her sleep regimen: the placement of pillows, the open windows, the cold air, the warm down comforter, its pattern, the room, the book, the cats, the feeling of it all. We also learned the details of her waking. And then, softly, as though it were a confession, she revealed: "Every morning, I wake up feeling crushed."

We learned that this profound and terrible first impression was invariable, depending neither on the degree of depression nor on the quality of remembered dreams. Whether feeling generally good or bad, she awoke feeling crushed. Something in the way she spoke and something in the emphasis she gave the word "crushed" instructed me that we needed to think freshly, even though she assumed, at first, that the feeling resulted from unremembered bad dreams. Now, this certainly could be the case. Kramer (1993) and others have demonstrated that a morning's mood is often contingent on the feeling state of the previous night's dreams. But as we continued, we learned that this feeling had been present most of her life, certainly from adolescence, and seemed unrelated to the kind of dreams she was having. We found further that the crushed experience remained with her most of each morning, slowly dissipating as the day's routines and duties filled her day. What is it like to wake each morning to such a feeling? What in her is crushed again and again?

As the session continued, we began to understand together that it was a sense of life as she knew it that was obliterated and snuffed out as she opened her eyes. How could that be? Usually, people feel a sense of life returning to them each morning as they open their eyes to the day. Ancient lore has always equated sleep with the soul's wanderings, with a touch or a rehearsal of death, and awakening with a return to the living. But this point of view takes the awake state as the standard from which one departs and returns. My patient was describing a different state of affairs, her own—one in which the standard or home base or sense of life is found not in being awake, but in the sleeping state from which she sadly departs and peacefully returns. To awaken is to lose her home, her place, her natural state. This suddenly revealed "upside down" view was recognized by both of us, in time, to be related to Freud's nirvana principle, to the Tibetan Book of the Dead, to Buddhist thinking, to the pleasures of nothingness, to unconsciousness, night life, and death. Her lifelong suicidal ambition began to seem more like a wish to return to her natural state, less a depressive threat to life than a fantasy of deepest life. In a psychotic depression, such thinking could seem dangerous, but in my patient it was more an effort to describe her deepest opposition to the domination of her life by the demands of daytime: the success world's repudiation of what she felt to be her softer, slower, and darker traits; her father's dominating power, his great success and his accompanying derision and contempt for his only child's more dreamy, internal, and artistic interests along with his contempt for her mother's darker side; the patient's difficulty in school competition, her sense of being crushed by the demands of linear and logical thinking, of ambition and sociability, all experienced as foreign and originating from without.

Sleep became her peaceful home in which the possibility of failure and a crushed self were eliminated and replaced by sweet nothingness, loving unconsciousness. Even dreams were potentially crushing when they touched on her profound fears of failure in the day world. For us to think together about the love of nothingness, without forcing a day world "remedy" for this "problem" was helpful and relieving to her. She had always been ashamed of these attitudes and had treated them as a further sign of failure and weakness, rather than as an effort to locate some realm where she might feel an "uncrushed" fuller self.

Many people yearn for a sense of home, a feeling of intactness, a psychological experience of an unharassed and natural breathing space. For some, this home exists away from the demands, pressures, and requirements of day life, in the shadows of night, where the increasingly relentless push of modern civilization slows and the ancient rhythms of nature assert themselves once again. Although some, perhaps even most of us, find this home in the day and push away the unfamiliarity and associated loss of control of night, some of us find this home only in the night, in sleep, in silence, in the underworld. Psychoanalysis, once upon a time, was a friend to this latter urge. Its interest in dreams, its use of the couch, its devotion to an understanding of the concealed self, all stood in contrast to the way in which more modern psychoanaly-sis began to align itself with social adjustment, success, consciousness, and purpose. We need to reexamine our values and our approaches so that our very own efforts do not further assist the crushing force of civilization, but instead provide a more sympathetic and a less patholo-gizing ear to those whose natural home lies in a realm closer to the psychology of sleep.

# ∝ 14 ∞

# WHY USE DREAMS IN
# PSYCHOANALYSIS AND
# PSYCHOTHERAPY?

*No one can practise the interpretation of dreams as an isolated activity; it remains the work of analysis.*

           –Sigmund Freud

*Dream analysis is the central problem of the analytical treatment, because it is the most important technical means of opening up an avenue to the unconscious.*

           –Carl Jung

Once we agree that dreams and dreaming are a significant human experience and that they hold interest for a psychology of mind, and special interest for a psychology of unconscious mind, the question can be raised: Of what use can dreams and dreaming be in psycho-analytically inspired psychotherapy, that is, in trying to understand and improve the psychological condition of persons who come for

treatment? Many therapists use some variety of dream analysis
without ever asking themselves the question: Why do this? In
addition, many patients and clients bring their dreams to the
"expert" without asking the question: Why do I do this? What is
the point? Simply that it is the tradition may be one good reason.
But this answer just leads to the obvious next question: Why the
tradition? How does it actually help people? That dreams are a
sample of human mental life and that everything brought into the
office is "grist for the mill," may also be another good reason, but
still it ignores the question: Is there anything special about dreams
that makes them worthy of particular attention and discussion in
psychotherapy?

Psychoanalysis has often engaged this question. Following the
enormous popularity of dream analysis in the first phase of psychoanalytic history, Brenner (1969) and others argued, as the structural
theory replaced the topographic model, and as transference interpretations replaced id interpretations, that dreams should be treated like
any other part of mental life and that their special purpose within
psychoanalytic theory and practice had already been fulfilled and
superceded. In a symposium on the Place of the Dream in Clinical
Practice (Waldhorn, 1967), a heated debate took place between the
followers of Brenner, who held that dreams were not special, and the
followers of Greenson and Khan, who held that dreams were special,
to no particular resolution. So we are left with the question: What
makes dreams potentially useful in psychoanalytic psychotherapy? In
this age of the "bottom line," what possible justification could there
be for talking about dreams? Why spend hard-earned money, of which
there is a limited amount, on dream discussion? Could it not be better
spent in other ways? Drug therapy, behavior modification, cognitive
restructuring, talking about concrete worries and goals—these are
ways of trying to help people in psychological trouble. Why talk about
dreams? They are elusive, insubstantial, possibly immaterial. Hobson
(1988) and other neuroscientists argue that they are probably nonsense of one sort or another to boot. There is hardly a science of
interpretation. There is hardly agreement about whether they can be
of help or how they can help. So, to argue for their usefulness at this
time is an uphill struggle. The following are some reflections on this
question.

## TRADITION

Let us return to tradition for a moment. Although tradition is hardly a sufficient reason for working with dreams or for expecting they can prove therapeutically useful, still the ancient tradition of telling dreams to a healer who interprets them and advises the dreamer accordingly is an extremely powerful piece of background. As described in earlier chapters, in every known culture, the dream found its way into healing in both the physical and the psychological realms. Dreams were told to shamans and other dream experts in the effort to cure illness and to understand the ways of the world above and the world below. In both ancient Egypt and Greece, dream temples were constructed as significant centers of knowledge, religion, and healing. And yet, since dreams have always been largely ambiguous, puzzling, metaphoric, symbolic, the dream translator or interpreter was called in to decipher the messages that might have been sent from central and mysterious sources. Thus, from the ancients in every era and on every continent, dreams have been looked into for information and meaning of a very special nature.

As we entered the 20th century, most in the West no longer believed much in mysticism and the occult traditions in which dreams were thought significant. The decline in the significance of religion, the effects of the Enlightenment, the growing power of scientific ideals, the effects of industrial materialism, the illumination of night, the domination over nature, all led to a decline in the belief in the power of dreams both to reflect and to influence the course of life. The modern dream expert, the high priest of the Enlightenment—the psychoanalyst—entered the scene with the assignment to bring this product of the ancient mind into modern times. This duty, I believe, was always part of the dream interpreter's role—to bring the dream, and with it the dreamer, into accord with the traditions, the customs and the needs of the culture. Thus, part of the dream expert's tradition has always involved the interpreter's review of the raw material of the dream in order to see what the particular culture has needed to see for its own maintenance and survival.

This old, revered, and occasionally reviled tradition of the dream interpreter is part of the relevant context, most often outside of awareness, shared by both dreamer and interpreter. The interpreter exists to make the irrational understandable, to make the puzzling clear, to make the particular dream manifestation of contact with the immensity of unconscious mind into something manageable, knowable, even familiar. The contemporary psychoanalytically inspired psychotherapist borrows on this vast tradition. The assumption is made that the experience of meaningfulness will in some way assist the sufferer and thus be of use in the therapeutic process. In addition to the ancient tradition, the contemporary therapist is also part of the 100-year tradition that began with Freud, and was joined by Jung and by generations of their followers. The patient's expectation that we will be interested in dreams, therefore, is based on two layers of tradition, the ancient and the modern.

## THE REQUIRED DREAM LISTENER

The patient's expectation may have nontraditional roots as well. In early individual development, small children tell their dreams to the older people who care for them. But I know of a 4-year-old child who would awake each morning to tell her dreams to her dog, a most sympathetic schnauzer. The dog made not a single interpretation, so far as I know. I know of an older child, an 11-year-old boy, who would confess his most difficult nightmares to a large granite boulder in his back yard. He considered the boulder a personal gift from God. He would climb onto the rock and whisper his dream into a small crevice. Most children, at one point or another, tell their dreams to mother, if she is available. This dream-telling is an important part of childhood and often requires the parent to inform the child about the difference between dream experience and regular experience as in "It's only a dream. Don't be frightened. There's no bear in the room. It was just in your dream." In addition to this reality-testing function, associated with children's difficulty on awakening from dreams, in distinguishing dream from reality, dreams may also have an effect on the dream listener. They may delight, amuse, worry, upset, or otherwise affect the mother. There develops a back-and-forth between child and mother in relation to dreams, until the child learns increasingly to keep dreams to him or herself. This step in development—keeping dreams to oneself—is a significant one, although as far as I know no research has been done on it.

Of course, dream-telling does not end in childhood. In many cultures, dreams continue to be told to one another throughout life, aside from those told a dream expert for relief of suffering or for some special information. People tell each other dreams, outside of psychotherapy, for many varied reasons. For some, to share with a friend or intimate an extraordinarily unusual experience, a sleep adventure, is a natural part of friendship and intimacy. That is what some people simply do as an act of bonding and closeness, like grooming in apes and monkeys.

I know of a young woman who phones her dreams each morning to an older sister across the continent. They have been dream-buddies from early childhood. The younger sister will continue to tell her dreams, she says, even after her ailing sister dies, to her sister in heaven. I have met people who e-mail dreams each morning to friends, chat rooms, dream groups. This busy new electronic sharing of dreams, this world of dreams being shipped back and forth across continents, reminds me of a fanciful notion I once had when I wondered what the world might be like if we all actually lived our dreams, all together, all night long. My own small town of Stockbridge would be a very strange and lively place with people and things flying about, driving through rivers, walking backward up hills that are not on our real maps, with wars and lovemaking breaking out all over, Norman Rockwell sitting in the lobby of the Red Lion Inn filled with Chasidim, tractors driven sideways by airline pilots, souls unknown to us rushing about, all at the same moment. But this surreal idea is only for the imagination; in the real world, the closest we come is the humming of thousands and thousands of dream descriptions on the internet. Or 15 different movies being shown in the darkened dream-theaters of cine-15. Or 100 TV channels telling 100 different stories all brought in from outerspace relay stations right into our living rooms.

For the most part, I have found that people are eager to relate their dreams, if only asked. Even if not asked, when some people learn of my interest in dreams, they are automatically inclined to tell a dream—a particularly interesting recent one, or an old repetitive one, or a puzzling one, or one their mother had, or a nightmare. Thus the tradition behind the dream listener meets up with the routines of dream telling both from childhood and from later life, and these combine in our offices. "I had a dream last night," and we reach for our notepads. I once reached for my notepad without any particular reason in mind and a patient instantly responded: "Oh, that reminds me. I had this dream last night." Reverse conditioning.

It certainly seems as though people have the idea that dreams are worth telling, and that they contain some special kind of information often requiring another to lend an ear or a hand. It is often true that the most experienced dream-interpreter has no idea what is contained in his or her own dream until another person, entirely naive about dreams and symbols, but familiar with the dreamer, says "That stranger in the dream, isn't that just like your brother? He's always been pretty strange." Or, "Sixteen pounds of grain? Your kid just had a sweet sixteen party, didn't she?" And the obvious then reveals itself to the dreamer through the listener. Although the dreamer creates and constructs the dream, and owns the dream, so to speak, the dreamer is often the last one to see and understand some of the meanings within the dream. Another mind is often necessary. It is crucial to help people value and appreciate their original creative expressions, and it is equally crucial not to take people's dreams away from them in rude and competitive interpretive zeal; at the same time, we must not be too shy to add our ideas to the mix. Whether we call it good interpretation or good dream conversation, many dreams await the listener for commentary in the implicit understanding that meaning is to be made not discovered.

In the Talmud, it is written that all dreams follow the mouth. This statement has been taken to contain a number of meanings including the idea that all dreams follow their interpretation, or that interpretation completes a dream. According to Frieden (1990), "Dream texts receive their meaning retrospectively, from the dreamer and from every interpreter called upon for assistance" (p. 73). The Talmud is unclear, however, whether "the mouth" refers to the dreamer telling the dream or to the interpreter telling the dreamer what is believed to be contained in the dream. It is left for us to combine these possibilities into the idea that dream and listener, both, have something to say about the dream.

Throughout this writing, I have repeated that the ambiguous dream invites the listener in for commentary, but I have insisted that the interpreter understand how much of his or her own projection is involved in dream interpretation. The interpreter must keep a light touch on the proceedings and be mindful of the capacity to turn a dream to the interpreter's own purposes. Now, however, it is time for a major amendment, assuming the interpreter is neither too anxious nor too arrogant in working with dreams.

Because there is no single and right interpretation to dreams, but rather a multitude of possibilities and a multitude of approaches, there is no longer any cause to fret that tests and failures abound in dream work or that a "real expert" could easily unravel the puzzle of a dream. Or that one is or is not an "expert." No such thing. All we have is an approach, a willingness to ask questions and to try out ideas as we go along. An expert, then, is not one who "knows," but is one who can assist in creating the conditions for good dream discussion and conversation, one who engages the dreamer in a process of collaborative play, of wondering and imagining together, one who finds matters of interest and curiosity in every turn. We start our stroll with dreamer and dream and see what lies around the bend. We become two colleagues in natural observation; no method; no tried and true approach; different every time. Once a Freudian, next time a Jungian. Once asking for clarification, next time offering one's own ideas. Once serious, next time humorous. Once seeking associations, next time seeking amplification. Once listening to transference, next time ignoring the relationship. Once being completely puzzled, next time being clear as day. Neither fearful nor arrogant, the dream listener is ready with notepad and "soft focus," as the Buddhists advise.

But the question remains: How does it help to work on dreams? First, the telling of a dream to a therapist may fall into the category of telling a dream to a friend or intimate. Such telling is often fun, pleasurable, filled with surprises and adventures. It often feels good to tell a dream and to talk about it together. This may seem like a superficial observation. But with Oscar Wilde, the superficial contains genuine depths. Certainly the telling of a frightening or shameful dream, if received with calm, interest, and respect, can be of important help. Some patients are terribly intimidated by their mind's products. A listener who can take in terrible or shameful images from another and, rather than turn away, can turn toward dream and to the very images that upset, and then lend his or her own mind to thinking about the dream, can be a source of strength and confidence. Also, a listener who, alongside the dreamer, can appreciate the artistry, or the humor, or the aggression, or the "funkiness," or the ridiculousness of a dream, is also strengthening a human bond in the therapeutic relationship. For some, the aloneness of life, joined to the solitary privacy of dreaming, calls out for another, a fellow being, to listen in, to share in the deeply personal creations of night. It can do the soul of both participants some good in coming together in this old way.

Also, the dream is not anybody's idea but the patient's. It originates from the patient's own sleeping mind. For those who fear that nothing original can issue from them, this fact can be quite restorative. For those who feel entirely dependent on the opinions, judgments and values of others, the originality of one's own dreams, of one's own mind, can come as a helpful discovery.

Secrets can be told better in dreams, for some, than directly. Because some secrets are also secret to the patient, dreams are often the only way that secret secrets can be revealed. If one can receive these without too much tumult, psychological pressure is often reduced. The virtues of calm receptivity are evident when the secrets are the patient's feelings about the therapy and the therapist. "You are fat, or Jewish, or ugly, or incompetent, or impotent, or stupid, or hateful, or self-centered or, conversely, brilliant, sexy, a savior, humble, lovable, a regular sweetheart." If the therapist can accept these judgments and talk about them, and can hear them, occasionally as transference and occasionally as reality, the patient can gain the confidence that you are not too defensive, that you will not collapse from attack or praise, that you might even have a textured idea of yourself such that the patient will not need to "carry" and be too guilty about you, and that other "secrets" can be shared. Dreams are often experiments, for both, in what can be told and heard. "It's only a dream," allows for taking risks with material that might be too "hot" in direct conversation.

## DREAMS CHANGE THE SET

Of special importance, as indicated earlier, dreams have the effect of changing the set. That is, practically no matter what the subject matter under consideration, no matter how much time or attention has been devoted to a particular topic or issue during the present or preceding session or for that matter during the past months' sessions, as soon as a dream is introduced, the subject matter usually changes in the direction of the dream. Thus the introduction of a dream and its subsequent discussion can have the effect of moving things about and by command of the unconscious joined together with the intention of telling it to the analyst. Permitting the unconscious, through dreams, to alter the proceedings as it wishes to, whenever it wishes to, represents an act of faith that the unconscious will guide us to essential matters. In my opinion, this act of faith in the unconscious is a defining characteristic of psychoanalytic therapy and is essential in our kind of psychological treatment.

For example, patient and therapist could be discussing the patient's failing marriage, or sexual dilemmas, or a feeling of improvement in depression, or illness, or how awful or terrific is the therapist, or was the last therapist, or the struggle for money, or anything at all, and at any degree of mutual involvement, and suddenly a dream is remembered from the night before and is told. The dream has in it that the patient's *Tante Rose is sitting in her old, frayed chair singing a portion of the aria, "la donna è mobile" from* Rigoletto, *while her cat with white eyes stares at the dreamer who is moved to tears. The tears become deep sobs mingled with the pleasure of seeing Tante Rose alive again.* It has been 40 years since Tante Rose died when the patient was 12 years old. And no matter what was the area of discussion before the dream was told, we are now led by the dream's manifest content to consider Tante Rose and the patient's experience of this beloved and long-dead great aunt, who has never been mentioned before. I may ask the patient later to consider the questions: Why Tante Rose and why now? I may hypothesize that this dream was dreamed in order to have the beloved dead relative brought to our consideration in therapy. I may like to think this way, it adds a dramatic or poetic aspect. But I have no way to test this hypothesis.

An alternative hypothesis would hold that this dream was not dreamt for our purposes at all, but for its own. And that our job is to follow it wherever it takes us, not to assume it comes to bring us anything at all. Meanwhile, however, our immediate subject matter prior to the dream, our habits of conversation, our topics, our designs, have suddenly been altered and we are face to face with a dead great aunt and with a child's magical love for an old woman. Actually not only the set of topic is changed, but an entire new configuration is present in the office. We have the patient at 12 and at 52. We have the great aunt alive in her 80s and now long dead paying a nighttime visit to her favorite nephew's daughter (my patient). We have me as I am and me always in her father's large shoes, especially in the evocation of the father's aunt who raised him when his mother (the aunt's younger sister) suddenly died in a train crash.

As we spoke for the entire hour about her feelings for this relative, whom she had not thought about for many months, at least since the beginning of the darkest part of her depression, she mentioned how her father was crushed by this death. I had the sense that her depression carried, in part, her father's grief and that I had been introduced deeply into this family's saga by the dream and the session of explication following the dream. Many new ideas flowed from this experience, hypotheses about the patient's depression, ideas about aspects of our relationship that seemed connected to her depression, and ideas about what areas needed airing. We may have gotten there some other way. We may have worked through this depression by other means.

Yet, this experience has been repeated with so many of my patients that I have become convinced that dreams can lead us, often in surprise, to essential aspects of the story, and are often connected in unconscious ways with the major aspects of the preceding or following contents and explorations. Such connections can emerge if we dare leave off where we are, no matter the "importance" of the discussion. and go where the dream takes us.

The cat's staring white eyes and "*la donna è mobile*" were left behind in this session, only to be recovered later when, during the report of a dream weeks afterward, there appeared a little bird whose coloring reminded her of the cat with the white eyes and also reminded her of the aria by Verdi. These images and their richly elaborated associations took us deeper into the family story, into early ambitions including a fervent, but forgotten, wish in childhood to become an opera singer, into the memory of certain repetitive dreams in childhood, into fears of dying, into ideas about God, into long-forgotten events in Katz's Delicatessen, into various meanings of the colors white and green (verdi) and black (the color of the bird and the cat), and into other matters of considerable interest and emotional importance for the patient and for our work together.

The importance of the change in set is particularly felt with rigid patient–therapist pairs who can't easily flow through ideas with one another, but who get stuck and influence each other to remain stuck. Obsessional patient–therapist pairs are particularly prone to this lack of movement as are depressive patient–therapist pairs. When both are present at the same time, as in depressive-obsessional patient–therapist pairs, there are many forces at work to keep surprise, change, and flow out of the picture. It can get deadly for both participants. Dreams can change things, can force movement, at least in topic, and can thus serve the purpose of stirring things up.

Now, there are situations between patient and therapist in which "stirring things up" can be a poor idea. In states of increasing disorganization, confusion, excitement, and disarray, it is sometimes best just to keep plugging at one note at a time for a while. Dreams, if they are pursued, may then upset the need for calm steadiness in the therapeutic environment, and for the slow development of islands of constancy and dependable habits. Such introduction of disarray can be a problem, unless one has a way of pursuing dreams without stirring the pot, in a way that itself instills calm and reduces the fever of confusion. It is possible but difficult to do. Dreams usually bring their own heat and new puzzlement.

It should also be mentioned that for some people, pursuing dreams and changing the set through a discussion of dreams may be used as ways of avoiding facing other, perhaps pressing issues. Dreams and their discussion can be used by patient and/or therapist to hide, avoid, or evade various kinds of anxieties. I think such avoidance, in part, was what Sullivan was grouching about in his criticism of Freud's dream methods. However, I have rarely found this to be a problem. If dreams are entered with an open mind by both, it is usually the case that whatever the anxious issues being avoided through a discussion of dreams, they will find no hiding place in a free-ranging discussion of dreams, or these concerns will find their way to the surface in their own time, later on. I have never yet heard myself say, "I don't think we should consider this dream that seems to be about your latest project at this time, because we have to discuss your having unprotected sex without telling your partner you are HIV-positive; or the fact that I mentioned a fee raise last week and you still haven't said anything about it; or the way the last session ended with your announcement at the door that you are moving to Seattle in 2 weeks; or that you are thinking of killing yourself before your next birthday."

I am never sure that what I think we should talk about is closer to the mark than what the dream may say about what and how we should be talking. I am usually willing to give the dream first crack, unless I figure that I am with a real trickster, in which event I will often be less polite.

## ACCESS TO THE UNCONSCIOUS

In addition to the virtues of breaking the set ways of thinking and talking in a particular psychotherapy, there is the broader and more fundamental role of dreams giving voice to the unconscious along with the general issue of the potential usefulness of knowledge of the unconscious in treatment. What differentiates psychoanalytic from other modes of psychotherapy is not so much the number of sessions per week, nor the use of the couch, but the idea in the analyst that the unconscious, the unknown, the shadow side of the mind is of singular significance in psychological life in general and in psychological treatment in particular. What also differentiates psychoanalysis from other psychological treatments is that the analyst's preoccupation with the unconscious aspect of the patient's psychology will guide his or her work with the patient. Dreams have from the beginning and continue to be a most important source of information about mental life beyond immediate awareness.

There are two aspects of our relationship with this great dark sea of mind that may be of specific benefit in psychoanalytic psychotherapy. The first is the original goal of psychoanalysis—to become aware of the unconscious, or to make the unconscious conscious. This giving voice to the unconscious was, in itself, deemed a healing experience. In today's rush to empathic and relational connectedness within contemporary psychoanalysis and to the expanding world of nontraditional healing and New Age psychologies, we do well to recall that the powerful impact of psychoanalysis was in large measure owed to its dedication to the study and understanding of the unconscious mind. To glimpse the extraordinary unconscious mind was to be changed forever—not necessarily healed, but changed.

Added to this orienting aim was also the effort to help the patient, and one's own self, to experience some emotional knowledge about the content, shape, and shading of one's conflicts. It was generally held that conflict was entirely inevitable in mental and emotional life. There was no nirvana in the real life in the real world. We can see how unpopular this view is. The more obvious it becomes that modern life is filled with conflict and difficulty, the more increasingly popular is the kind of wishfulness found in fundamentalism and in parts of the New Age healing communities. In addition to pointing to the deep inevitability of conflict on many levels, psychoanalysis also showed the brave, foolish, and poignant quality of the unconscious mind's ingeniously created compromises, such that one need not necessarily abandon whole aspects of the self in order to survive. Through unconscious compromise together with secondary-process thinking, we survive.

Psychoanalysis was, thus, interested in helping the uninitiated become initiated primarily into the culture of awareness of the unconscious. Secondarily, the newly initiated could also catch sight of some of the goings-on within this unconscious mind. And that was that! The treatment had achieved its purpose. On to the next! One went on with one's life. One's life was where the action was, not in the analyst's office, but in the real world.

Further, and of considerable importance, "ordinary" people could, through psychoanalysis, have the kind of access to an experience of the unconscious world that had been reserved for artists, writers, mystics, drug users, bohemians, and the privileged class. Through dreams and free association, almost anyone could gain the strength that comes of living through and learning from contact with knowledge of the existence of powerful unconscious forces. Thus the growing middle class, even the least creative among them, could be shown the immense creativity of their own unconscious minds. Add to this enlightenment the great Greek tragedies of Oedipus, Narcissus, and others and the profound conflicts raging in them. It was almost enough to make one proud to be a neurotic. It goes without saying that the psychoanalytic view, contrary to Freud's insistence that narcissism was diminished by an awareness of unconscious motivation, must have been enormously flattering for ordinary people. Although I don't think that visual artists much delighted in learning that their labors were believed to be the compromise results of an unconscious mind transforming feces, most people could feel larger than their lives permitted if they could see themselves as part of a Greek tragedy. Of course, Jung carried this flattery much further, into the host of archetypal heroes and giants. I am not arguing that such large ideas are invalid or unhelpful—just that they are flattering.

The early method, without the therapeutic zeal we see practiced today, did not stress a profoundly relational or a particularly time-consuming procedure. One was not to dot the i's and cross the t's of personality quirks. That could be endless as well as fruitless. Show patients the unconscious and the particular conflicts involved and they will get better, or at least they won't expect perfect happiness, and they will get on with their lives. A capacity for self-analysis including dream analysis would eventually, inevitably, and economically replace the relatively brief analytic treatment. In addition, discovery of the unconscious would lead to renewed aliveness, partly as a result of a liberation of the energy that would otherwise be used to keep things hidden in the unconscious. That is, just "knowing" about the unconscious freed up energy previously bound in the patient's resistant efforts to maintain ignorance of the unconscious. Thus, there was no need for the extensive complexity and depth of emotional and intellectual work that one can find in contemporary psychoanalytic therapy.

There are many different kinds of people in very different kinds of psychological difficulty who come for treatment. Certainly no single statement about the usefulness of knowledge about the unconscious or about the dream's role in all this will do. Persons who are seeking help in sorting through a failed relationship or the death of a loved one or the causes of emotional exhaustion or an oncoming breakdown or decisions about career or marriage or whatever, whether they are 17 or 70 years old, whether frail or robust, whether in an emergency or seeking psychoanalytic training, will be in varying degrees affected by and in need of information about and contact with the unconscious, the unknown, the shadow sides and layers of the mind—or not. Not everyone needs to uncover unconscious patterns of living and thinking and not everyone needs dreams to lead them to such knowledge. But I believe no matter what the patient's circumstances, it is well for the therapist to have some idea about the place and range of unconscious motivation, both in general and in reference to this specific patient. In addition, it is well for the therapist to have some idea of the impact of unconscious ideas in his or her own experience as therapist, in general, and with this patient, specifically.


## MULTIPLICITY, COMPLEXITY, LAYEREDNESS

In addition to demonstrating the existence and importance of the unconscious, dreams are particularly meaningful in therapy, because they lead directly to an appreciation of layeredness, of multiple meanings, and of the many-sided complexity in mental life. Dreams show the mind as the major meaning-maker and creator of intricate webs and systems of interconnected meanings. The mind will connect the dots, almost no matter what. Call to mind any two stimuli, nonsense syllables, words, pictures, planets, whatnot—and the mind will create connections between them. The urge to meaning and meaningfulness is a powerful one. Without connections and patterns, the mind gets very edgy. It would rather be paranoid than bereft of meaning.

But let us keep to the question: How can it benefit a patient to come to some experience and understanding of the complexity of unconscious processes? I am here focusing on that aspect of unconscious life that shows itself in the possibility of compressing more than one meaning into an image or idea, as in condensation. Considerations from neuropsychology and cognitive psychology lead us to think about the remarkable economy of mind, existing as it does in a three-pound brain housing billions and billions of interconnections, perhaps in numbers greater than the number of stars in the universe. It must pack so much information into so small a space that any process that reduces the need for more space would be most helpful. Thus, if one image can represent multiple ideas, or has more multiple meanings, we are doing well. In other words, the more meanings that can exist in a single image, the better. This interest leads directly to considerations of multiplicity, multicausation, many-sidedness, many-layeredness, complexity of organization, and in Freud's term: overdetermination. Still, of what use is a patient's coming to know about these matters?

First and of greatest importance: such a point of view seems consistent with what we know to be true of psychological life—that it is many-sided, prismatic, layered, and multidetermined. If a dream or some part of a discussion of dreams in therapy leads both participants, but particularly the patient, to a realization of multiple meanings within a dream, a good result has been achieved. Dreams compress information, emotion, memory, evaluation, and all sorts of mental operations into parts of single images and bits of story. By the time we have multiple and complex images and stories, there has been the artful compression of huge amounts of cognitive and emotional living as seen from the inside. To become aware of this compression operation is to become aware of one's own extraordinary mind, as it is. To the extent that psychoanalysis aims at the truth of things, it is of value for the patient to see his or her mind at work, as it is.

Second, the idea of more than one meaning has several positive implications. It means one doesn't have to decide between whether one hates mother or loves mother, whether one wishes to be a child or an adult, whether one means ill or means well. There is more than one possibility at a time. Also, multiple causation is more consistent with what we learn from the sciences—many layers, many and complex causes. Many possibilities guaranteed by an amazingly complex brain and mind. We need not be reductive in our explanations. The contemporary "dumbing down" and oversimplification of psychological life deserves rebuttal. Dreams, taken seriously and entered into with an open mind, can often assist in resisting some of the more egregious cause-and-effect simplifications now popular.

"This dream-image of your sister has in it your brown eyes, your mother's look, your husband's name, your daughter's problem, your analyst's chair." Were we to look still more closely, were we to follow all the associations, we might discover a score of other persons and archetypes and shadows and associated meanings, enough to fill a village green. The acceptance of the fact that the dream image seems more often than not to contain within it ideas, memories, and feelings about many matters squeezed into a single frame, is a matter of some consequence, and allows for a necessary fluidity in the experience and discussion of the many dimensions to one's psychology. The sister, the patient, the mother, the husband, the daughter, the analyst converge for an instant—and then go their separate ways. But at that instant, what comes next in association or in description is critical because it often contains a wealth of preconscious and unconscious material about the patient's experience of all these persons. That is, the next bit of description or action is likely to contain a great deal of information condensed in the dream image. Thus, "my sister, back from church, looks unhappy and disheveled, and turns away in disgust." The sister who is also, in varying degrees, the patient, the patient's mother, husband, daughter, and analyst, all look away from the patient in disgust, all are depressed, all are trying to return from some kind of house of religion. When many objects, including representations of the self are condensed, it is sometimes desirable to begin with the represented figure itself (sister) and then proceed to the patient herself, assuming the affects and actions are hers. Therefore, I begin to reflect on the patient's disgust—in life, with her sister, in her marriage, with her daughter, with her analyst. If there is time, one might learn more about each of the dream's occupants; if not, simply opening a discussion of her experience of disgust could well be of interest.

The multiple meanings begin to create room to move about in the process of discovering the dimensions and ingredients of mind and self in relation to itself and in relation to the social and natural worlds. With work on multiple possibilities, one has a chance to expand unidimensional judgments of self, world, and other. This work is especially useful in depression, paranoia, obsessional states, narcissistic vulnerability, and in borderline conditions in which splitting is a primitive and positive effort to deal with a confusingly and painfully multidimensional world. For most all people, patients and otherwise, an awareness of the multidimensionality of dreams can provide a sense of pride in the complexity of one's experience of living, in one's capacity to respond from within, and a feeling that one's own complex mind is usually attempting to assist as best it can in the task of creating a meaningful life.

## THE DREAM SEMINAR

Just recently, I was again reminded how extraordinary is the experience of a dream when it is discussed in a seminar in which a participant presents a patient's dream for the group's consideration. The flow of ideas in such a group from dream to patient's unconscious wishes, to the patient's private sex life, to the analyst's self, to feelings toward the surrounding physical world, to political aspects of the dream, to parallel processes, to the relation between males and females, between young and old, to considerations of psychoanalytic theory, to the specifics of this patient's problems in interaction with this analyst—these are only the headlines of intricate discussion flowing from different therapists' reactions to this dream. A dream is such that the more people involved with it, the larger is the set of interconnecting thoughts that emerge from its consideration.

In such a discussion, one is able to experience the dream as organic life with its roots as the many sources into the construction of the dream, through its telling to the analyst and then branching out to the several listeners who have their own multiple reactions. Like mirror opposites, the complex creation of a dream ends in the complex discussion of a dream. The pleasure is certainly, in part, in this group sharing, which allows for an appreciation in the external world of the architecture of the internal world. So, when it goes well, understanding a dream together seems to parallel the experience of the creation of a dream. For dream appreciators, coming close to dream creation is as close as it gets to heaven. For Freud, the process of dream deconstruction through associations was the opposite of the process of dream creation through associations; aesthetically pleasing, at the very least. I am adding that the discussion of a dream in analysis by many analyst listeners can be as richly complex and fruitful as the process at the other end—the creation of a dream from very many sources.

For the solitary dream-listener, the therapist, without a chorus of colleagues to make things interesting, with only the dreamer and dream as companion, it is a different kind of experience, but much of the pleasure for both can be similar. The evocation of meanings, the conversation about this and that piece of the dream, the range of associative connections, the introduction of material from the day and the therapy, all of it back and forth between dreamer and therapist, provides an immense harvest of ideas, images, and feelings. For the therapist, the capacity to let go, to open up, to feel one's way into the crevices of a dream, to share one's innermost responses, to grow the dream in one's own mind, all of this is often a compelling and meaningful way to work. Recall that Freud once complained to Fliess that it was a pity one could not make a living interpreting dreams. Well, we may not be able to make a living at it, but it makes us rich in spirit and for many patients, the dream connection to the unconscious mind is crucial for an effective therapy.

Thus, working with dreams in therapy can provide an abundant harvest of experience. The reasons for engaging with dreams just described—that it's in the oldest tradition, that it keeps things flowing by changing the set, that it is part of a bonding experience between dreamer and listener, that it shows the ways of the unconscious mind, that it allows secrets to be shared, that it shows interest in and respect for the complexity and multiplicity of psychological life in the hope that the patient will follow suit, and finally that there is interest and fun in it—these reasons may no longer provide a satisfactory or cost-efficient basis for work with dreams. However, dreams will continue to be communicated in analytic therapy, although without the centrality of days gone by, and as long as they are being communicated to us, we can greet them happily and respectfully.

A former patient, with whom I spent many hours in discussion of dreams, recently wrote: "I have an almost inexhaustible avalanche of dreams which I, however, do not preserve or even use as inspiration. It is difficult to do alone." I suppose this feeling is at the center of our work with dreams. It is difficult to do alone.

# ঞ 15 ৯০

## The Companionship of Dreams

*We are the music makers*
*And we are the dreamers of dreams . . .*
                              —Arthur O'Shaughnessy

*Music when soft voices die,*
*Vibrates in the memory.*
                              —Percy Bysshe Shelley

My topic is the companionship of mind and of the imaginary. As psychologists, as psychoanalysts, and as all others interested in the dream, our goal is to be keen observers of the imaginary. James Cowell (1997) describes just such a path in his recent novel, *A Mapmaker's Dream,* concerning the meditations of a certain monk, Fra Mauro, cartographer to the Court of Venice in the 16th century. It is the story of a mind poised between the ancient and the modern, as are we. The path requires that to be a keen observer of the imaginary, to look carefully, to look with intense interest and clarity of mind into the heart of unseeable mystery, it is necessary to gather all one's faculties, as mapmakers, geometers, scientists, naturalists of the mind and to accept no turning back from enthusiastic efforts to get as close as possible to the actualities and realities, to the wrinkles, the sounds, the smells of the imaginary, as they are, in their own right.

Now this is not particularly easy to do. There are, of course, extraordinary interweavings between the realms of the material and the invisible, between the physical and measurable universe, on the one hand, and the universe of mind, imagination, spirit on the other. One hundred years ago, Sigmund Freud embarked on a journey into the inner world in which the voice of the imaginary prevails. It is our journey still, although of late, many of us have lost heart and speak only in the language of behavior, relationship, and other observables. Lacan found it necessary to torture language as part of an arduous, and often obscure, effort to turn our energies back to the imaginary. He even turned the word "real" on its head, perhaps to confuse the modern mind, which seems to have forgotten its own rightful home within.

## An Education in Psychology

The interrelations between the real and the imaginary are extraordinary and have been the subject matter of philosophy, poetry, art, and some science. I remember my undergraduate courses as a psychology major at the City College of New York (CCNY) shortly after the long and illustrious tenure of Gardner Murphy as chairman of the psychology department. His open-minded embrace of all of psychology still filled the spirit of the corridors of Townsend Harris Hall. I had no specific path in mind in turning to psychology as a major. I had, earlier in life, moved toward and then away from piano, baseball, history, economics, teaching, dance, and poetry as potential careers. I liked the way psychology was taught at CCNY. I enjoyed the mix of science, politics, philosophy, humanism, mathematics, humor, and an uncertain searching filled with a sense of being on the verge of something momentous that characterized the atmosphere in the psychology department in the early 1950s. I wasn't particularly headed toward psychoanalysis. I had read a little Freud, more Fromm. Earlier I mentioned that I remember my father, when I was very small, reading Freud in Yiddish to my mother—perhaps from *The Interpretation of Dreams*—from the Yiddish newspaper that serialized great works of literature and philosophy for the education of hard-working and poor Jewish intellectuals. I remember my father loved reading to my mother and she loved being read to. I enjoyed hearing the articles, more for the sounds of closeness between my parents than for the content of the articles. They were lovers at such moments. So part of their love, which I took in like milk while I played nearby, was Freud in Yiddish, rather than Talmud; Marx in Yiddish rather than Torah.

But I wasn't clearly headed toward psychoanalysis in those early days at CCNY. Rather, I had fallen in love with psychology. Lehrman, Birch, Barmack, Peatman, Clark, Hertzman, and Hartley, who were social, physiological, comparative, experimental, and clinical psychologists, were my models for the life ahead. I loved the story of psychology, its history, its systems, its scope, its range. It was European and American all at once, intellectual and practical all at once. And it might even offer a way to make a living, because I seemed to be good at it as a student. Traveling by bus, ferry, and two subways from our candy store in Staten Island to uptown City College and back again, which provided plenty of time for reading and assignments, I fell in love with psychology and have been faithful ever since.

The courses that generated the most anxiety and excitement were those in experimental psychology. I recall the time-consuming and arduous experiments in psychophysics in which, following Fechner and others, we measured the just noticeable differences in responses to auditory tones or weights or the timing of lights, and then attempted laboriously and carefully to measure some externally quantifiable indicators of sensations and other presumed internal mental states. We new experimenters, we youthful scientists, we raw empiricists, we eager recruits to the psychologists' version of "hard science," had no idea, at the time, that Gustav Fechner, pioneer in the world of "just noticeable differences" and psychophysics had been a notorius dreamer, a visionary, a mystic who was attempting in his way to "measure the soul."

Some of us within the psychoanalytic world are still trying to measure the soul. To be a keen observer of the imaginary means to watch, to note carefully, and to record—as we did in our psychophysics experiments—the emanations of mind in language both verbal and nonverbal, in body states, in all the various creations of the human mind, and especially in dreams.

As I think back to the courses in experimental psychology, I am reminded that they proceeded beyond psychophysics to other aspects of the study of mind. I remember experiments in learning, particularly in learning and memorizing lists of nonsense syllables. These stimuli, found in randomized tables, were used to eliminate the possibility of social influence or of the influence of past learnings. We found again and again, however, that there were no such things as genuinely "nonsense" syllables. Our subjects, other students cajoled from the tables of the CCNY cafeteria, repeatedly demonstrated an insistent habit of finding meaning in, through, and around the nonsense syllables, of turning the nonsense into sense. Thus, as with Woody Allen, "gub" was thought of as "gun" or "grub" or "bug." "Lek" became "lick," or sounded just like "lack" with a Yiddish accent. Clearly the compilers of such lists never spoke Yiddish or other languages that were the background languages for many of us children of immigrants. And certainly there was a profound underestimation of the relentless and unceasingly capacity to find meaning in all things.

Further, the Gestalt psychology of Koffka, Kohler, and Wertheimer was taken seriously in the psychology department at CCNY in the 1950s. Their contributions to our understanding of perception and thinking seem less revolutionary now, but 40 years ago their emphasis on "meaningful wholeness" was a powerful antidote to the growing influence of behaviorism's atomistic and mechanistic approach. The group at City College took special pleasure in debunking the small-mindedness of the behaviorists, and the Gestalt thinkers were made to order in this effort. Despite some relative experimental weakness of the Gestalt argument, an emphasis on meaningful wholeness in our basic perceptual capacities along with a built-in urge to complete the incomplete, went hand in hand with the growing conviction that meaning making is an essential function and property of mind.

In addition to psychophysics through Fechner, learning experiments through Ebbinghaus, and the Gestalt approach to perception and thinking through Koffka and Kohler, we studied the principle of association of ideas in our thick bible: Woodworth and Schlossberg. We entered the world of Jung's association experiments with stopwatch in hand and learned the myriad ways that ideas can connect with one another. Through similarity, contiguity, contrast, and linkages of various sorts, ideas cling to or are repelled by other ideas, like iron filings in a magnetic field. Images of connecting ideas still seem relevant, especially in classical psychoanalytic theory and in the use of more-or-less free associations in following the "basic rule," and in work with dreams in psychoanalytic psychotherapy. Although entering Jung's association experiments, we steered clear of Jung, that bad boy of psychoanalysis, mystic, supporter of Nazi mythology, and had no idea of his larger scientific contributions. For example, we knew nothing of his profoundly influential work on "complexes."

One further aspect of undergraduate experimental psychology is worth mentioning. Introspection was once an honored method in psychological investigation. Midway between philosophical speculation and psychological self-examination, the methods of introspection and introspectionism were an important aspect of our experimental efforts. Early psychologists attempting to develop an experimental science saw no reason to exclude the human's capacity for self-observation and self-report. The introspective aspect of psychology affords a direct link to psychoanalysis and to clinical efforts with patients.

## THE MIND AS ASSOCIATIONAL RAIN FOREST

These studies and points of view left an indelible impression on me and served as a foundation for the repeated observation and conclusion that it is in the nature of mind to make connections, to create meanings, to project and find order and familiar coherence out of disorder and incoherence. When in ancient times we looked to the stars, we automatically "saw" hunters and bears and faces and other familiar forms. Most every child knows that clouds take on meaningful shapes, or more correctly, that we impose meaningful forms onto clouds. Long before Rorschach, humans have been seeing the familiar in the unfamiliar, the formed in the unformed. Whether as with Hobson, the cerebral cortex imposes coherence and meaning onto randomly activated memory fragments, or with dream interpreters who from the beginning have imposed coherence and meaning on the obscure and enigmatic dream, a serious consideration of dreams and dreaming recognizes the brain's and mind's capacities to discover, impose, and recognize coherent patterns in our encounter with the external and internal realms. It seems to be in our nature to assemble meaning and to live in a subjectively meaningful universe.

In thinking about the way in which ideas and images are interwoven in mind, according to principles of association, I find it useful to imagine a rain forest of intimately, intensely, and endlessly interconnected trees

and vines, in which dizzying, as well as harmonious, designs of thickly
interwoven leaves and branches represent the interconnections between ideas and images. Seen from above, especially during intense
mental activity, it looks as though the rain forest of ideas lights up here
and there, viewed through brain imaging technology, as a result of
oxygen being burned up in the neurons. Ideas entering the rain forest
interconnect with associated ideas through roots, trunks, and branches
and flow along pathways together. Swarms of Tarzans and his apes
swing along the vines. In REM dreaming, the rain forest of thickly
interconnected ideas and images is ablaze, on fire, a fever in the
mindbrain, as connections are sought and found, made and unmade
within the thick jungle of associations. Like the wonderfully impossible
Chinese encyclopedia written about by Borges and Foucault and described by States (1997), associations are developed according to every
conceivable possibility, every physical, cultural, and personal experience that can put ideas and images in proximity. Thus entirely predictable and unpredictable possibilities exist side by side. States writes:

> Among other things, it (the Chinese encyclopedia) divides ani-
> mals into such bizarre categories as those belonging to the em-
> peror, stray dogs, tame, innumerable, suckling pigs, fabulous,
> drawn with a very fine camelhair brush . . . and having just broken
> the water pitcher. An impossible melange! . . . Now the dream is,
> if anything, even more exotic than the Chinese encyclopedia . . .
> a veritable Alexandrian library of Chinese encyclopedias [pp.
> 29–30].

It is not only within dream life that such unpredictable and ex-
otic—or according to Hobson, bizarre—occurrences take place. Day life,
if looked at up close, is as filled with unlikely juxtapositions. Long
before the advent of television channel browsing that produces jar-
ringly different sets of manufactured images, stories, sounds, and
events, people were being subjected to seemingly arbitrary and unrelated events that become associated with one another. The window
rattles from the wind, just as the bird sings, just as dad comes home,
just as the phone rings, just as a car horn is honked, just as the cat enters
the room, just as the smell of dinner is strongest, just as the toilet is
flushed, just as a headache begins, just as the knee hurts, just as one
remembers an event from yesterday, just as the rash reappears, just as

the newspaper headline about floods is spotted, just as . . . and so on. I watch my baby granddaughter whirl about in her play seat and be lifted up by her daddy while life goes around her: sounds, discussions, visual changes, radio music, a cacophony of external and internal sensations, all of it entering her mind connected by—who knows what? The idea that daytime secondary-process thinking is coherent, rational, and linear may not have much to do with the way stimuli actually enter the rain forest of a mental system of associated forms and contents. The chaotic, random, arbitrary, "bizarre" nature of many associations is kept largely out of focal awareness, but exists nonetheless as an accurate mirror of the way life happens. If dreams are "bizarre," could it not be that life is similarly bizarre, but is "fixed up" somehow by aspects of our capacity for screening and sorting for the necessary experience of coherent and meaningful focal consciousness.

At night, with a shutdown of input from this strange external life and with inhibition in our capacity to move our muscles, the relaxation in the requirements for coherent focal consciousness may allow us to reexperience life in its usual and normal bizarreness, in its ordinarily discontinuous and enigmatic fashion, held together by the structures of the mind's extraordinary associational forests. The dynamics and structures of conscious awareness, therefore, fix up the "messiness" that follows from the relative chaos of the sensations of everyday life. Dream life, in this view, may accurately reflect the relatively discontinuous messiness of psychological life prior to its organization within conscious awareness, prior to the organizing that filters, selects, chooses, and "cleans up" the clutter. Experimental subliminal studies (e.g., Bornstein and Pittman, 1992) demonstrate that much more enters the psychological system, a process termed *registration outside of awareness,* than ever enters conscious awareness and perception. Studies of dreams (Fisher, 1960) showed that such registered material remains in the mental system and can appear in dreams, an outcome thought to be a subtype of indifferent impressions within day residues.

Working with dreams in psychoanalytic therapy gives us the opportunity to reenter the associational rain forest from whence the dream originated and thus gives us an up-close look at the mental structure of the dreamer, at the way in which the personal Chinese encyclopedia is constructed. This, to me, is the great gift left us by Freud. While the pre- and nonpsychoanalytic history of writings about dreams is filled with an impressive array of understandings, it is in Freud's contribution that we find dreams in their fullest relationship to all of mental life. In a psychoanalytic interpretation of dreams, the full use of associations places the dream in the center of a throng of radiating meanings, some from the day before, the day residue, some from earlier memories, some from distant and infantile memories, some emanating from current concerns, some from ideas and feelings related to future concerns, some in which affect-connections dominate, some in which mundane worries intersect with spiritual understandings, some including highly creative moments, some reflecting important philosophical concerns. The variety of radiating meanings further interconnect with one another to the point that one can experience a remarkably complex and aesthetically intricate, often harmonious architecture. For example, one need only review Freud's Irma dream (Freud, 1900), along with his commentary on its antecedents, along with our subsequent knowledge of the actual and highly dramatic history surrounding it, along with the letters to Fliess, along with Schur's, Erikson's and Grinstein's perspectives, to achieve a sense of a dream as a piece of mental life at the center of an exraordinary interweave of history, personality, culture, childhood, ambition, love life, loyalty, disguise, and conflict. The thick density of the dream in its associational and historical context gives one the feeling of the absolute complexity of life itself.

## DREAM AS COMPANION TO THE SOUL

There is, I believe, a side of the mind that sits alone, in its own realm, away from the light, unseen by casual observation. Let us call it the innermost private self. Or let us call it the underside of the psyche. Or let us call it soul. Particularly in modern times, where disconnection from nature, from community, and from spiritual life seems the rule rather than the exception, the innermost qualities of the self exist more and more in solitude. In this center, images are held and created, images of what it is to be alive in this place, in this time, in this body, in this culture. The images are various, layered and complex, but sometimes they organize and cohere in central images of the innermost experience of oneself. These self-experience images are hard to put into words. They are mostly a sense of things, a metaphoric approximation, a wisp of one's being.

I believe there are times when this central and hidden self requires connection with other aspects of the self, with other sides of the mind, when it craves seeing itself in some way. Perhaps embodied in another person, perhaps in a bit of nature, a song, a look, it scans for company, or for contrast. Put more simply, the soul, like all living things in nature, sometimes requires companionship. Sometimes this matching of a side of oneself with something other, can take the form of an image, a picture of some piece of this innermost sense of oneself, a reflection of inner being. I believe this search goes on day and night.

During the day, the matching process includes a host of experiences. A person in some indefinable agitation sits oceanside, watching, listening, taking in, feeling the surging surf. The state of internal agitation diminishes and, gradually, an inner calm takes its place. One way to think about this experience is that the agitated soul feels calmed when it "sees" or senses itself in the outside world, when it finds a match, an equivalence, a mate, a twin for itself. It is then not so alone, not so trapped in alienated isolation. Or a troubled and isolated soul walks in the woods and slowly feels less troubled and isolated, in part for having found companionship in the silence of the trees, bushes, shapes. The outer quiet is in some parallel with, some match with, the inner silent aloneness, and the person feels less alone. Or it could be said that the inner soul has found, in this silence, not so much a lonely union as an internalization of a calming surround. Either is possible. Or a lonely soul sees in a particular face, in a sea of faces on a city street, that particular look, those special eyes, and feels a sense of connection, a lessening of isolation, a momentary mating. Or an angry soul seeks and finds an urgently needed counterpart in a violent moment in a television boxing match or football game or crime show. Or a sadistic soul slows next to a car crash, scanning, staring, seeking a glimpse of bloody disaster, an external connection to the hidden inner state of mind.

The inner being, thus, has many ways of seeing itself, or hints and versions of itself, in the world around. It is less isolated, less alone in this coupling with the selfsame in the outside. This is the matching work of daytime or of wakefulness. The match is found not only in seeking, but in all forms of expression. Thus the inner soul sings out or writes out or dances out or paints out or speaks out its inner designs. This myriad and full range of expressiveness is, most often, performed in the hope that someone or some spirit or some god or some other being will "get it," feel it, understand it, relate to it, resonate with it in some fashion that will leave the inner soul in some connection with the world outside. So through searching and expressing, the inner being matches its innermost wisp and nature with events and beings outside itself. That which religion and community once helped to accomplish, we are left to our own devices to bring about in the modern world.

But what of the night? What of sleep? Does the loneliness of the inner soul lead to a continuation into nighttime and sleep of the search for a twin, a mate, a companion? I believe, with Hillman (1979), that dreams can serve the function of keeping the soul company. Entirely automatically, without intention, dreams provide a continuous stream of images both emanating from and, at the same time, accompanying the soul in its solitariness. Object relations theory posits that the soul is filled with the influences and memories of others and parts of others. Yet, the inner world is also one's very own and can feel, in experience, disconnected from both the residues and realities of relationship. This innermost self is at the heart of the one-person psychology that is being replaced in our theories by relational considerations. But I believe linking a poetic-spiritual dimension to the one-person intrapsychic emphasis adds interesting and challenging ideas to our repertoire. For example, the mind can be thought of as reflecting on itself. Conflicts between self and other and self and world can also be thought of as conflicts between aspects of the self.

Such ideas are enormously compelling, interesting, and helpful to many patients who have little idea of the complexities of the world within and feel a vast inner emptiness while facing difficulties in the outer world. So it is of interest to a patient to learn that a dream of a fight with a boss may also reflect an inner struggle between subservient and bossy aspects of self. Or, a man's dream of making love with a lower class girl may also reflect ideas about commingling with a demeaned female aspect of the self. These examples are not particularly refined but show that the inner world of a one-person psychology still has most important information. All of this must seem backward, regressive, reactionary, given the dominant move toward relationalism. But dreams, although often considering life with others, are primarily from, of, and about the world of one's own mind and self.

The solitary soul can feel companionship, recognition, and connection in dream images about anything under the sun. The inner mind has taken in the whole world and exists in terms of images of sky, buildings, God, others, automobiles, colors, clothing, gnomes, animals, music, language, and so on. Any dream image that presents itself to sleeping consciousness arises from and connects with some piece of that inner mind. All night long, the inner mind keeps company—the company of its own reflections. A patient reported a dream of *a flying garbage truck settling quietly down between two parked cars.* Our conversation brought us to the way her own mind and body often felt like garbage and that her private and lonely adolescent food rituals had been her life's secret. It felt important for her to see herself thus reflected. Now, why not a more specific and unambiguous image of bulimia for companionship with the inner state? Sometimes metaphor is a favorite way of communicating with the self in dreams; that is to say, from the side is better than head-on. The shy soul feels better when it is not bombarded frontally with its own nature; it handles self-recognition and reflection better when ideas are alluded to, hinted at, implied, made kind of clear. The use of the couch helps in this sidewise approach. Just as the mind does not open if one yells into the ear, neither does it open with direct, glaring, neon, confrontational "truths."

Another patient reported a dream in which an old, worn, weather-beaten shawl knitted by his grandmother found its way into a dream's postscript. The shawl still had its lovely colors but these could hardly be made out. It could still provide warmth, but it was frayed. It did not take long for him to fill with feelings at the sense of self within the shawl, as he faced aspects of his unexpected aging. The inner soul felt less lonely in the experience, first by virtue of the dream itself and then by virtue of our conversation about it. But these dream companions, these imaginary alteregos, for the most part disappear on awakening, and the companionship is most fleeting.

## On Waking Without a Dream

Sometimes, a wisp of a dream returns to memory as the day goes on. But usually, we awake with no memory for dreams, although we might know that we dreamt a lot. Quite apart from the patient in psychoanaly-sis who is remembering and forgetting dreams within the context of the treatment relationship, people more often awaken with amnesia for the dreams that have flowed forth throughout the night in REM and nonREM states. For many, such amnesia is felt to be quite natural, and there is no evidence that this lost night life matters at all. But for some, it seems to make a difference that wakefulness comes with a diffuse sense of missing something. I propose that such a regular occurrence may serve as one of the unconscious roots of a pervasive sense of a life lost. I am suggesting that built into the human experience is the fact of a lost, missing, irrevocably absent side of one's life. Following a night of cavorting with fishes or ghosts, of conversing with friends and enemies, of witnessing and participating in strange and wondrous happenings, of music and murder, of all manner of events and possibilities—all this is gone and lost forever, suddenly with the new day, no more.

I believe that this "no moreness" may serve as a companion to a host of related experiences of lost life. The belief in a lost continent of Atlantis, the belief in a lost tribe of Jews, the belief in a lost Eden, of a lost holy grail, all this mystical "lostness" may refer, in part, to the omnipresent actuality of lost experience in morning's wakening. Further, the repeated experience of waking without a piece of oneself, without a remembered self, may be considered, for some, the basic underpinning of castration experience, understood most broadly to include loss of mind, loss of self, loss of other, loss of one's own experience, loss of life.

A woman patient, mentioned earlier, wakes each morning to the experience of "feeling crushed" by the awakening itself. Being thrust into the world of conscious wakefulness and with it, into the day's problems: cleaning, checkbook balancing, shopping, working, problems with the boyfriend, with the office mate. And with this crushing set of day problems, there is a surge of necessary competitiveness, aggression, push, and mighty effortfulness. In contrast to the feeling and meaning to her of sleep and dreaming, the awakening is horrendous, enough to bring forth the wish to die rather than to arise. What is lost in her is more than a dream, it is her soul. Thus, the shadow side to waking with a song is waking to a nightmare of waking. Although not remembering one's dreams is hardly in the same class as waking with a feeling of being crushed, and for some there may even be a sense of relief at "losing" the memories of one's dreams, for most of us awakening involves a large shift from fluid dreaming to drier thinking, and with it a loss of the magic of life within the imagery of dreaming.

Dreams in their interweavings can provide deep companionship, connection of self with self. Dreams can also leave the dreamer more alone. For example, in a pleasurable dream of companionship, the dreamer awakens to the solitariness of a lonely life, and feels worse and more bereft than before. Remembering and not remembering one's dreams also can provide a sense of mental companionship or aloneness. The entire way dreams are experienced and thought about provides an entire world within one's own mind for one's own experience. When added to the relationship of dreamer and therapist through discussion of dreams and through the entire therapeutic engagement, one's own life with dreams is deeply enriched and made more complex. This is difficult to do alone.

# ୧ 16 ୨

## On Two Kinds of Dreams

*Mirrors should reflect a little before throwing back images.*
                                                        —Jean Cocteau

*Two roads diverged in a wood, and I*
*I took the one less traveled by,*
*And that has made all the difference.*
                                                        —Robert Frost

There are two kinds of dreams, most interesting in my opinion, that
have occasioned little notice in the general dream literature. One has
to do with dreams about dreaming; the second with dreams about "the
path not chosen." An awareness of both will enable us to develop a
more open idea about the extraordinary breadth and potential range
of dream subject matter.

### On Dreams About Dreaming

First, consider dreams about dreaming. In view of the two-sided
nature of thinking—the view from daytime thinking and the view

from nighttime thinking—we understand that our ideas about dreams and dreaming are the expression of daytime thinking. Our various views of the dream develop from the perspective of the kind of thinking that derives from awake consciousness, from relatively rational, linear, coherent, grammatical, secondary process, consensually validated thought. But the other side, the sleep and nighttime side of our thinking, can also be directed at dreams and dreaming. Because the mind can potentially consider just about anything and is so constituted that it can turn around and view even its own operations—the mind considering the mind—it should come as no surprise that it will, on occasion, think about its daytime ways in its awake mode—thinking and imagining about thinking and imagining. It will also think about its daytime ways in its sleep mode of thinking—dreaming. It will also think about its nighttime ways—dreams—in the awake mode as in awake ideas about dreams and dreaming. And finally it is capable of thinking about its nighttime ways—dreaming—in the sleep mode as in dreams about dreaming and about sleeping.

We can draw on two kinds of evidence for the existence of dreams about sleep and about dreaming. First is the direct experience and expression, without interpretation, of dreams actually about sleep and dreaming. Let us begin with the experience of dreaming that one is sleeping. There are many direct examples of this class of dream. For instance, there are many reported dreams about sleeping within the dream.

> *One dreams that she keeps falling asleep in the dream of watching her girlfriend. Another dreams that she is asleep and wakes up in the dream. A third dreams that he is watching his mother make his bed and he lies down and dreams that he is asleep while his parents move about. He wakes up when he wakes up. Another person, moderately well educated and not involved in dream research, reported a dream in which he watched his EEG and REM recordings appearing on a monitor. He watched as his recordings indicated changes in his sleep state.*

In addition, one can easily interpret various dream experiences as metaphors for sleeping; dreams of lying down, of floating, of darkness, of body parts in different states of inactivity, of motor paralysis or inhibition, and of any of the myriad ways the dreaming mind can conjure up, report, imagine, and dramatize the experience and the effect of sleeping. If we hypothesize that dreaming is potentially a commentary about anything under the sun, then why not about itself sleeping? In addition, there is the possibility of clinical relevance particularly in regard to actual and symbolic problems in sleeping. By paying attention to the manifest content of sleeping in a dream, we may provide an opportunity, based on the dream itself, for patients to give voice to problematic concerns that may not have otherwise been accessible to discussion. In addition, and outside of problematic concerns, there is intrinsic interest in what the sleeping mind may have to say about its own conditions.

Dreaming about sleep also has its metaphoric possibilities. People may dream about sleeping as a general comment on their psychological state of mind at that moment or as a more characteristic situation. In the former instance, the person may be signaling a special self-consciousness that can speak of its own experience, often a very good sign for deeper work together. Or the dream of sleeping can also be signaling a crucial absence, not necessarily a good sign, although its dream communication could be the beginning of a conversation about such things. Or the dream of sleeping could conceivably be simply a noticing and mentioning its own condition—sometimes a cigar is just a cigar. How the dreamer thinks about and plays with you about the dream will provide more than enough information about which way to go at this point in the conversation. At a further step, particularly if you sense the dream of sleep is pointing to deeper themes, and if you should feel that some interpretive activity is called for, one might say: "Could it be possible that you might be dreaming about your own mind—or heart or self or soul—being in a sleeping state?" And see how the dreamer reacts.

Of greater complexity and potential interest than the category of dreaming about sleeping is the category of dreaming about dreaming. We begin with direct evidence. For instance, one dreams that, in the midst of a dream, the dreamer goes to sleep and has a dream, and may even wake up in the dream. This is the dream within a dream.

*Someone dreams he is playing in a basketball game with his two brothers and several others. The game being played on an indoor court with people watching is vigorous, reminding him in the dream of his high school varsity days. He is excited and "sees" the court and its action the way he used to. A yellow haze hangs over the basketball rims. His team is losing by 4 points.*

*He becomes very tired after running up and down the court for what seems
like hours. He finds a bed on the side of the indoor court, lies down, goes to
sleep, and has a dream in which his dead father appears and is crying for
him. He becomes angry and demands that his father stop crying about him
and wakes from the dream to find the other basketball players gone and
replaced by strangers. He awakens feeling slightly agitated, confused, and
annoyed.*

There are so many ways to go with such a dream following a request
for the patient's view. At some point in the discussion, my only
comment was: "You said your father was crying for you, but you were
later angry that he was crying about you. What is the difference between
his crying for you and crying about you?" It sounds a bit obsessional
out of context, and it probably was, but it also turned out to be
productive of good discussion about the dreamer resenting his father
feeling sorry for him, particularly from his father's unenviable position
of being dead. The idea of the father crying for him, which the patient
altered in subsequent communication, was filled with anger and grief
and our conversation, initiated by the dream, served to open deeply
significant themes. However, in dreaming that he is dreaming, we have
more an example of dreaming within a dream than dreaming about
dreaming.

The second kind of evidence for dreams about dreaming is seen
through the lens of interpretation. These can be more interesting and
complex, but it is difficult to find secure anchoring given the subjec-
tivities of interpretation. With a minimum of interpretation, it is
possible to think about dreaming of a curtain going up and a play or
film being presented, as potentially also about dreaming in addition to
being about a play or film. The dream then states: "This is what I am
about to experience right in front of my eyes, and for now I am making
the point that I am audience." I suppose that because the earliest film
makers used dreams as the model for their infant art, made hundreds
of films about dreams, and described their project as the creation of
public dream theaters (Gamwell, 2000), dreamers can return the favor
and use movies to describe the workings of their dreaming minds.
Furthermore, it is fun to think that dreams may have inspired most art
forms and that dreamers now use those same art forms (film, theater,
painting, ballet, opera, story telling, poetry) as background or focus for

their dreams. We see a similar process in relation to religion (Young, 1999). A never-ending cycle—dreaming to living and back again.

A patient *dreamt of making a film, assembling the story, the cast, the props, the entire production. She was producer, director, writer, and one of the actors. She dreamt that she was trying to create a role for a popular contemporary modern ballet director.* In addition to the dream referring to the creation of a film, it may also have reflected a description of dream-making itself, since it involved a discussion of the scene behind the scene. The latent content of this dream is not so much a different and underlying story as the story of how the manifest content is assembled.

There are dreams and fragments that seem to reflect the underlying creation of the final dream in bits and pieces of sleep-thinking architecture. We can sometimes see names and faces in the process of being altered, thought about, replaced, played with, and so on. We sometimes see the kind of thinking that goes on behind the scenes in various choices and competitions for final product. I have myself experienced and have learned of others experiencing brief glimpses of dream material in the making, during waking thinking. Momentary dreaming while awake and introspective commentary within dreams while asleep—both reflect a natural fluidity between the two states.

*A patient dreamt of a red bird flying into and out of a cage. What made the dream unusual was that within the dream, the patient woke and slept and dreamt the dream three times. In the dream, the patient fell asleep to dream of the bird and the cage, then woke up within the dream and again fell asleep to dream of the bird and cage, then woke up and fell asleep again, to dream a third time of the bird flying into and out of the cage.*

Through associations and discussion, we thought we were engaging with a dream that spoke of dreaming, as experienced by this patient. Each flight from the cage—a dream image going free—and return to the cage—a dream image captured and held—involved a tiny difference as the dream was being shaped over and over. We were being given a glimpse of the gradual shaping of a dream's image. Again, in a sense, the manifest dream was the finished product; the latent dream represented the prior drafts. This patient's internal visual representation or image of holding onto and letting go of an idea (with the red bird representing the idea or emotion or some other variety of mental content?) reflected considerable thinking about caging and freedom in many realms. Although we believed that the dream reflected some ideas about dreaming itself, it may also have reflected ideas about reading (red) and thinking more generally.

A patient dreamt of *waking up within a dream and not wanting to go into the nearby room where "someone" was asleep. The patient, in the dream, did not wish to awaken the nearby sleeper.* Because dreams occasionally "waken" a sleeper—waking is here defined as awareness of involvement in dreaming—this dream could be thought of as reflecting a wish not to dream, or at least not to waken within a dream. This assumes that the "someone" is a sleeping version of the self. Questions were directed to information about the dream-sleeper, whose characteristics seemed significantly to reflect "shadow" sides of the dreamer, and also sides of the therapist. Both ideas were of interest to the participants and led to good discussion.

A patient dreamt several times about a particular species of monkey; the associations were to an Asian culture with which the patient was very familiar and in which this species of monkey is regarded as symbol for the mind. The patient and I thought that, in addition to other possible meanings, the monkey dreams reflected dreams about the mind in various states: the mind alive, the mind in play, the mind in death, the mind in interaction with other minds, the mind in sleep and in dreams. These dreams taught us about the vast variety and richness of possible ideas about the mind within the confines of the sleeping mind.

In addition to such monkey-equals-mind symbolism, there are undoubtedly countless other metaphors of mind within dream imagery. I mentioned earlier a vivid dream *about standing onboard a fishing boat and watching a school of flying fish emerge from and return to the ocean's waters perhaps 50 yards away. The flying fish spread their fins like wings and they were airborne for a while. Within the dream, I recall being pleased by this symbol for dreams.* Birds, in mythology, are often symbols for the mind or the soul in flight. The creatures in my dream emerged from the sea, as from the unconscious, like fish, and fly, like birds, through the air before returning to the sea, again to the unconscious as in the forgetting of dreams. *While I was focused on the flying fish and thinking about casting out and trying to catch one*—fishing for a dream—*one of the fish flew overhead and hovered there, allowing me to look at it carefully.* What came next was omitted from the earlier chapter, but now that I think we are better acquainted,

I can add the following: *As the fish hovered overhead and as I was watching, it opened its anus and released its waste above me just as I woke up both fearful of being defecated on and yet still pleased by the earlier image.* I believed at the time, within the dream and also on awakening, that the dream was about dreaming. The possibility of being defecated on by the dream flying fish suggested to me Crick and Mitchison's (1983) garbage hypothesis, and the dangers of looking too closely into dreams, and also the potential for a nasty, ugly, smelly, dirty side of dreams—a good corrective for a too positive view of dreaming.

Alongside the aforementioned examples of the possibility of dreaming about dreaming is the frequent instance of reference being made within a dream to another, usually earlier, dream or series of dreams, sometimes even to a catalogue of dreams. Another subtype includes the making of an interpretation of a dream, or having an understanding of the dream, while still within the dream. Thus, because the waking introspective mind contemplating itself and its own nature is at the center of a psychoanalytic psychology, the sleeping introspective mind contemplating itself and its own nature, as in dreams about dreaming, is also of major interest.

## On Dreams About the Road Not Taken

The second type of dream I wish to call attention to concerns dreams about the road not taken. The title of Robert Frost's (1916) poem offers a good starting point. I propose that alongside the many, many possible purposes of dreams, one additional purpose is to dramatize, experience, amplify and explore choices not taken. Life as lived offers a limited number of possibilities. We turn left rather than right; we choose this rather than that path; we take this rather than that job; we have one and not two children, or we have no children instead of the four we imagined. Or what if she had lived? Or what if I had not said "Go away"? And so on. The examples are endless. I am suggesting that the mind explores all manner of experience, including the experience of what if? It is particularly interesting when this exploration goes on in the expansively imaginative realm outside of awareness, as in unconscious fantasy or dreams. Rather than occupy oneself consciously with the infinity of what might have been, the mind outside of awareness seems a better home for this proposed activity.

This category is of course filled with a certain kind of wish fulfillment—the wish to experience everything. Some minds are exceedingly greedy for possibility, and this may be particularly true of students of the mind, who reside as long as possible in the land of omnipossibility—a cognitive manifestation of the pleasure principle. This allows some minds to live through and explore the other side of experience. Sleep thinking is ideally suited to this task because it already contains many elements of "the other side" of things.

A patient dreams *he is yelling at an acquaintance who is always late for appointments, never returns calls, and treats others with disrespect.* The patient recalls that he, himself, is just such a person. The dream provides him with the valuable opportunity of feeling enraged at being treated so poorly—as poorly as he treats others. He is being given the experience, in the dream, of what others feel at his hands. It helps him to "get it" about how others might feel toward him from time to time. It also helps him to understand some of the hurt and rejecting behavior of others in response to his disrespect.

A patient dreams *she is running away from home, with ensuing strange adventures.* She did not run away from home in her day life, but her dream provides the safe-enough environment for such a thought experiment. It should be mentioned that dreams are not only of the positive variety. Some dreams highlight awful experiences, as when a patient dreams *her beloved child is dead.* Whether or not she is expressing a wish or a fear may be secondary to the dream's natural exploration of that which has not happened. Such experiments probably have many motives: perhaps for rehearsal, perhaps for a "greedy mind," perhaps out of curiosity, perhaps for the experience of pain or pleasure within or on awakening from the dream. I propose that such dreams, in addition to having other meanings, also explore the vast realm of the life not lived, of what might have been, of the "if" of life.

A patient experienced a repetitive dream over many years *about his dead father returning to the rooms of childhood. In the dreams, the father was always disheveled, unhappy, lonely, sickly, agitated, and angry at the patient's mother who was also long dead.* The patient, a man of Caribbean ancestry, interpreted these dreams as a sign that his father's soul had not yet found a peaceful afterlife, and was returning in disarray as a sign and a punishment to the patient who felt responsible and guilty both during and after each of these dreams. Wishing that his father's soul and he himself could find rest, the patient was eager to talk about just such a dream that appeared during our work together. Following some good dream discussion, we believed we had uncovered the mystery of this repetitive and unhappy dream. When the patient was 9 years old, the father, a hard-working civil servant, came home early from work one day to discover his wife with another man both in a state of undress. The father immediately made plans to leave the family. The 9-year-old panicked and pleaded desperately with him to stay, warning the father that he (the patient) would write to his oldest sister, who was working for a family in the United States, to tell her that their father was leaving the family—a message that would surely lead to the sister's suicide, the 9-year-old threatened. The father, yielding to his son's pleas (or so the patient believed), stayed and the marriage improved over time. All agreed things turned out for the best. The patient, however, many years after his father had died, began to dream his uneasy dream in which, we came to believe, the patient was experiencing the "what if?" side of the situation. What if his father had left them instead of staying? What if the patient had been left fatherless to take care of his younger brother and sister? What would have become of his father, and of them all? The patient, we came to believe, was exploring and experiencing in the repetitive dream a piece of what might have been had the patient not interceded and had father actually left the family. Unshaven, unhappy, angry, and lost, the father wandered in and out of the patient's dreams as he might have appeared had he left home, not so much a dead soul wandering about, but a divorced father wandering about; or so we concluded. The patient always felt a mixture of pride, grandiosity, and guilt about his persuasive capacity to alter the family's destiny by this deed of desperation. I should mention that following this dream discussion and the revised view of the nature of this dream, the father twice again returned to the patient's dreams, but in a happier frame of mind, which signaled to the patient that his father's soul was now able to show that it had always been more at peace than the patient realized. The painful repetitive dream, he came to believe, had less to do with the condition of his father's soul than with the patient's own conflict and need to experience over and over the life that might have been. With this hypothesis in mind, we looked at several other dreams and saw a number of times the patient's need and capacity to experience others of life's what ifs. In a recent letter, many years after treatment, the patient was pleased to inform me that his father was certainly still in paradise, looking fit and trim in the latest dreams, appearing happy together with the mother and not the angry and lonely man the patient felt the father might have been had the patient not intervened.

There are countless examples of dreams about the road not chosen, and countless ways in which such dreams are useful, sometimes with, often without, interpretation. In the playground of dreams, it could turn out that a great many dreams share the idea that, although we live out our choices in the day world, in the night world, with our eyes closed, we look around without blinders to see what might have been.

# ɔȝ 17 ೞ

## ON FREEDOM AND DREAMS

*Between what I see and what I say*
*Between what I say and what I keep silent*
*Between what I keep silent and what I dream*
*Between what I dream and what I forget:*
*Poetry.*

—Octavio Paz

*Newsweek* (1999) magazine, a major summarizer of current news and trends, recently announced that psychoanalysis will not survive far into the new century. It will disappear from view and sink back to its roots in mysticism, the implication being that it was a fad of the mad 20th century. *Newsweek* is not alone in its prediction; this idea is not new. Psychoanalysis has been buried many times in its tumultuous life. But, like Yiddish, Freud's mama's-*lushn* (his mother's tongue), its death has been prematurely announced. On the one hand, psychoanalysis grows— new institutes, new and more open policies, more diverse theories of practice, more women, more psychologists and social workers, and more committees with more guidelines about more policies. On the

227

other hand, psychoanalysis shrinks—fewer patients, fewer candidates, lower incomes, less influence in the world of "mental health," less to say about significant cultural matters, less of a meaningful beacon to young students and intellectuals.

All in all, it is not good news, unless one's basic oppositionalism causes celebration at our drop from high status to the original position of outsider. We are not favored by the new era. We are on the outs with the global market, with rampant materialism, with some central aspects of the enormously powerful new electronic universe, with the erosion of the private realm, and with the rush to fundamentalist religion as response to the weakening of many basic values. Psychoanalysis does not fit well with these developments. Nor should it! What fits better is the *Diagnostic and Statistical Manual* (*DSM*) mentality, the drug mentality, the HMO profit mentality, the management mentality, and along with these, the abhorrent simplifications of human psychology.

At a recent meeting of the American Psychoanalytic Association, I heard four panelists, all serious artists of one kind or another, attribute their artistic work to trauma, to alcoholic fathers, unempathic mothers, difficult childhoods. Although I had no doubt about the sincerity of their descriptions of earlier difficulties and how trauma can have a powerful effect, I winced because they seemed to think that psychoanalysts would be at home with such simplistic reductionism, just as the shameless confessional television shows could leave us analysts embarrassed at so horrendous an outcome of aspects of our contribution. The reductionistic narrowing of vision that robs human attainment of its complexity and its dignity, both on television and at the psychoanalytic meeting, requires our attention. If we rush to join these trends, we deserve our burial. There is still time for us to study and learn about, to stand apart from, and, when necessary, to stand in vigorous opposition to the damaging effects of powerful developments that increasingly stand in the center of our culture and that make good use of the dumbing down of ideas about the human condition.

## PSYCHOANALYSIS AT THE NEW CENTURY

We need to devote our energies to considering the effect on the individual human psyche of the extraordinary changes that are fast shaping our world. We are being influenced, changed, organized, shaped in ways that are difficult to detect, both because of the lightning speed of contemporary change and because of the subtlety of the system's functioning. We are losing our connection with the natural world and are being increasingly shaped to a virtual world. We little understand the electronic technology that runs things. We are losing physical connection with others and find ourselves relating, communicating, learning, shopping, even loving, more and more through the external screen. We are unable to maintain a private world. Our air, water, and food supplies are increasingly contaminated. We are too many. We are beginning to suffer from new and dangerous viral and bacterial diseases. Some of us, including our children, are murderously violent in new and frightening ways. On the other hand, in this fortunate part of the globe, most of us live longer, have decent food and shelter, are not at war, can connect instantaneously with people around the globe, are able to select from over 100 television channels—and can still maintain some of the elements of individual freedom.

All of us, psychoanalysts and therapists, daily sit in extended meetings with troubled individuals. We listen to their complaints, their miseries, their failures, their wishes, and, occasionally, their dreams. We collect a massive amount of information about the human situation in our times, about the way things are on the inside. It should come as no surprise that the system is not interested in this dimension, will not support its investigation, and would rather close us down than pay heed to what we are learning daily in our offices. Up close and in the inner world, something is terribly the matter, even while the system constantly advertises its wondrous benefits along with the vision that the entire world desperately wants these benefits. In our private offices, we are learning of the cost in individual psychological life of our good times, of our position at the top of the world: for example, job loss, forced retraining, the misery of farmers, part-time employment without benefits, loss of neighborhoods as family businesses and local downtowns turn into malls and then into internet shopping, loss of friends as families move about, all of us working too hard, not having time for relaxation, loss of family ties, the burdens of being a "successful" woman, the complexities of increased "weakness" in men, spending a lifetime paying off student loans, parents' fears of environmental illness in their infants and children, along with fears that violence will descend in their children's classrooms, the fear of lonely aging, of an inability to conceive, of the dangers of having an "imperfect" body. We gather this information daily, information about profound social dislocation and personal alienation. We, as persons and as a profession, are part of this new world and suffer the advantages and disadvantages along with our patients. Yet we are silent on all this.

Things are complicated. There are great benefits as well as great difficulties with the emerging 21st century system of social, economic, and technological reorganization. But as a profession, we often seem more interested in our own credentialing concerns, in who will be called "training analyst," and under what conditions we should or should not disclose where we are going on vacation. Our narrowing concerns, despite our new self-advertising as more relational and relevant, include our own participation in simple-minded reductionism. We are not consistent or strong enough in our criticism of an increasingly powerful view that floods popular mental health discussion and that includes a faddish use of ideas about trauma, addiction, abuse, PTSD (posttraumatic stress disorder), alcohol and drugs as the cause of all problems, OCD (obsessive-compulsive disorder), ADD (attention deficit disorder), panic disorder, MPD (multiple personality disorder), the "correct" and "healthy" order in which to grieve loss or deal with trauma, and along with these an army of "healers" and counselors ready to descend on disasters at a moment's notice.

These problems are symptoms of a larger disorder than Alice Miller dreams of. Narcissistic and unempathic mothers, distant and absent fathers, abusing grandfathers, parentified children as explanatory concepts will just not do as reasons for everything that goes wrong, from anorexia to shooting up a schoolroom. Such ideas merely compound the problem. For example, from the beginning of time, many children have taken care of distressed parents in subtle and profound ways. Our mental health culture treats children as though they have no power, no mind, no capacity except to be damaged and to feel bad about some presumed loss of childhood as though the correct way to be a child is known. Furthermore, such a view guarantees a lifetime of self-absorbed, self-pitying justification for one's own failings along with deeply felt babble about one's inner child. I believe these simplifications have more to do with psychotherapy's business needs: creating customers and creating ourselves as better mothers, fathers, and caretakers than the original ones so that our customers will continue to need and pay us. We don't parentify our patients, because this is considered sin. We are not sure whether to let them know we have a cold. Thus, we are in concert with the view of patients as well as children as weak and two-dimensional. This view is disgraceful, both as theory and as practice. We can do better.

Psychoanalysis, at its best, has a complex vision of psychological life. We daily come to know people in depth as they try to survive their difficulties. Narrow and reductionist views contain nothing but a vision of weakness, frailty, an inner emptiness that can be shaped and worsened or helped by a loving therapist. Nonsense. People have enormous capacity to endure, to transform, to expend a life of energy in survival, to create their own conditions, to suffer through hard times, defeat, and indignity with great patience, forebearance, and dignity. Slavery, the Holocaust, the horrors of war, the oppression of women, human disasters such as famine and pestilence, all have evoked the power and strength of our capacity for survival. Poor people, starving people, hard-working people at the bottom of the new economic order, are not found in our practices for the most part. We tend more to work with the upper and middle classes and their problems. But we need to learn from the way many people at the bottom do not so easily succumb or find themselves destroyed by experiences like "mothers who are not empathic enough."

We have, more and more, developed a psychology of weakness. In contrast, we require a psychology, not only of disorder, but of endurance, fortitude, and strength, both for meaningful analytic work and for the hard times ahead. Freud provided the seeds of such an approach, as did Erikson, Fromm, and the socially aware analysts of Fenichel's Rundbriefe group. We find ideas about strength also in Adler, Frankl, Reich, and others and in many corners of intellectual life outside of psychoanalysis.

Freud's instinct theory, although superseded by much of the politics and science of the 20th century, does have the advantage of trying to grapple with life and death issues, with powerful conflict, with biology and destiny, with love as well as the darkest and strongest aspects of aggression. Contemporary psychoanalysis, by reducing many of our struggles to emotional failures in the nursery, I think is too weak in conception, and therefore may be missing an opportunity to struggle with the kinds of developments in humans that lead to resilience, to toughness, to grit, to stubborn holding on, to humor, and to love in the midst of catastrophe, even death. Our contribution to a psychology of the victim is of no help. The sort of hope that is called for comes from a richly layered understanding of life. Defeat, despair, depression, hopelessness are always at the door, while within we need maintain some sense of hope, some basic narcissism, some wish to survive. We are, after all, the descendants of those who have survived, more than we are of those who gave up hope. So we have it in us to struggle against resignation.

## PSYCHOANALYSIS AND FREEDOM

In reflecting on my experiences as a psychologist and analyst, I realize that over the years there has been a single and central guiding theme that has become clearer with time and that brings together many aspects of my views on theory and practice. Simply put, mainly I have been concerned with the implications of freedom in its many manifestations. Although I doubt all pronouncements, especially my own, yet, the spirit of freedom in human affairs and in intrapsychic life has been at the center of how I think and feel about my work and my interests.

*Freedom* is a quality and a state with many possible meanings and definitions. By freedom, I do not mean "the quality of being free from the control of fate or necessity," nor do I mean "the state of being able to act without hindrance or restraint" (Brown, 1993, p. 1023). By freedom, I mean a combination of qualities best described by synonyms like "open, unchained, with latitude, range, elbowroom, scope, play" (Rodale, 1978, p. 438). In psychological affairs, for me, freedom has to do with motion, with the capacity and ability to move among alternatives, to experience the complex layeredness of potential meanings. It points to the capacity to hold more than one thing in mind at a time. It relates to the potential for being in touch with and moving among life's many-sided aspects. It is closely related to spaciousness in thought and feeling, to breadth, scope, range, to the ability to think close up and far away at the same time. Opposite the chair in my office is a landscape painting showing sixteen layers of earth, mountain, and sky. It helps remind me of layeredness in all things in the midst of working with patients who sometimes wish for and demand a kind of certainty.

Most times, the best I can offer my patients is a complex, multiple, prismatic point of view. Since God has not yet whispered "the answer" into anyone's ear, as far as I know, and since it seems we are all extraordinary experiments in nature and in evolution, it may be that this view of the complexity of our nature is the best we can do.

Psychoanalysis, in its beginnings, offered an enormous range of thought, particularly in its extension of the human mind to include the vast domain of experience outside of awareness—the unconscious. Together with Freud's thoroughgoing insistence on multiple causation and on conflict and compromise in psychic life, new realms of thought were opened that spoke with the spirit of freedom; that is, the freedom to consider that human behavior is complexly determined, born from several roots, and often not what it seems to be. Psychoanalysis and freedom, in the sense just described, were in many ways connected. As a theory of mind, it offered spaciousness as the boundaries of psychic functioning were broadened from the narrower confines of conscious and rational thought. As a method of treatment, psychoanalysis listened carefully to the utterances of its patients, who were instructed to go wherever the spontaneous movement of associated thinking led them in "free association."

Further, psychoanalysis instructed the expert to give up the pretense of knowingness and instead listen in the spirit of a Buddhist meditation—in "evenly hovering attention." Both patient and analyst, as equals in an important sense, were encouraged to enter together a realm of play guided by the spirit of freedom in thought. They were encouraged not to prematurely evaluate their mental activities in this play–work as it unfolded, rather they were to give free rein to whatever entered consciousness, without selection and without prior judgment. The unconscious meanings would best show themselves when conscious considerations and focal attention were relaxed.

Because the mind does not often allow itself to be entered by yelling in the ear, as direct as that may seem, an indirect route was recommended for reaching the underside of the psyche. Don't think too hard. Don't try too hard. Like a river, just flow along, allowing whatever comes to enter the mind, allowing whatever enters the mind to be spoken aloud. For the analyst: Don't think too hard. Don't try too hard. Like a river, just flow along, allowing whatever comes to enter the mind; thus would the unconscious minds of the two be brought into correspondence and harmony. One can come to know the other most deeply by not trying, by allowing oneself the freedom to think on whatever comes to mind. There are, of course, in psychoanalysis, other ways and other forms of instructing patient and therapist, other styles of opening the mind and of therapeutic relationship that are not dependent on couch or free association, but these too aim toward freedom in communication and toward increasing freedom in the patient's self-experience.

No matter which of the many methods of therapeutic engagement one uses, clearly the mind is a wondrous part of nature in that it allows an extraordinary degree of mental activity to go on at the same time. The mind of the traditional analyst, for example, at the same time as it proceeds in evenly hovering attention, concurrently sorts through the themes of the last session, keeps track of the patient's associations, registers aspects of countertransference, always trying to find a place for them, compares one experience with others, and so on. The freedom of association in both analyst and patient is, of course, a relative thing, an ideal, an attempt.

Thus, the idea of freedom is central to the earliest development of psychoanalysis. The capacity to move freely within the complex and layered realm of mind–psyche represents an ideal. Psychoanalysis and the psychotherapies that draw their inspiration from psychoanalysis all represent attempts to increase the freedom of movement both in its practitioners, in part through training analyses, and in those who come for psychological assistance.

Freedom as a fundamental and guiding idea in psychoanalytic psychotherapy, both in its method and in its goal, brings us to the experience of dreaming and the analysis of dreams. Dreams, in my opinion, stand in the center of a reordering of our work in line with the new era in which the external screen (RAM) competes with the inner screen (REM) for a say in how our minds are to function. Dreams are the voice of unwilled freedom in the human mind. Dreams show, from the inside, how things look and are experienced. Our interest in them and our work with them, from the beginning, spoke of our devotion to the most private corners of human experience and to the creative potential of the mind, even in sleep, to search out ways of coming to grips with life as best we can.

For the past 25 years, I have had the good fortune to teach the advanced seminar on dreams at the William Alanson White Psychoanalytic Institute in New York City. This opportunity has allowed me ample time to explore, together with many students, the relationship between dreams and psychoanalytic treatment. We have found that the freedom of dream life and the freedom in the spirit of psychoanalysis can best meet and join forces in the work on dreams within psychoanalytic psychotherapy—especially within an atmosphere, such as at White, where the tradition of freedom of thought continues to be highly valued.

There are many ways one comes to an interest in dreams. My own childhood nightmares led to extended periods of blocking out dreams. This antagonism to dreams was relieved decades later through intellectual and artistic interest stimulated largely in the clinical situation. That is, patients told me their dreams because they often thought an analytic therapist would or should be interested. Over time, I began to relax and to allow dreams their play time. And then, I could begin to relax with my own. I come to the study of dreams through the clinical interpersonal tradition in New York City. But, also, at the Austen Riggs Center, where I was a postdoctoral fellow in the early 1960s, the spirit of David Rapaport's chapter seven seminars still echoed. If you can imagine putting these together, you have an approximation of two of the analytic roots of my thinking about dreams.

In the interpersonal approach, that is, at the William Alanson White Institute, there never was a theory of dreams, never a particular clinical approach to dream interpretation, and certainly much divided opinion on the nature of the unconscious, all of which led to an atmosphere of relative freedom in thinking about dreams (Eisold, 1995). To this was joined the quality of the dream seminars of Fromm, and later Tauber, in which playfulness, intuition, and open-mindedness were seen as primary virtues. I learned to find my own way with dreams within a general clinical approach that was not doctrinaire, that was as attuned to the real world as to the inner world, that allowed the therapist considerable individual latitude, including the possibilities of direct engagement with the patient, that was closer to patients' experience than to theory, and that anticipated many of the recent changes in modern psychoanalysis, on the one hand. On the other hand, there was Rapaport's Freud, from which I derived an appreciation for mental architecture. This appreciation involved a growing awareness of layered, complexly interwoven psychological themes in which drives, defenses, day residues, and infantile experience join together in carefully constructed yet remarkably fluid ways. It gave me a sense of the universe within each dream image—including the distinct possibility that it could all make sense, if one had the desire and the patience to apply Rapaportian learning to Freudian creation—or Talmud to Torah, from which much of the spirit of psychoanalysis arose. There is, I suppose, an oppositional quality that required this interpersonalist to move to Freud. I am sure if I came from a Freudian atmosphere, I would be Jungian, and vice versa. Oppositionalism, it might be said, is the rough edge of an attachment to freedom. Yet oppositionalism can be helpful in working with dreams insofar as one is constructed to look at the other side of things. For with dreams, there is nothing but other sides.

<h2 align="center">DREAM CONVERSATION</h2>

Throughout, I have made reference to the relatively mundane concepts of "dream conversation" or "dream discussion" in place of the more traditional "dream interpretation." This reference is not meant with any lack of respect or appreciation for the significance, both historical and practical, of interpretive work with dreams. Opening a dream to its layered meanings and to the possibility of broad and deep under-standings can be richly rewarding. It is simply that there are often more helpful things to do in psychoanalytic therapy than interpretation. Talking together about dreams certainly does not sound as lofty as interpretation, but it comes closer to the spirit of what I have in mind. Thus, "dream conversation" or "dream discussion" may be a more useful term.

Among other responses to a dream that might encourage good dream conversation are appreciation, aesthetic discussion, spending adequate time with dream associations, elaborations and amplifica-tions, each interwoven with some question or reaction or elaboration from the dream listener, if he or she cares to. It is not so much that one eschews interpretation, although the knowing tone can be tiresome and offensive. Rather, one makes efforts to help create the conditions from which interpretations will show themselves if they wish. The meanings within a dream will open to good conversation. One literally makes the effort to enter a back and forth, in which one thing leads to an-other—similar to the conditions of dream construction itself. In this sense, Brenner (1969) is close to and enlarges on Freud: Do not treat a dream differently from any other communication. I believe this advice to be correct in method. Although, in my view, the range of possible activity with or without a dream is much broader in an interpersonal perspective than in Brenner's classical approach or in modern Freudian psychoanalysis, the basic idea in how to approach a dream is that one uses one's good clinical sense as one would with all communication in therapy.

Many people are frozen in some idea of how they "should" interpret dreams. Their inhibition often stimulates similar inhibition in the dreamer in the ensuing conversation. Better, if possible, is a more mobile reaction in which the listener is able to feel, think, react in any way, in any direction, guided by increasing familiarity with the story and the ways of the dreamer. This recommendation of freedom in responsiveness of the dream receiver assumes that the therapist has some good training and is generally capable of intelligent considerateness and reasonableness. In the absence of these, I don't know what to recommend, except perhaps to mumble: "I don't do dreams."

For the rest of us, one could feel inclined, in beginning to respond to a dream presented to us in the clinical situation, to mention a single piece of the dream, because it interests you, because it puzzles you, because of the way the dreamer mentioned it, or for whatever reason. One could remain quiet for a bit, but not stubbornly so. One could tackle the entire dream at once and ask the dreamer what he or she thinks. One could begin at the end or in the middle or at the beginning. A good way to begin is to ask of dreamers how they felt during and after the dream, what they think about it, how they felt telling it, and so on.

The point is, the analyst must be in a state of adequate freedom to work well with dreams. Otherwise, why bother? The time could better be spent in talking about the patient's life these last days or about other day life experiences, rather than in engaging in a lifeless exercise with a dream. A deadly spirit in conversing about dreams is doubly deadly. Unless that deadly feeling itself is the point of the dream and its exchange. Otherwise, try as best you can not to be dulled or mentally half asleep or bored or thickheaded or depressed when a dream comes your way. A patient once told me, when she felt I was elsewhere while she was talking about her dream, that a dream is like a bird chirping "wake up, wake up!" As is often true of patients, she was right. What I was thinking about during her recounting of her dream was the patient's congenitally blind 3-year-old child in contrast to my granddaughter: I felt so grateful that my daughter's daughter could see. It had been the opening words of my patient's dream description that had sent me away from her dream's images and to my own thankfulness: she said, "I saw this dream . . ."

I have been writing mostly about how dreams must generally be treated in order for them to show themselves most fully. Here, however, I am discussing more specifically the aspect of work with dreams that is located within therapy. With Freud, Brenner, and practically all analysts, the therapy comes first. To the simple truth, "It is a pity that one cannot make a living on dream interpretation," one could add, "Especially if the person has come to you at the end of his or her emotional rope." The dream conversation must serve the therapy. One hopes the two goals can be served at the same time, and that there will not be too great a disparity between the two interests; but sometimes there is.

Let us consider a hypothetical patient who launches into the description of a dream from some nights earlier, which turns out to be about many interesting things. Contrary to some of the orienting ideas expressed earlier, I might ignore the dream and bring her attention to any of the following mutually exclusive hypothetical possibilities: (a) that her tied-up dog was howling continuously outside my office window; (b) that her phone call the previous night about her daughter's suicide attempt called for clarification; (c) that she was cleaning the mud out of the cleats of her boots onto my rug while describing the dream, and that she should cut it out; (d) that she casually mentioned at the very end of the last session, for the first time, the probability that she was moving to California next week; (e) try to learn quickly whether she was playing and testing about my interest in dreams in the midst of a genuine crisis of one sort or another. Or I might work with the dream, following her lead whether well intentioned or not, to see how we would come out. Or I might ask: "Do you believe the dream touches on any of the possibilities just mentioned?" Or I might just put my notepad down and try to find out something about the disjunction between our talking about dreams and about life as it bursts around us.

I should confess, at this point, that I have a very hard time writing about technique in working with dreams. It is not hard to write about how not to work with dreams, or about ideas about dreams, but ideas about how to do it go against the grain in several ways. First, there is the distinct possibility that advice and instructions could impinge on therapists' necessary freedom in working with dreams. This essential freedom in the heart and mind of the dream-listener is, I believe, aesthetically and architecturally equal to the aesthetic and architectural freedom of thought within the construction of dreams. Both resonate with one another in good dream conversation. The playful, creative, zany, irreverent, free, and informed spirit in the interpreter is, thus, entirely necessary.

Although it is not difficult to understand that people like hints about how to do things, for instance, whether to write or not write down the dreams a patient is relating, or whether and when to ask or not ask for associations to the dream's sections from beginning to end, or end to beginning, or whether to focus on verbs or feelings or action or people or the transference or whatever. There is something self-defeating about these sorts of technical instructions. Following Freud, it is probably best to trust in the character and training (i.e., analysis) of the therapist and have him learn by doing. Telling people how to work with dreams will backfire according to the basic principle of oppositionalism near and dear to almost every analyst's heart. For example, the idea that the first dream in therapy reveals all—an interesting idea though untested as far as I know—has created all sorts of mischief. Some therapists get too nervous when they hear that first dream, because if they don't get it, all is lost.

Getting nervous in dreamland is a problem for therapists. How not to be nervous, but rather ready for ideational play about even the grimmest matters, is the point. How can one help others not be nervous in dream-work? Well, first by not making recommendations. Further, it may help to stress that there is no one answer to a dream; one can also point out the multiple ways of approaching a dream and of understanding a dream. Then, it may help to emphasize that dreams mostly do what they need to do without the interpreter anywhere near. You are not the beginning and end of things in relation to dreams, but rather a listener, maybe an appreciator, certainly a guest and not the main action. Finally, it helps to read a lot about dreams, both in and out of the professional literature, both in the science and art of dreams and their interpretation. It is a wonderful literature.

The second confession is that I do not like to write about my patients' dreams. I don't mind telling some of my own, or those of friends and family, but patients' dreams are told in privacy. Telling a patient's dream in a book, even with permission, would be a very complex thing to do, even more so than revealing other facets of a patient's life. While dreams might seem less personal to some than details of the patient's marriage or sex life, I think of them as more personal. We all have complex lives, but each dream is a unique creation. Well, I suppose our personal relationships are also unique creations. But dreams feel more so, especially because I don't think of my relationships as narrative constructions. Dreams are.

There are several reasons I do not like to write publicly about my patients' dreams. Because I work in a small town within a small professional community, some of my patients, a good number of whom are younger colleagues, could be identified. And I believe that well-intentioned changing of information to conceal identity seems a poor way to conduct a science. The best way to show how to work with dreams would be to open a dream slowly, as did Freud. But he used his own dreams to do that, and, therefore, his dream analyses omitted the way a dream actually might be used in therapy. Given these reservations, at the conclusion of this book, as at its beginning, let us return to patients' dreams, for instruction and inspiration. Here are some examples of working with dreams in which the possibilities for patient recognition have been largely eliminated.

Jack was a man of 62 who had been actively homosexual until at 49 he met the woman who would become his wife. They married and although he often thought of male lovers during intercourse, he was happily sexually mated. That was not his problem. He had just learned he had incurable cancer and needed to talk about things. We had been meeting once weekly for 2 months since the bad news, when he reported the following dream at the beginning of a session.

> I am in bed with my wife and I awake to find a big and powerful horse in the doorway. The horse looks just like one I rode in my childhood. But he had no business being in the house. I try to get him out before my wife could waken. Then, I'm riding him in a parade. Like one of those we used to have in our town: Memorial Day or July 4th. I like the spurs I have on and I like the reins; they're sparkly as though made of precious stones, like diamonds. There are many people around. It's confusing because I don't know which way to go. The parade is going up the main street. My horse, his name was Topper, wants to go elsewhere. You ever ride horses?

"Yes," I said, "a bit." I wanted to tell him about it. I wanted him to know how this old Brooklyn Jewish boy had come to play cowboy and that I knew about the pleasures of riding bareback on our horse in the snow with my children when we were all much younger. But, I didn't. His pain at not having children was profound. Some other day, we could talk horses, perhaps. Actually, we did later on that day.

He continued:

*Then you know what it's like when you sense a horse's wish. You can feel what they want, where they want to go. It's in their body. But they sometimes hold back cause you're the boss, sort of. It's not a big deal. Everybody who rides knows it. Well, all I could feel was his body telling me he wanted to go home, the other way than the parade. So home we went. I know there was more, but that's what I remember. What do you think?*

He was a proud man and didn't like to show when he was tearful. But he was while telling the dream. After a bit—here I notice this is the second time the word "bit" is used in this description, and that a "bit" is the metal mouthpiece on a horse's bridle that connects the reins—I asked, with feeling in my voice, because something in the dream also left me in sadness: "How did you feel in the dream?" "Did you like having the dream?" "How was it for you when you woke up with this dream?" I didn't ask these questions all at once, but they were the questions that initiated and kept our discussion going.

The rest was fine conversation. He spoke of feeling wonderful in the dream, to be with Topper again, a favorite horse of his youth. I thought that "Topper" could refer to the top, to his brain, where cancer had spread. I thought the big powerful "Topper" could refer to parts of his homosexual life. But these ideas seemed too "shrinky" and might be for later, or not at all. It is as important to shelve, to table, and to forget some ideas as to have them. A discussion opened about his life with horses, his childhood out West where his grand-uncle owned a share in a large working ranch and where the patient learned some of the ways of the cowboys, actually living and working as one for several years. The arduous and pleasure–pain life of a cowboy, until then, had gone unmentioned by the patient, who made his livelihood in aeronautics, and who didn't much like talking about his past, for several reasons. The reasons included shame at aspects of his homosexual life, but also as we learned in this dream discussion, an incident with a horse that came after Topper which led to great upset. He feared he was responsible, through laziness and stupidity, for the untimely death of this second favorite horse. He could hardly bring himself to talk about it.

But Topper was the bridge to a whole past life and to a deeper and more feelingful discussion of dying. He felt that through laziness and stupidity, he was responsible for his cancer—for not seeing a doctor soon enough, for not taking care of things. And now he was about to part from his beloved wife and companion and couldn't bear the guilt.

We spoke quietly, slowly, and softly of these things, and returned to the dream many times through the session-and-a half meeting times we had arranged these past months. He felt "going home" referred to his wish to die, his exhaustion with living, and how hard it was to talk about these central feelings with his wife, who only wanted him to keep living, to take up positive visualization practices, to be hypnotized, to have me help him to want to go on and "fight the big fight."

He had become angrier with his wife these past weeks, and frustrated with her urgent positiveness. Lately, he had spoken by phone with an old male lover, living in another country, about his need to begin to sum up his life, to think about things, to set things right, and to die with some grace. The patient believed this old lover showed up in the dreams in the sparkly reins; he always wore sparkly jewelry. Before, we had focused on how badly things were going in his body and how upsetting was his dying. But now, things changed. He wanted to think about his life and to prepare for death. And Topper was leading the way; his body, his memory were pointing home. Together we considered his guiltiness about his wish to begin to prepare to die until it abated somewhat and he could proceed with a clearer conscience. Joint sessions with his loving and frightened wife helped them both begin to say goodby.

There was much in the back and forth about details in this dream that were interesting and helpful, but I'll not report them, except to say that "the bit" turned out to be most important as we spoke sessions later about the relation between his dying and a horse taking the bit, accepting and allowing itself to be directed. The feeling of the bit in a horse's mouth was connected in several ways with the bitter acceptance of going the way "the main man" leads, and allowing death to lead. The point is that, with many dreams, if you allow yourself to relax in regard to your own ideas and reactions, you may be able to be open to what the dream means to the patient, and in so doing, most of the work is done.

The importance of allowing a dream its own way was also true with a young woman I worked with in jail. She had been given excessive pelvic exams by the prison doctor and concluded the exams were an attempt on the part of the prison authorities to terminate her wanted pregnancy. She asked for help in speaking to the authorities to have them stop this abusive practice. And she asked for a therapy session because she had been increasingly agitated and was starting to forget things necessary for her legal defense. During one session, in a crowded visiting room, she told me the dream she had had the night before in which she was once again in her grandfather's church down South. It was a nightmare and awakened her in fright. The dream of the church brought her grandfather to mind. In our discussion, partly buried memories resurfaced. This giant of a grandfather, a renowned preacher, when no one was around, in a room in the back of the church, would put his hand on top of her head, the fingers of his other hand in her vagina, and yell repeatedly: "Be healed! Be healed!" The dream that led to the discussion of the memory of her grandfather's abuse connected with the prison doctor's hand in her private parts trying to "heal" her of her pregnancy. Her rage at the grandfather of the old days and the prison doctor of the present joined; her anxious symptoms began slowly to abate; and she was able to use her good mind in better ways in her own legal defense. And with the help of another doctor, I was able to stop the abusive efforts to abort her baby. Sometimes, a dream, memories, and real life action come together to lead to a good outcome.

Another brief example. A young woman patient dreamt of flying. The question "What would it be like to fly?" opens the conversation in a meaningful way for this person. She takes it and flies with it, into a world of wish, pleasure, and physical opposition to the gravity and depression of her background, and into a sense of spaciousness and power. Often, taking the dream into real life imagination is the way. A man dreamt a complex dream of *standing on a ladder fixing something on a roof.* There were countless ways to go, but in this instance, I found myself asking him about his "life on ladders," and off we went, learning lots about his psychological life.

A man in his late 50s, a successful raiser of bulls, came to my office after calling from a nearby telephone. He was on his way to Vermont to declare the Kingdom of Christ, with himself as the Messiah. One of his children recommended he speak to a psychiatrist or psychologist before taking off. Afraid of and hating psychiatrists, he looked in the phone book, saw my name listed under psychologists, called, and here he was. A big man, handsome, weatherbeaten, farm boots on, smelling of animals, speaking in a soft and gentle voice. After talking openly and proudly about his mission, he shamedly told a dream from the week before *in which he was inside a large round room, making love to one of his bulls, and liking the feeling.* My question, "What would it really be like to make love to one of your bulls?" surprised him and led to an extraordinary discussion of sex, animals, his occasionally frightening perversions, his unhappiness with his home life, his growing depression, his fear of going mad, his rages, his need to start a new life where he could be boss, his relation to "bullshit," his past heroic exploits, his self-loathing as a weak man, his dislike of Jews, his love and hatred of his animals, and mostly, his relation to Jesus and to Christ, which for him entailed two very different experiences. Good dream conversation. He was interested in talking more, delayed his journey and entered therapy for about a year, at the end of which he felt better; he later quit his business, which he felt was driving him mad, and enrolled in divinity school, a slower route to the Messiah.

I am reminded here of a young woman who dreamed *that she was looking down from above and saw a crowd of people, some laughing, some crying. Out of the corner of her eye, she saw a large piece of wood, like an old beam in a barn.* Her associations and our conversation soon wandered into her deep identification with Christ (more than Jesus). She was Jewish and therefore somewhat startled to find herself dreaming that she was on the cross. She understood that this previously unconscious identification was connected with her complete lack of feeling of sin when she did bad things like shoplifting, hanging out with car thieves, dealing drugs, and other crimes. For this was taking from the rich, now understood in a broader sense, in unconscious fantasy, to connect with her lack of original sin. Likewise she did not feel guilty for hating her mother, in general, for not being as loving as her imagined real mother—who now turned out, in the fantasy, to be the Virgin Mary; nor for being disgusted by her mother specifically for having had sex. But in addition, her lifelong wish not to be Jewish, to be Catholic, to be a boy, to take on other people's sins, to be famous and beloved coalesced in the unconscious fantasy of being Christ and finally showed itself in this dream of finding herself on the cross in Christ's space. The dream opened the way; it was truly a royal road to the main action—the unconscious. Our subsequent discussions continued to reveal a profoundly imaginative and terribly guilty soul.

Dreams and therapy go together. There is no better way to the soul's secrets. In psychological pain, the soul's secrets are still the ones that count. And in the relative freedom of dreaming and of dream-listening, it is still possible, despite the "death of psychoanalysis," to talk together—with dreams at the center—toward self-understanding and the relief of psychological suffering.

We have traveled a ways in this book, from a stroll with Odessa, to ancient dream interpreters, to our exploration of dreams and their use in psychotherapy. The world of dreams and of dream interpretation has provided an enormous harvest for the ancients and for us contemporary dream listeners. What lies ahead around the bend? Can dreams help us locate ourselves in this new, rapidly emerging electronic universe? Can dreams and their understanding have relevance for modern explorations of consciousness? Can the private and social nature of dreams lend meaning to life in our new market culture? Did psychoanalysis abandon the dream too soon? We have just completed a remarkable 100 years of engagement with dreams. I think there is more than enough to wonder and learn about for the next 100 years.

# REFERENCES

Adler, A. (1936), On the interpretation of dreams. *Internat. J. Indiv. Psychol.*, 2:3–16.

Anzieu, D. (1989), *The Skin Ego.* New Haven, CT: Yale University Press.

Aserinsky, E. & Kleitman, S. (1953), Regularly occurring periods of eye motility and concomitant phenomena during sleep. *Science*, 118: 273–274.

Berakoth (1948), *In the Babylonian Talmud: Seder Zera'im, Vol. 1,* ed. I. Epstein, trans. M. Simon. London: Soncino.

Blechner, M. (1995), The patient's dreams and the countertransference. *Psychoanal. Dial.*, 5:1–25.

Bonime, W. (1962), *The Clinical Use of Dreams.* New York: Basic Books.

Bornstein, R. F. & Pittman, T. S., ed. (1992), *Perception Without Awareness: Cognitive, Clinical and Social Perspectives.* New York: Guilford Press.

Boss, M. (1958), *The Analysis of Dreams.* New York: Philosophical Library.

Brenner, C. (1969), Dreams in clinical psychoanalytic practice. *J. Nerv. Ment. Dis.*, 149:122–132.

Brown, L., ed. (1993), *The New Shorter Oxford English Dictionary*. Oxford, UK: Clarendon Press.

Bulkeley, K. (1994), *The Wilderness of Dreams*. Albany: State University of New York Press.

Cartwright, R. (1986), Affect and dream work from an information processing point of view. *J. Mind Behav.*, 7:411–428.

Casey, E. (1976), *Imagining*. Bloomington: Indiana University Press.

Cortina, M. & Maccoby, M., ed. (1996), *A Prophetic Analyst*. Northvale, NJ: Aronson.

Cowell, J. (1997), *A Mapmaker's Dream*. New York: Warner Books.

Crick, F. & Mitchison, G. (1983), The function of dream sleep. *Nature*, 304:111–114.

Dee, N. (1984), *Your Dreams and What They Mean*. New York: Aquarian Press.

Dement, W. (1978), *Some Must Watch While Some Sleep*. New York: Norton.

Eisold, K. (1995), Clinical uses of dreams. In *Handbook of Interpersonal Psychoanalysis*, ed. M. Lionells, J. Fiscalini, C. Mann & D. Stern. Hillsdale, NJ: The Analytic Press, pp. 709–728.

Ellman, S. & Antrobus, J., ed. (1991), *The Mind in Sleep*. New York: Wiley.

Erikson, E. (1950), *Childhood and Society*. New York: Norton.

Erikson, E. (1954), The dream specimen of psychoanalysis. *J. Amer. Psychoanal. Assn.*, 2:5–56.

Fisher, C. (1960), Introduction. In *Preconscious Stimulation in Dreams, Associations and Images*, ed. O. Potzl, R. Allers & J. Teler. New York: International Universities Press.

Fosshage, J. & Loew, C. (1978), *Dream Interpretation: A Comparative Study*. New York: Spectrum.

Fraiberg, S. (1959), *The Magic Years*. New York: Scribner.

Franklin, G. (1992), The contributions of being unknowing to psychoanalysis. *Psychoanal. Psychother.*, 11:127–141.

Freud, S. (1900), The interpretation of dreams. *Standard Edition*, 4 & 5. London: Hogarth Press, 1953.

Freud, S. (1911), The handling of dream-interpretation in psychoanalysis. *Standard Edition*, 12:91–96. London: Hogarth Press, 1958.

Freud, S. (1923), Remarks on the theory and practise of dream-interpretation. *Standard Edition*, 19:108–121. London: Hogarth Press, 1961.

Freud, S. (1925), Some additional notes on dream-interpretation as a whole. *Standard Edition,* 19:125–138. London: Hogarth Press, 1961.

Freud, S. (1932), New introductory lectures on psycho-analysis. *Standard Edition,* 22:5–183. London: Hogarth Press, 1964.

Frieden, K. (1990), *Freud's Dream of Interpretation.* Albany: State University of New York Press.

Fromm, E. (1951), *The Forgotten Language.* New York: Grove Press.

Gamwell, L., ed. (2000), *Dreams 1900–2000.* Ithaca, NY: Cornell University Press.

Goldstein, J. (1997), Embracing the random in the self-organizing psyche. In *Nonlinear Dynamics, Psychology and Life Sciences,* Vol. 1, No. 3. Human Sciences Press.

Greenson, R. (1970), The exceptional position of the dream in psychoanalytic practice. *Psychoanal. Quart.,* 39:519–549.

Grünbaum, A. (1984), *The Foundations of Psychoanalysis: A Philosophical Critique.* Berkeley: University of California Press.

Hall, C. (1966), *The Meaning of Dreams.* New York: McGraw-Hill.

Hall, C. & Van de Castle, R. (1966), *The Content Analysis of Dreams.* New York: Appleton-Century-Crofts.

Hall, J. (1991), *Patterns of Dreaming.* Boston, MA: Shambhala Press.

Hartmann, E. (1995), Making connections in a safe place: Is dreaming psychotherapy? *Dreaming,* 5:213–228.

Hillman, J. (1979), *The Dream and the Underworld.* New York: Harper & Row.

Hobson, J. (1988), *The Dreaming Brain.* New York: Basic Books.

Hunt, H. (1989), *The Multiplicity of Dreams.* New Haven, CT: Yale University Press.

Jouvet, M. (1980), Paradoxical sleep and the nature–nurture controversy. In *Adaptive Capabilities of the Nervous System,* ed. J. McConnell. Amsterdam: Elsevier.

Jung, C. (1974), *Dreams,* trans. R. F. C. Hull. Princeton, NJ: Princeton University Press.

Kerr, J. (1993), *A Most Dangerous Method.* New York: Knopf.

Kilborne, B. (1987), Dreams. In *Encyclopedia of Religion,* ed. M. Eliade. New York: Macmillan, 4:482–491.

Kramer, M. (1993), The selective mood regulatory function of dreaming: An update and revision. In *The Functions of Dreaming,* ed. A. Moffitt, M. Kramer & R. Hoffmann. Albany: State University of New York Press.

Krippner, S., ed. (1990), *Dreamtime and Dreamwork*. Los Angeles, CA: Tarcher.

Lewin, B. (1954), Sleep, narcissistic neurosis, and the analytic situation. *Psychoanal. Quart.*, 23:487–510.

Lewin, B. (1955), Dream psychology and the analytic situation. *Psychoanal. Quart.*, 24:169–199.

Lippmann, P. (1996a), On dreams: Greatness and limitations of Fromm's thought. In: *A Prophetic Analyst,* ed. M. Cortina & M. Maccoby. Northvale, NJ: Aronson, pp. 133–150.

Lippmann, P. (1996b), On dreams and interpersonal psychoanalysis. *Psychoanal. Dial.*, 6:831–846.

Lippmann, P. (1996c), The dream's challenge to psychoanalysis. Presented at symposium on Creativity in Dreams at spring meeting of Division 39, American Psychological Association, New York City.

Lippmann, P. (1997), A return to dreams. *The Round Robin,* Fall:1, 10–13.

Lippmann, P. (1998), On the private and social nature of dreams. *Contemp. Psychoanal.*, 34:195–221.

Masson, J., ed. (1985), *The Complete Letters of Sigmund Freud to Wilhelm Fliess.* Cambridge, MA: Harvard University Press.

Natterson, J., ed. (1980), *The Dream in Clinical Practice.* New York: Aronson.

Perls, F. (1969), *Gestalt Therapy Verbatim.* Moab, UT: Real People's Press.

Rapaport, D., Gill, M. & Schafer, R. (1945), *Diagnostic Psychological Testing,* 2 vols. Chicago: Year Book Publishers.

Rodale, J. (1978), *The Synonym Finder.* New York: Rodale Press.

Rupprecht, C. (1990), Our unacknowledged ancestors: Dream theorists of antiquity, the Middle Ages, and the Renaissance. *Psychiat. J. Univ. Ottowa,* 15(2):117–122.

Rycroft, C. (1979), *The Innocence of Dreams.* London: Hogarth Press.

Sanville, J. (1991), *The Playground of Psychoanalytic Therapy.* Hillsdale, NJ: The Analytic Press.

Schafer, R. (1948), *The Clinical Application of Psychological Tests.* New York: International Universities Press.

Schorske, C. (1980), *Fin-de-Siècle Vienna: Politics and Culture.* New York: Knopf.

Shafton, A. (1995), *The Dream Reader.* Albany: State University of New York Press.

Shapiro, D. (1965), *Neurotic Styles.* New York: Basic Books.

Solms, M. (1997), *The Neuropsychology of Dreams*. Mahwah, NJ: Lawrence Erlbaum Associates.

Spock, B. (1957), *Baby and Child Care*. New York: Pocket Books.

States, B. (1997), *Seeing in the Dark*. New Haven, CT: Yale University Press.

Stevens, A. (1995), *Private Myths: Dreams and Dreaming*. Cambridge, MA: Harvard University Press.

Sullivan, H. (1938), The data of psychiatry. In *The Fusion of Psychiatry and Social Science*, New York: Norton, 1964.

Sullivan, H. (1953), *The Interpersonal Theory of Psychiatry*. New York: Norton.

Tauber, E. (1963), The dream in the therapeutic process from the therapist's standpoint. In *Dreams in Contemporary Psychoanalysis*, ed. E. Adelson. New York: Society of Medical Psychoanalysts.

Tauber, E. & Green, M. (1959), *Prelogical Experience*. New York: Basic Books.

Tedlock, B., ed. (1992), *Dreaming: Anthropological and Psychological Interpretations*. Santa Fe, NM: School of American Research Press.

Ullman, M. (1978), Foreword. In *Dream Interpretation: A Comparative Study*, ed. J. Fosshage & C. Loew. New York: Spectrum.

Ullman, M. (1988), Dreams and society. In *The Variety of Dream Experience*, ed. M. Ullman & C. Limmer. New York: Continuum.

Van de Castle, R. (1994), *Our Dreaming Mind*. New York: Ballantine Books.

Waldhorn, H. F. (1967), Indications for psychoanalysis: The place of the dream in clinical psychoanalysis. In Monogr. 2, *The Kris Study Group of the New York Psychoanalytic Institute*, ed. E. D. Joseph. New York: International Universities Press.

Williams, W. C. (1984), *The Doctor Stories*. New York: New Directions.

Young, E., ed. (1960), *The Paintings of Henry Miller*. San Francisco: Chronicle Books.

Young, S. (1999), *Dreaming in the Lotus*. Boston, MA: Wisdom.

Zborowski, M. & McNamara, P. (1998), Attachment hypothesis of REM sleep: Toward an integration of psychoanalysis, neuroscience, and evolutionary psychology and the implications of psychopathology research. *Psychoanal. Psychol.*, 15:115–140.

# Suggested Reading

Adelson, E., ed. (1963), *Dreams in Contemporary Psychoanalysis*. New York: Society of Medical Psychoanalysts.

Altman, L. (1975), *The Dream in Psychoanalysis*. New York: International Universities Press.

Alvarez, A. (1995), *Night*. New York: Norton.

Antrobus, J. (1977), The dream as metaphor. *J. Ment. Imagery*, 2:327–338.

Arnold-Foster, M. (1921), *Studies in Dreams*. New York: Macmillan.

Bettelheim, B. (1990), *Freud's Vienna and Other Essays*. New York: Knopf.

Bloom, H., ed. (1987), *Sigmund Freud's* The Interpretation of Dreams. New York: Chelsea House.

Blum, H. (1976), The changing use of dreams in psychoanalytic practice. *Internat. J. Psycho-Anal.*, 57:315–324.

Bonime, W. (1978), The culturalist approach. In *Dream Interpretation: A Comparative Study*, ed. J. Fosshage & C. Loew. New York: Spectrum.

Bootzin, R., Kihlstrom, J. & Shacter, D., eds. (1990), *Sleep and Cognition*. Washington, DC: American Psychological Association.

Boss, M. (1977), *I Dreamt Last Night*. New York: Wiley.

Bower, B. (1998), All fired up: Perception may dance to the beat of collective neural rhythms. *Sci. News,* 153:120–121.

Bulkeley, K., ed. (1996), *Among All These Dreamers.* Albany: State University of New York Press.

Caligor, L. & May, R. (1968), *Dreams and Symbols.* New York: Basic Books.

Castoriadis, C. (1997), *World in Fragments.* Stanford, CA: Stanford University Press.

Ellman, S. (1992), Psychoanalytic theory, dream formation, and REM sleep. In *Interface of Psychoanalysis and Psychology,* ed. J. Barron, M. Eagle & D. Wolitzky. Washington, DC: American Psychological Association.

Epel, N., ed. (1994), *Writers Dreaming.* New York: Vintage Press.

Fiss, H. (1986), An empirical foundation for a self psychology of dreaming. *J. Mind Behav.,* 7:161–192.

Flanagan, O. (2000), *Dreaming Souls.* Oxford, UK: Oxford University Press.

Flanders, S., ed. (1993), *The Dream Discourse Today.* London: Routledge.

Foulkes, D. (1985), *Dreaming: A Cognitive-Psychological Analysis.* Hillsdale, NJ: Lawrence Erlbaum Associates.

French, T. & Fromm, E. (1964), *Dream Interpretation: A New Approach.* New York: Basic Books.

Fromm, E. (1980), *The Greatness and Limitations of Freud's Thought.* New York: Meridian.

Gaines, R. (1994), Interpersonal and Jungian dream interpretation. *Contemp. Psychoanal.,* 30:855–867.

Gill, M. & Brenman, M. (1959), *Hypnosis and Related States.* New York: International Universities Press.

Globus, G. (1987), *Dream Life, Wake Life.* Albany: State University of New York Press.

Green, M., Ullman, M. & Tauber, E. (1966), Dreaming and modern dream theory. In *Modern Psychoanalysis,* ed. J. Marmor. New York: Basic Books.

Grinstein, A. (1983), *Freud's Rules of Dream Interpretation.* New York: International Universities Press.

Harris, M. (1994), *Studies in Jewish Dream Interpretation.* Northvale, NJ: Aronson.

Hill, C. (1996), *Working with Dreams in Psychotherapy.* New York: Guilford Press.

Hillman, J. (1989), *A Blue Fire*. New York: Harper & Row.

Hobson, J. (1989), *Sleep*. New York: Scientific American Library.

Holt, R., ed. (1967), *Motives and Thought: Psychoanalytic Essays in Honor of David Rapaport*. New York: International Universities Press.

Jacobi, R. (1983), *The Repression of Psychoanalysis*. New York: Basic Books.

Jones, R. (1970), *The New Psychology of Dreaming*. New York: Grune & Stratton.

Jung, C. (1933), *Modern Man in Search of a Soul*, trans. W. Dell & C. Baynes. New York: Harcourt Brace Jovanovich.

Jung, C. (1965), *Memories, Dreams, Reflections*. New York: Vintage Books.

Khan, M. (1974), *The Privacy of the Self*. London: Hogarth Press.

Khan, M. (1976), The changing use of dreams in psychoanalytic practice: In search of the dreaming experience. *Internat. J. Psycho-Anal.*, 57:325–330.

Langer, S. (1948), *Philosophy in a New Key*. New York: Mentor Books.

Lasky, M., ed. (1992), *Essential Papers on Dreams*. New York: New York University Press.

Lavie, P. (1996), *The Enchanted World of Sleep*. New Haven, CT: Yale University Press.

Levenson, E. (1983), *The Ambiguity of Change*. New York: Basic Books.

Lippmann, P. (in press), Dreams and psychoanalysis: A love–hate story. *Psychoanal. Psychol.*

Lohser, B. & Newton, P. (1996), *Unorthodox Freud*. New York: Guilford Press.

Marcus, S. (1984), *Freud and the Culture of Psychoanalysis*. New York: Norton.

Marmor, J., ed. (1968), *Modern Psychoanalysis*. New York: Basic Books.

Melville, H. (1851), *Moby Dick, or The Whale*. Chicago: Great Books Foundation, 1956.

Mendelsohn, R. (1990), *The Manifest Dream and Its Use in Therapy*. Northvale, NJ: Aronson.

Mitchell, S. (1988), *Relational Concepts in Psychoanalysis*. Cambridge, MA: Harvard University Press.

Navratil, C., ed. (1997), *In the House of Night*. San Francisco: Chronicle Books.

Palumbo, S. (1978), *Dreaming and Memory: A New Information Processing Model*. New York: Basic Books.

Pontalis, J. (1974), The dream as an object. *Internat. Rev. Psycho-Anal.*, 1:125–133.

Reiser, M. (1990), *Memory in Mind and Brain.* New York: Basic Books.

Roszak, T., Gomes, M. & Kanner, A., eds. (1995), *Ecopsychology.* San Francisco: Sierra Books.

Rothstein, A., ed. (1987), *The Interpretation of Dreams in Clinical Work.* New York: International Universities Press.

Rupprecht, C., ed. (1993), *The Dream and the Text.* Albany: State University of New York Press.

Russo, R., ed. (1987), *Dreams Are Wiser Than Men.* Berkeley, CA: North Atlantic Press.

Sharpe, E. (1949), *Dream Analysis.* London: Hogarth Press.

States, B. (1988), *The Rhetoric of Dreams.* Ithaca, NY: Cornell University Press.

States, B. (1993), *Dreaming and Storytelling.* Ithaca, NY: Cornell University Press.

Ullman, M. & Limmer, C., eds. (1988), *The Variety of Dream Experience.* New York: Continuum.

Von Franz, M. (1991), *Dreams.* Boston, MA: Shambhala Press.

Winnicott, D. (1971), *Playing and Reality.* London: Tavistock.

Wittgenstein, L. (1966), *Wittgenstein: Lectures and Conversations,* ed. C. Barrett. Berkeley: University of California Press.

Woods, R. & Greenhouse, H., eds. (1974), *The New World of Dreams.* New York: Macmillan.

Zweig, P. (1968), *The Heresy of Self-Love.* Princeton, NJ: Princeton University Press.

# INDEX

257